A VOLUME IN THE SERIES
VETERANS

EDITED BY
BRIAN MATTHEW JORDAN & J. ROSS DANCY

SERVICE DENIED

MARGINALIZED VETERANS IN MODERN AMERICAN HISTORY

EDITED BY JOHN M. KINDER &
JASON A. HIGGINS

UNIVERSITY OF MASSACHUSETTS PRESS
Amherst and Boston

Copyright © 2022 by University of Massachusetts Press
All rights reserved
Printed in the United States of America

ISBN 978-1-62534-653-7 (paper); 654-4 (hardcover)

Designed by Deste Roosa
Set in Garamond Premier Pro and Trade Gothic
Printed and bound by Books International, Inc.

Cover design by adam b. bohannon
Cover photo by Jeff Albertson, *Moratorium to End the War in Vietnam: African American World War I veteran in front of Marsh Chapel at Boston University, October 15, 1969*. Jeff Albertson Photograph Collection (PH 57). Special Collections and University Archives, University of Massachusetts Amherst Libraries.

Library of Congress Cataloging-in-Publication Data
Names: Kinder, John M. (John Matthew), 1975– editor. | Higgins, Jason A., 1985– editor.
Title: Service denied : marginalized veterans in modern American history / edited by John M. Kinder and Jason A. Higgins.
Description: Amherst : University of Massachusetts Press, [2022] | Series: Veterans | Includes bibliographical references and index.
Identifiers: LCCN 2021054323 (print) | LCCN 2021054324 (ebook) | ISBN 9781625346544 (hardcover) | ISBN 9781625346537 (paperback) | ISBN 9781613769317 (ebook) | ISBN 9781613769324 (ebook)
Subjects: LCSH: Veterans—United States—History. | Veterans—United States—Social conditions. | Marginality, Social—United States. | United States—Armed Forces—Minorities—History. | United States—Armed Forces—African Americans—History. | United States—Armed Forces—Women—History.
Classification: LCC UB357 .S46 2022 (print) | LCC UB357 (ebook) | DDC 362.860973—dc23/eng/20220121
LC record available at https://lccn.loc.gov/2021054323
LC ebook record available at https://lccn.loc.gov/2021054324

British Library Cataloguing-in-Publication Data
A catalog record for this book is available from the British Library.

This book is dedicated to Jenny Gowen, who remains my closest confidant, my partner in life, and (the last I checked) the very best librarian I know.

—JK

I offer my dedication to Danyelle, who enabled me to complete my doctorate amid the pandemic, while also working virtually and caring for our two children, Maya and Ian.

—JH

CONTENTS

III. IN THE SHADOW OF A LOST WAR

IV. CENTERING MARGINALIZED VETERANS IN A TIME OF FOREVER WAR

ACKNOWLEDGMENTS

I want to thank my co-editor Jason Higgins, who proved to be an ideal partner on this project; the individual chapter contributors, who graciously agreed to lend their expertise; and Matt Becker and the other good folks at the University of Massachusetts Press, who supported this book from the start. I also want to acknowledge my colleagues in the American Studies Program and the History Department at Oklahoma State University, who somehow manage to put up with my early and inevitable slide into grumpy-old-manhood. Finally, I want to recognize the millions of marginalized veterans who didn't make it into this book. I can only hope that other scholars will carry on where we left off.

—JK

I acknowledge the support and mentorship provided by the History Department at UMass Amherst and my doctoral advisor, Christian G. Appy. Additionally, Kay J. Walter, Ron Brooks, and John M. Kinder each had a unique influence on my editorial approach. John: I am grateful for your collegiality and your mentorship. I express a special thanks to each of the contributors for this extraordinary opportunity to work with them, especially Kara Dixon Vuic, who generously shared sources, and David Kieran, who served on my dissertation committee. Finally, thank you to Matt Becker, editor in chief at UMass Press, and series editors Brian Matthew Jordan and Ross Dancy, for believing in this collection and for supporting our efforts to center marginalized people in the field of veterans studies.

—JH

SERVICE DENIED

Veterans in the Margins of Modern American History

JOHN M. KINDER & JASON A. HIGGINS

In April 2020, as the first wave of COVID-19 swept across North America, a group of military veterans logged onto their computers for a virtual buddy check. The participants were all veterans of US wars who had been deported after their military service. Over the course of the meeting, the group's founder, Hector Barajas-Varela, discussed efforts to obtain emergency hygiene kits and encouraged his fellow deported veterans to stay home, if possible. An army veteran of the 82nd Airborne Division, Barajas had been deported to Mexico in 2004, after serving time in prison on a weapons charge. From Tijuana, Barajas launched the Deported Veteran Support House (DVSH) in 2012.[1]

Nicknamed the "Bunker," the DVSH functions as a "shelter and resource center for veterans who need assistance."[2] More than that, DVSH is a community of veterans living in exile, excluded from the benefits of their service, isolated from their families and former lives in the United States, and reliant on one another. "At the house, we're able to help guys connect with rehab centers. We have volunteer counselors. Sometimes, we have toy drives, Christmas dinners, Thanksgiving dinners, birthday celebrations," says Barajas. "I think that helps— that hope can keep you alive for that day."[3] According to the group's mission statement, the DVSH has a political aim as well, advocating for "legislation which would prohibit the deportation of United States service personnel, both former and current."[4] After several years of effort, Hector Barajas received a full pardon and gained US citizenship in 2018. Since the 1990s, however, the federal government has deported hundreds of US military veterans, many of whom had enlisted as an opportunity to earn their full citizenship.[5] To this day, deported veterans (also known as "green card" vets) live precarious lives, exiled to countries they barely know and rejected by a nation for which they fought.

Deported veterans are only one group among many that we call "marginalized veterans." We use this term to describe former service members who, for various reasons, have been denied by veterans' institutions, ignored by the public, or overlooked by scholars. Wartime military service has been idealized as a marker of civic duty, patriotism, and manhood, yet the rewards of veteran status have never been distributed equally. Women, people of color, LGBTQ people, those with other-than-honorable discharges, veterans with "shameful" conditions, and other stigmatized groups have been both denied much-needed state recognition and excised from official histories. None of

Hector Barajas-Varela, Bronx, New York, August 12, 2019.
Courtesy of Jason A. Higgins.

this is accidental. Veteranhood is an intrinsically and historically unequal social construction, propping up the status of certain groups of ex-military personnel while denying acknowledgment and equal rights to others.

CENTERING MARGINALIZED VETERANS

The very concept of a "marginalized" veteran might strike some readers as contradictory. After all, veteranhood remains a privileged status in American culture—celebrated on holidays, valorized by politicians, and enshrined in our patriotic rituals. Indeed, by some measures, no single group has benefitted more from the nation's largesse and goodwill than military veterans. This sentiment emerged, to a large degree, in the aftermath of the Civil War. At a time when Americans were expected to pull themselves up by their bootstraps, Union veterans claimed the most extensive social safety net at that point in US history. By the end of the nineteenth century, roughly one-quarter of the federal budget went toward providing pensions and other care for Union vets, thanks in no small part to the advocacy of the Grand Army of the Republic, a Union veterans group whose membership eventually topped four hundred thousand.[6]

Not all military veterans benefitted equally within this system. With the expansion of state-sponsored racial segregation following Reconstruction, African Americans were locked out of the burgeoning veteran's state, their claims of veteran status largely denied, if not actively, silenced. As James E. Sanford, a Black World War I veteran, observed of his poor treatment at a Virginia rehabilitation farm, "The fact is that we are invariabl[y] received as a colored man and not as a disabled soldier."[7] Even as the armed forces began to desegregate in the late 1940s, the further expansion of structural racism via the Veterans Administration and other federal agencies continued to marginalize Black veterans, who—along with other people of color—increasingly played outsized roles in the grunt work of military operations abroad.[8] At the exclusion of African Americans, by the mid-twentieth century, the United States had forged a unique social and economic compact with military veterans, one that afforded them opportunities and access to programs (e.g., the GI Bill, federally backed home loans) above and beyond those offered to nonveteran civilians.[9]

The fact that the vast majority of military veterans were (purportedly) straight, white men only added to their social, economic, and political capital. At various points throughout US history, postwar governments established hiring schemes, job preference initiatives, and educational opportunities specifically aimed at veterans.[10] Military experience can also help launch candidates into the higher echelons of American politics. The late John McCain (R-AZ), who spent decades developing a reputation as maverick in the Senate, routinely invoked his ordeal in Vietnam at the start of his career. The same was true of his political rival John Kerry (D-MA), who famously opened his presidential acceptance address at the 2004 Democratic Convention by saluting the crowd and announcing that he was "reporting for duty."[11] (This was from a founder of the Vietnam Veterans Against the War, who, when testifying before the Senate Foreign Relations Committee in 1971, had described the war in Vietnam as a "filthy obscene memory."[12])

Well into the twenty-first century, claiming a veteran identity—no matter what branch of service—remains politically useful, both as a stepping stone to higher office and as a means of legitimizing one's political vision. During his 2020 presidential campaign, Pete Buttigieg, the mayor of South Bend, Indiana, invoked his status as a war veteran to highlight his commitment to public service. "I was packing my bags for Afghanistan while he was working on Season 7 of 'The Apprentice,'" Buttigieg said of then-president Donald Trump, the scion of a rich family who famously sought medical deferments to escape service in Vietnam.[13] At the opposite extreme of the political spectrum, senator Tom Cotton (R-AK), weaponizes his military service to claim authority on security matters and bludgeon his ideological opponents. During protests of the 2020 police murder of George Floyd, Cotton called for "no quarter," threatening to mobilize the 82nd Airborne against predominantly Black protesters.[14] In an era of hyperpartisan gridlock in politics, conservatives and liberals seem to agree on at least one thing: veterans represent the best of society, emblems of self-sacrifice and icons of national service.[15]

However, veterans are not a monolithic group and never have been. Historically, who "has counted" as a (real) veteran depended on a range of other factors, including a person's branch of service, exposure to combat, and contributions to a particular military campaign. This rich diversity is reflected in the make-up of major veterans groups, such as the Veterans of Foreign

Wars, the Disabled American Veterans, and Vietnam Veterans of America, which distinguish between veterans eligible and ineligible for admission. But veteran populations are diverse in other ways as well. As this volume makes clear, factors such as race, gender, sexuality, disability, and politics have played determinative roles in shaping veterans' public recognition and treatment by the state. Put another way, former military personnel are never *just* veterans. They exist within intersecting networks of privilege and oppression, the status of some veterans meted out at the expense of others.[16] Consequently, like other socially constructed populations, veterans are less a homogenous group than an unacknowledged hierarchy—with some garnering the bulk of attention and others ignored by the public and denied by the state.[17]

In describing this hierarchy, we've chosen to deploy the sociological concept of *marginalization*. Marginalization is a process of sorting and ranking in which certain individuals or groups are assigned a position of relative powerlessness. At times, marginalization can appear quite literal, as in the case of Hector Barajas-Varela and other veterans deported beyond the boundaries of the US nation-state. However, marginalization is perhaps best understood in metaphorical terms as a process of social exclusion and denigration, one that relegates chosen groups beyond the realm of social concern.[18] Deployed by scholars across the critical humanities, the concept of marginalization is a useful tool for describing and, in part, explaining socially constructed differences in status and public recognition.[19]

Processes of marginalization affect individual veterans in different ways. In some cases, marginalization among veterans can be a matter of *spatial exclusion*, as Jason Higgins shows in his chapter on incarcerated veterans since the American war in Vietnam. All too often, the histories of veterans take place on the margins of society—in prisons, asylums, and hospitals, institutions of containment and social erasure. Veterans in such spaces are, quite literally, out of sight and out of mind, trapped in biopolitical regimes that frequently equate punishment and cure.[20] Marginalization also functions as a process of *intragroup stratification*, a means of drawing distinctions among the broader veteran population. This book shows how veteranhood is both an exalted and exclusionary identity from which large numbers of former military personnel benefit while others are barred. Barbara Gannon's chapter, for example, reveals how Great War veterans viewed their counterparts from the Spanish-American War as "paper" veterans, unworthy of recognition due to the brief nature of their military service.

Marginalization additionally functions as a kind of *collective forgetting*, a historical amnesia that clouds both popular memory and scholarly imagination alike. To this date, Hollywood spotlights a relatively narrow population of young white men who spend their war years firing guns. Historians, with some notable exceptions, have followed a similar impulse. Yet, as the chapters by Kara Dixon Vuic, Heather Stur, and Robert Jefferson make clear, the history of American veterans extends far beyond the "coming home" clichés we often encounter—especially if the veterans are women, queer, or Black.[21] In other cases, the military can uplift previously marginalized communities, as Steven Rosales reminds us in his chapter on Mexican American veterans and the GI Bill.

Marginalized veterans also experience *stigmatization,* the process by which certain traits or affinities are deemed deviant and socially discrediting, as John Kinder and Evan Sullivan show. "Part of the power of stigmatization lies in the realization that people who are stigmatized or acquire a stigma lose their place in the social hierarchy," writes Lerita M. Coleman. "Consequently, most people want to ensure that they are counted in the nonstigmatized 'majority.' This, of course, leads to more stigmatization."[22] In many cases, stigma is associated with race, gender, sexuality, or what sociologist Erving Goffman called "abominations of the body."[23] However, as John Worsencroft points out, some Americans will take extraordinary steps to avoid becoming any type of veteran—even if it means abandoning the draft during a time of war.

Of course, marginalization and social exclusion do not begin when service members leave the military. Marginalization, as we understand it, reflects and reinforces already-existing social inequalities in American society. These distinctions persist throughout service members' military careers, despite the armed forces' admirable, albeit long overdue, attempts to redress structural prejudices within its own ranks.[24] For this reason, several of this book's contributors—most notably Juan Coronado and David Kieran—devote ample attention to individuals' (and groups') experiences *during* service, when the processes and justifications of marginalization were already at work.

To some degree, all veterans experience the kinds of ranking, devaluing, denying, and misremembering at the heart of marginalization. Yet the lives of some veterans remain especially out of focus, obscuring the social problems many encounter after their discharge. Veterans of the "forever wars" experience excessively high rates of homelessness, suicide, substance use, and mental health issues.[25] After being discharged, many veterans feel dissociated from their former lives, finding it difficult to transition between two increasingly separated worlds, being disconnected from their military units and isolated within the civilian population. The widening gap between the public and the military fosters distrust on both sides of the military-civilian divide. Meanwhile, pop culture continues to revel in stories of dangerous, delusional, or otherwise deranged military veterans. Keeping them at a comfortable distance, we've been taught to "thank" veterans for their service, all the while ignoring war's radiating effects on many veterans' daily lives.

Recent history continues to expose the precarity of many veterans. Throughout 2020, the twin onslaughts of racial injustice and the pandemic shattered countless veterans' lives. The economic fallout of 2020 left large numbers of veterans out of work and dependent on state resources to survive. Yet, as always, some veterans remain more vulnerable than others. This reality hit home throughout the year—in hospitals, in prisons, and on the streets. In one particularly devastating outbreak, over one hundred veterans died from COVID-19 at Holyoke Soldiers' Home in Massachusetts.[26] Paradoxically, it seems, an automatic deference to "the troops" has emerged in a time of cultural indifference to actual veterans, particularly those who—because of age, sexuality, disability, race or ethnicity, or politics—have been marginalized to the fringes of American life.

THE MYTH OF THE "VETERAN'S EXPERIENCE"

In telling the histories of marginalized veterans, this book seeks to debunk what we call the myth of the veteran's experience. Intellectually lazy, at best, the "veteran's experience" is a kind of descriptive shorthand constructed from Western tropes and heroic narratives.[27] It serves as a general reference to the various formal relationships that ex–service personnel share—transitioning from military to postmilitary identities, lingering connections to the state, and the performative rituals of martial manhood, among others. According to the myth, all veteran narratives follow a similar set of patterns, share a similar set of struggles, and stand for a similar set of values. Gatekeepers of the myth of the veteran's experience frequently point to archetypical veterans—Homer's Odysseus, the Roman statesmen Cincinnatus, and even George Washington—as exemplars of the ahistorical nature of veteranhood.[28] More often, however, the prototypical veteran exists as a broadly generic figure that somehow encapsulates thousands, if not millions, of former personnel.

References to the "veteran's experience" pervade American history and popular culture. Writing shortly before the end of World War II, Columbia University sociologist Willard Waller offered what would become the text-book account of the "veteran" as a sociological figure. In the more than 340 pages of his book, he returns numerous times to the singular veteran and his various qualities (e.g., he is like a "motherless child"; he "doubts his ability to love"; he is "bitter—and with reason"). Though Waller, at times, acknowledges some differences, he clearly views the veteran as a normative figure—an abstraction that represents the vast majority of ex–service personnel.[29]

Invocations of the "veteran experience" remain popular, especially among politicians and veterans' groups, who conjure the plight of the veteran in service of their respective agendas. Launched in 2017, for example, the video streaming service VET Tv makes little effort to acknowledge the diversity of perspectives among active and former military personnel. VET Tv advertises itself as the "Comedy Central of the military . . . the first veteran television network full of dark, perverted, inappropriate, controversial, and irreverent military humor—created by and for veterans, without civilian influence."[30] Yet viewers of the network quickly learn that VET Tv is aimed not at *all* veterans but at a specific type: hypermasculine, misogynistic, bawdy, and casually racist. Those who don't fit this narrowly prescribed set of characteristics (women, homosexuals, transgender people) are objects of ridicule.[31] Even the Department of Veterans Affairs—a government institution that should know better—routinely deploys *the* veteran as a rhetorical figure in its public messaging.[32]

For all its apparent clarity, the myth of the veteran's experience obscures the diversity and complexity of veterans' lives after leaving the military. More than that, it functions as a kind of ideological muzzle to silence and delegitimize social protest and criticism of US foreign policy. In reaction to the revival of Black Lives Matter activism in the summer of 2020, politicians and conservative media decried protestors as un-American, drawing an uncrossable line between "heroes" (soldiers, police, and first responders) deserving of praise and "criminals" (protestors) deserving of violent control. Within this framework, Black, female, queer, disabled, antiwar, or "liberal" veterans don't count as heroes, denying their place in national consciousness. Veterans studies must not repeat these false dichotomies. If historians are partly to blame for these erasures, then it becomes our responsibility to rewrite the narrative. As W. E. B. Du Bois wrote, "Nations reel and stagger on their way; they make hideous mistakes; they commit frightful wrongs; they do great and beautiful things. And shall we not best guide humanity by telling the truth about all of this, so far as the truth is ascertainable?"[33] This book represents our collective efforts to move marginalized veterans closer to the center of modern American history.

No moment more clearly illustrates the sharp divide in veterans today than the US Capitol insurrection on January 6, 2021. On the furthest fringes of veteran groups, fourteen-year veteran of the US Air Force Ashli Babbitt—who became a radicalized MAGA (Make America Great Again) follower and QAnon conspiracy theorist—was shot and killed by police as she breached the US Capitol.[34] On the other end, Eugene Goodman, an African American veteran of the Iraq War, single-handedly faced a mob and lured the violent crowd away from the Senate Chamber just in time.[35] The tectonic plates of white nationalism and American democracy—the contradictory historical forces that Du Bois well understood—collided violently on that fateful day in the Capitol, as one veteran became a martyr for MAGA and another the savior of democracy. Outside the Capitol, police, national guardsmen, and veterans clashed under the chaos of waving flags and smoke.[36] One police officer was mobbed and beaten with the pole from an American flag.[37]

Between these extremities, the very concept of veteran identity is stretched to its breaking point. We might ask what, if any, value can be ascertained from their shared experiences and common history? We attempt to answer this question by studying the historical processes that shape and uphold the structural order that ranks veterans by race, gender, class, ability, politics, and place in modern American history.

GOALS

In compiling this book, we recognize its limitations. We do not pretend to address the histories of all marginalized veterans. Far too many people have been left out of the historical records to give us a full picture of the history of marginalized veterans in America. We also acknowledge that the majority of US military veterans have led productive and successful lives after service. But to measure the social costs of US wars and their impact on the survivors, veterans studies must center the histories of the most marginalized—not the most generalized.[38]

With this in mind, *Service Denied: Marginalized Veterans in Modern American History* is driven by four distinct goals.

The first is to offer a glimpse into the lives of some of the most marginalized veterans in modern US history: people of color, women, gays and lesbians, people with "shameful" conditions, and formerly incarcerated veterans such as Hector Barajas-Varela. We do so not simply to recover the voices of the voiceless. Integrating these stories allows us to reconsider veterans' history—indeed, all of modern American history—in a new light. When we move beyond the "veteran's experience," scholars challenge the monochromatic national narratives about American war, spotlighting diverse motivations and unequal aftermaths.

Second, we ask questions about the denial of rights, status, and claims of veterans in history. We seek to show how state apparatuses and intersectional systems of oppression have exacerbated the social and political marginalization of various groups of veterans throughout the twentieth century. In doing this, we must reckon with the complicity of scholars in the past. As Michel-Rolph Trouillot argued, power affects the process and production of history at formative moments: the making of sources; the assembly of facts and archives; the construction of narrative; and the determination of "retrospective significance."[39] In other words, marginalization occurs at each stage in the writing of history; so, in editing this book, we turned our attention to veterans mostly unwritten into the annals of war and society.

Third, we aim to showcase a variety of methodologies and lines of inquiry for future scholars of veterans' history. In tracing the histories of marginalized veterans, we've been led to look beyond the archives and rethink old paradigms. Consequently, we hope to inspire future scholars and students to seek out (to paraphrase historian Philip Deloria) unexpected veterans and the unexpected places they inhabit.[40] Marginalized veterans are everywhere—in universities, hospitals, government, police forces, courtrooms, prisons, local neighborhoods, schools, and online. Advocate groups such as the Deported Veterans Support House, Minority Veterans of America, the Black Veterans Project, SERVICE: Women Who Serve, Protect Our Defenders, Veterans for Peace, and many more organize on social media and engage the public in film, journalism, and grassroots activism. In an emerging field such as veterans studies, historians have an opportunity (and an obligation) to seek out marginalized communities and ask critical questions about veterans' ever-evolving status in American society.

Above all else, we hope to use this book to "unsettle" assumptions about the status of military veterans in American history.[41] If we wish to grapple with the marginalization of certain groups of veterans, we must first acknowledge America's long history of social inequality at home and violence abroad. Only then can we begin to address the lingering effects of this history in the present, for it has been too long denied.

NOTES

1. Deported Veterans Support House, "About," *Facebook*, accessed April 30, 2020, https://www.facebook.com/DeportedVeteransSupportHousePage/; Catherine E. Shoichet, "A Deported Veteran Just Became a US Citizen. Wait . . . What?," *CNN*, April 13, 2018, https://www.cnn.com/2018/04/13/politics/deported-veterans-explainer-hector-barajas/index.html; Aaron Nelsen, "Hector Barajas Served in the American Military. We Was Deported Just the Same," *Vice*, September 11, 2019, https://www.vice.cm/en_us/article/qvgdn7/hector-barajas-served-in-the-american-military-he-was-deported-just-the-same-v26n3.

2. Deported Veterans Support House, "About."

3. Hector Barajas-Varela, Incarcerated Veterans Oral History Project, interview by Jason A. Higgins, August 12, 2019, Bronx, NY.

4. Deported Veterans Support House, "About."

5. The US military recruits approximately five thousand noncitizens each year. As of 2016, the Department of Defense estimated that more than 109,250 "green card" veterans have gained US citizenship through military service. Department of Defense, "Military Accessions Vital to National Interest (MAVNI) Recruitment Pilot Program, Factsheet," 2016, DOI: https://dod.defense.gov/news/mavni-fact-sheet.pdf. The

Department of Justice does not track the number of veterans deported, but Barajas has connected with hundreds of US military veterans deported around the globe.

6. For more on the the Grand Army of the Republic's influence on American politics, see Stuart McConnell, *Glorious Contentment: The Grand Army of the Republic, 1865–1900* (Chapel Hill: University of North Carolina Press, 1997); and Brian Matthew Jordan, *Marching Home: Union Veterans and Their Unending Civil War* (New York: Liverlight, 2015).

7. Quoted in John M. Kinder, *Paying with Their Bodies: American War and the Problem of the Disabled Veteran* (Chicago, IL: University of Chicago Press, 2015), 136.

8. See also Rhonda Y. Williams, *The Politics of Public Housing: Black Women's Struggles against Urban Inequality* (New York: Oxford University Press, 2004); Richard Rothstein, *The Color of Law: A Forgotten History of How Our Government Segregated America* (New York: Liveright, 2017).

9. For more on the GI Bill, see Jennifer Mittelstadt, *The Rise of the Military Welfare State* (Cambridge, MA: Harvard University Press, 2015); Kathleen J. Frydl, *The GI Bill* (New York: Cambridge, 2009); Glenn C. Altschuler and Stuart M. Blumin, *The GI Bill: A New Deal for Veterans* (New York: Oxford University Press, 2009).

10. See also *Veterans' Policies, Veterans' Politics: New Perspectives on Veterans in the United States,* ed. Stephen R. Ortiz (Gainesville: University Press of Florida, 2012).

11. John Kerry, 2004 presidential acceptance speech, July 29, 2004, *C-Span,* https://www.c-span.org/video/?c4849735/user-clip-reporting-duty.

12. "Transcript: Kerry Testifies before Senate Panel, 1971," *NPR,* April 25, 2006, https://www.npr.org/templates/story/story.php?storyId=3875422.

13. Quoted in Steve Hendrix and Joshua Partlow, "How Pete Buttigieg Went from War Protestor to 'Packing My Bags for Afghanistan,'" *Washington Post,* July 29, 2019, https://www.washingtonpost.com/politics/2019/07/29/how-pete-buttigieg-went-war-protester-packing-my-bags-afghanistan/.

14. Tom Cotton, "Send in the Troops," *New York Times,* June 3, 2020, https://www.nytimes.com/2020/06/03/opinion/tom-cotton-protests-military.html.

15. Serving in the military does not necessarily lead to political success. This is especially the case when attitudes toward a particular war are conflicted (e.g., Vietnam, Iraq) or if the would-be veteran-politician is a member of a historically marginalized group (e.g., a person of color, a disabled person, a woman, a trans person). In 1978, Lewis Puller Jr., a former marine who suffered multiple amputations in Vietnam, ran on his veteran status only to lose to a war drum–beating right wing candidate with no military service. More recently, Amy McGrath, the first woman to fly a marine combat mission, failed in her 2020 campaign to oust Kentucky senator Mitch McConnell.

16. On the concept of intersectionality, see Kimberlé Crenshaw, "Mapping the Margins: Intersectionality, Identity Politics, and Violence against Women," *Stanford Law Review* 43 (July 1991): 1241–99.

17. Foundational works on this matter include David A. Gerber, ed., *Disabled Veterans in History* (Ann Arbor: University of Michigan Press, 2000); David W. Blight, *Race and Reunion: The Civil War in American Memory* (Cambridge, MA: Harvard University Press, 2001); Jennifer Brooks, *Defining the Peace: World War II Veterans, Race, and the Remaking of Southern Political Tradition* (Chapel Hill: University of North Carolina Press, 2004); Steve Estes, *Ask and Tell: Gay and Lesbian Veterans Speak Out* (Chapel Hill: University of North Carolina Press, 2007); Christopher S. Parker, *Fighting for*

Democracy: Black Veterans and the Struggle against White Supremacy in the Postwar South (Princeton, NJ: Princeton University Press, 2009); Kinder, *Paying with Their Bodies*; Benjamin Cooper, *Veteran Americans: Literature and Citizenship from Revolution to Reconstruction* (Amherst: University of Massachusetts Press, 2018); Robert F. Jefferson, ed., *Black Veterans, Politics, and Civil Rights in Twentieth-Century America: Closing Ranks* (Lanham, MD: Lexington Books, 2018).

18. In many cases, both literal and metaphorical marginalization are deeply intertwined, as Susan M. Schweik details in her analysis of "ugly laws" in nineteenth-century America. See Susan M. Schweik, *The Ugly Laws: Disability in Public* (New York: New York University Press, 2009).

19. For more on "marginalization" as a tool of social analysis, see Joan G. Mowat, "Towards a New Conception of Marginalisation," *European Education Research Journal* 14, no. 5 (2015): 454–76.

20. On the concept of "biopolitics," see Thomas Lemke, *Biopolitics: An Advanced Introduction* (New York: New York University Press, 2011).

21. In fact, the contributors of this collection have spent their careers seeking to move beyond soldier-centric understandings of military history. See, for example, Heather Marie Stur, *Beyond Combat: Women and Gender in the Vietnam War Era* (New York: Cambridge University Press, 2011); Kara Dixon Vuic, *Officer, Nurse, Woman: The Army Nurses Corps in the Vietnam War* (Baltimore, MD: Johns Hopkins University Press, 2010); and Kara Dixon Vuic, *The Routledge History of Gender, War, and the US Military* (London: Routledge, 2018).

22. Lerita M. Coleman, "Stigma: An Enigma Demystified," in *The Disability Studies Reader*, ed. Lennard J. Davis (New York: Routledge, 1997), 218.

23. Erving Goffman, "Selections from *Stigma*," in Davis, *Disability Studies Reader*, 205.

24. See also *Integrating the US Military: Race, Gender, and Sexual Orientation since World War II*, ed. Douglas Walter Bristol Jr. and Heather Marie Stur (Baltimore, MD: Johns Hopkins University Press, 2017).

25. See also David Kieran, *Signature Wounds: The Untold Story of the Military's Mental Health Crisis* (New York: New York University Press, 2019).

26. "The Latest: State Reports 100 Resident Deaths at Holyoke Soldiers' Home," *Western Mass News*, July 15, 2020, https://www.westernmassnews.com/news/the-latest-state-reports-100-resident-deaths-at-holyoke-soldiers-home/article_88b3a4d8-791d-11ea-b3b7-f37420fe3e63.html.

27. See Jason A. Higgins, "Through Star-Spangled Eyes: Lew Puller's *Fortunate Son* and the Problem of Resolution," *War, Literature & the Arts: An International Journal of the Humanities* 30 (2018): 1–25.

28. This includes influential works such as Jonathan Shay's *Achilles in Vietnam: Combat Trauma and the Undoing of Character* (New York: Scribner, 1994/2003) and *Odysseus in America: Combat Trauma and the Trials of Homecoming* (New York: Scribner, 2002).

29. Willard Waller, *The Veteran Comes Back* (New York: The Dryden Press, 1944), 159–75.

30. Quoted in Rina Raphael, "Does This Controversial TV Network for Vets Help or Hurt Those Who Served?" *Fast Company*, October 11, 2017, https://www.fastcompany.com/40450439/does-this-controversial-tv-network-for-vets-help-or-hurt-those-who-served.

31. Christopher J. Gilbert, "Bawdy Blows: VET Tv and the Comedy of Combat Masculinity," *Women's Studies in Communication* 42, no. 2 (2019): 181–201.

32. See US Department of Veterans Affairs, "Own The Moment—Voice of the Veteran," April 18, 2019, https://www.youtube.com/watch?v=ChXhPLXm2pc&list=PLY7m RNUcQyMTjhSvG6RYWQWoFdkYRICX. This tendency to collapse all veterans into a singular type persists among veterans studies scholars as well. According to the *Journal of Veterans Studies*, "Veterans studies, by its nature, may analyze experiences closely tied to military studies, but the emphasis of veterans studies is the 'veteran experience,' i.e., what happens after the service member departs the armed forces." See "About this Journal," *Journal of Veterans Studies*, accessed September 4, 2021, https:// journal-veterans-studies.org/.

33. W. E. B. Du Bois, "The Propaganda of History," in *Black Reconstruction: Toward a History of the Part of Which Black Folk Played in the Attempt to Reconstruct Democracy in America, 1860–1880* (New York: Harcourt: 1935), 714.

34. Ellen Barry, Nicholas Bogel-Burroughs, and Dave Philipps, "Woman Killed in Capitol Embraced Trump and QAnon," *New York Times*, January 7, 2021, https://www.nytimes. com/2021/01/07/us/who-was-ashli-babbitt.html. Babbitt's embrace of right-wing extremism is not unique the Trump era. As Kathleen Belew has shown, the modern history of white supremacy and domestic terrorism among veterans groups dates back to the Vietnam War, if not earlier; see *Bringing the War Home: The White Power Movement and Paramilitary America* (Cambridge, MA: Harvard University Press: 2018).

35. Rebecca Tan, "A Black Officer Faced Down a Mostly White Mob at the Capitol: Meet Eugene Goodman," *Washington Post*, January 14, 2021, https://www.washingtonpost .com/local/public-safety/goodman-capitol-police-video/2021/01/13/08ab3eb6-546b -11eb-a931-5b162d0d033d_story.html.

36. Tom Dreisbach and Meg Anderson, "Nearly 1 in 5 Defendants in Capitol Riot Cases Served in the Military, *NPR*, January 21, 2021, https://www.npr.org/2021/01/21 /958915267/nearly-one-in-five-defendants-in-capitol-riot-cases-served-in-the-military.

37. Since January 6, 2021, several veterans, active service members, and police have been arrested in connection with the insurrection. See Gina Harkins, "National Guardsman Is 1st Current Service Member to Be Arrested after Capitol Riot," *Military Times*, January 14, 2021, https://www.military.com/daily-news/2021/01/14 /national-guardsman-1st-current-service-member-be-arrested-after-capitol-riot.html; Alex Horton, "Why Service Members Charged in the Capitol Riot Are Staying in Uniform—for Now," *Washington Post*, May 22, 2021, https://www.washingtonpost .com/national-security/2021/05/22/military-capitol-riot/.

38. In this sense, we are guided by legal theorist Kimberlé Crenshaw's insight that a "focus on the most privileged group members marginalizes those who are multiply-burdened and obscures claims that cannot be understood as resulting from discrete sources of discrimination." Kimberlé Crenshaw, "Demarginalizing the Intersection of Race and Sex: A Black Feminist Critique of Antidiscrimination Doctrine, Feminist Theory and Antiracist Politics," *University of Chicago Legal Forum*, no. 1 (1989): 140.

39. Michel-Rolph Trouillot, *Silencing the Past: Power and the Production of History*, with a new forward from Hazel V. Carby (Boston, MA: Beacon Press, 2015), 26.

40. See Philip J. Deloria, *Indians in Unexpected Places*, Culture America (Lawrence: University Press of Kansas, 2004).

41. According to Cynthia Fabrizio Pelak, "Decolonization scholars use the term *unsettled* to refer to the uncomfortable feelings and processes associated with non-Native people acknowledging settler colonialism and recognizing their own colonial blinders." Cynthia Fabrizio Pelak, "Teaching and Learning about Settler-colonial Racism: A Case for 'Unsettling' Minoritizing and Multicultural Perspectives," *Sociology of Race and Ethnicity* 5, no. 2 (2019): 2.

I.

COMING HOME IN THE GREAT WAR ERA

So-Called Disabilities

Spanish War Veterans and the
New Deal's Economy Act

BARBARA GANNON

At the dawn of the twentieth century, the United States started its ascent to world power fighting in the Cuban and Philippine jungles. The men who volunteered for these conflicts made up the first generation of modern American veterans. Subsequently, US involvement in world wars, small wars, counterinsurgencies, cold wars, and hot wars ensured that every generation had its own war. This high tempo of overseas involvement began in 1898, when the United States fought and won a war against the dying Spanish empire in the Caribbean. After a longer, more deadly, counterinsurgency in the Pacific, the United States claimed the Philippines outright. The "Spanish Wars"—the Spanish-American and the Philippine-American War—created a new generation of veterans who lived alongside other veteran cohorts spawned by America's rise to world power. In time, Spanish War soldiers' service was forgotten, or at least minimized, by generations of Americans that came after them. Ironically, they may have been the first generation of marginalized American veterans in the twentieth century, but sadly not the last.[1]

The generation of 1898 belonged to two veterans' organizations. The first still exists, the Veterans of Foreign Wars (VFW); the other, the largely forgotten United Spanish War Veterans (USWV), does not. A notable distinction between these groups may explain why Americans minimized the service of Spanish-American War veterans: most men who enlisted to revenge the USS *Maine* never went overseas. These men joined the USWV because they could not join the VFW, which, as its name suggests, accepted only those with overseas service. The VFW later welcomed overseas veterans of World War I and World War II, and it continues to admit veterans of twenty-first-century wars. Though forgotten, the USWV was long-lived; it formed in 1904 and folded in 1992 after the last Spanish War veteran passed away. At the height of its membership in 1933, it had 126,000 members.

This chapter examines Spanish War veterans after World War I, particularly in 1933, when the Roosevelt administration's Economy Act targeted Spanish War veterans' benefits. Government officials singled out Spanish War veterans partly because of their marginalized status compared to other veterans. Americans depreciated their service for several reasons. First, fewer American served in these wars, and by 1918 a much larger veteran cohort had replaced the men of 1898 in the American public's mind. (The same phenomenon affected later generations of veterans; World War II veterans overshadowed those of the Korean War, for example.) Second, the Spanish Wars were smaller than the wars that bookended American memory in this era—the Civil War and the Great War. To veterans of these larger conflicts, the Spanish Wars did not compare to their own epic clashes, an impression that exacerbated Spanish War veterans' plight. Finally, veterans of other wars and nonveterans alike remembered the Spanish Wars as conflicts that incurred few battle casualties. As a result, Americans believed that these men were less worthy of the nation's gratitude and financial largesse.

However, such arguments failed to grasp the Spanish War's decades-long legacies to the men who served. Consider, for example, the lingering effects of debilitating disease. Because of poorly planned and underresourced mobilization efforts, thousands of soldiers sent to Cuba and the Philippines contracted tropical illnesses. The case was the same closer to home, where large numbers of Spanish War volunteers were sickened in hastily built and unsanitary training camps. They would pay for the nation's penury and lack of foresight. Overburdened and ill equipped, military medical staff struggled to provide adequate medical care and often neglected to document soldiers' illnesses. Consequently, a number of Spanish War veterans were forced to apply for non-service-related pensions, despite the fact that their disabilities stemmed directly from wartime illness. Nonveterans scorned Spanish Wars veterans who received these payments because they believed that their pensions had nothing to do with their military service. Thus, when the Great Depression created a budget crisis, officials targeted marginalized Spanish War veterans and their supposedly "non-service-connected" pensions.

In addition to being marginalized, one of the Spanish Wars, the Philippine-American War, has been largely erased from the official record. According to the Department of Defense's online tabulation of US war casualties, the Spanish-American War resulted in 385 battle deaths; 2,061 deaths from disease; and 1,662 nonmortal wounds. Notably absent are US casualties of the war in the Philippines—the 4,200 Americans who died (1,053 in battle, more than 3,000 from disease) and the 2,900 who were wounded. While the dead of any war need no help, soldiers who are sick and survive—uncounted in any record of any war—often require government assistance. In the case of the Spanish Wars, government officials undercounted disabled veterans of both the Spanish- and Philippine-American Wars because their illnesses were undocumented.[2]

Scholars have also dismissed Spanish War veterans. No single study exists documenting their service and their postwar organization—the United Spanish War Veterans. I wrote the first published article about the USWV, and even then, it was not solely about Spanish War vets; instead, it chronicled the USWV's troubled relationship with the larger and better-known Civil War veterans' group—the Grand Army of the Republic. In a broader study of twentieth-century veterans and nationalism, *Peerless Patriots: Organized Veterans and the Spirit of Americanism*, Rodney G. Minott asks of the generation of 1898, "Who remembers, much less cares, about them now?," reflecting an American amnesia about these men and their wars. Similarly, when Stephen R. Ortiz identified the relationship between the 1933 Economy Act, the rise of the VFW, and the emergence of "New Deal Dissent," Spanish- and Philippine-American War veterans received one brief mention because of a contemporary cartoon titled "Some Call This Economy." In it, three veterans, a Spanish War veteran, a Civil War veteran, and a World War I veteran, stood against a wall and were about to be executed by men in top hats and tuxedos; the artist drew the words "US Chamber of Commerce" on one executioner's back to indicate who they held responsible for these economies.[3]

While government erasures, scholarly neglect, and businessmen's willingness to sacrifice Spanish War veterans may seem understandable, Theodore Roosevelt's disdain for these wars and, by extension, the men who fought them, is more surprising. Colonel Roosevelt's political career, which ended in his improbable rise to the presidency, began in the Spanish-American War when his volunteer regiment, the "Rough Riders," charged San Juan Heights alongside, or perhaps behind, African American Regular Army cavalry troopers. In fact, the memory of Roosevelt's service and that of his "Rough Riders" eclipsed that of all other Spanish War veterans, white or Black. Once president, Roosevelt declared major combat operations over in the Philippine-American War after four long years of war, even before operations ended.

It must have been surprising to his comrades when Roosevelt asked the indulgence of his fellow Spanish War veterans, whom he called "Comrades, of a lesser war" at a 1910 dinner attended by both Civil War and Spanish War veterans. Instead of lauding the sacrifice of his generation, he exalted the "deeds of valor and heroic devotion done by men who wore the blue and those done by the men who wore the grey, alike from a common heritage of honor for all Americans, no matter in what portion of the country they dwell." Roosevelt greeted the veterans of the Civil War as "the men of the big war," to whom he had to "admit that our war was not very big, but it was all there was." (His description of a short war was protested by at least one member of the audience listening to these remarks, who shouted, "Long enough over in the Philippines!") Roosevelt shared many Americans' belief that the Spanish War began in April 1898 and ended in a cease-fire three months later. While the war with Spain concluded with a peace treaty in December of that same year, the United States fought a brutal counterinsurgency for nearly four years in the Philippines. Including all operations in Cuba and the Philippines, the Spanish Wars lasted longer than the Civil War—April 25, 1898, to July 4, 1902. Roosevelt the politician may have understood that Civil War veterans and their families cast more votes than Spanish War veterans, who likely already supported him because of their shared service. The size of the veteran's cohort and the political power they wielded mattered.[4]

Lesser-known veterans disputed the notion that these men sacrificed little in small wars. Congressman George Huddleston served in the 1st Alabama Infantry during the Spanish-American War. Stationed in Miami, his unit suffered during the summer of 1898 from too little sanitation and too many insects. Eventually, Huddleston and many others became ill; however, he reported to his congressional colleagues that "medicines and supplies [were] almost wholly lacking, and medical attention largely a pretense. There were no nurses and no suitable food for the sick. I lay for 30 hours, after admission to the hospital, upon a bare board, with my blouse folded under my head for a pillow, without seeing a doctor or receiving the slightest attention." Eventually, he testified that half of his unit sickened, "racked by malaria, typhoid, and other diseases of the semi tropics[.] Within 60 days there was scarcely a sound man in the pestilential camp, and deaths had risen to an appalling figure." Huddleston's unit never went overseas; their war ended in Miami—or did it only begin there? According to the congressman, "These men came away to be discharged without a medical examination, and without any adequate record having been made of their disabilities . . . discharged to their homes gaunt and fever-stricken, and bearing the seeds of disease to plague them throughout their lives."[5]

Huddleston understood why his generation suffered long after the war ended: Spanish War veterans had survived wartime diseases with little medical intervention. At least twenty thousand Spanish-American recruits experienced typhoid fever in stateside camps, and 7 percent died. Volunteers with no military training and little discipline suffered more than regular army soldiers because they failed to practice appropriate hygienic measures. Once a soldier became ill, there was no treatment. The best-known medical text of the day advised that the medical "profession was long in learning that typhoid fever is not a disease to be treated with medicines." Instead, the experts advised a special diet of barley-gruel and antiseptics including "carbolic acid and iodine." Even if these treatments had been effective, typhoid fever was often misdiagnosed. Walter Reed, the famous army doctor, and his colleagues examined typhoid fever in every unit mobilized for the Spanish-American War. He and his team found that army physicians diagnosed only 50 percent of the typhoid fever cases they later identified. The twenty thousand figure represents Reed and his teams' estimate and not an actual number based on medical records; the toll may have been greater. Inadvertently, this report documented another disease that had long-term chronic implications: malaria. According to a contemporary (1924) medical specialist, individuals "who have malaria attacks and who do not undergo sufficient treatments to destroy the infection frequently have subsequent attacks . . . and these constitute malaria relapses." Given the limited availability of medical treatment for Spanish War soldiers, many veterans of these conflicts likely endured chronic relapses due to poor health care. In addition to the typhoid fever and malaria, Spanish War soldiers who served at home and overseas encountered a number of diseases that, left untreated, led to chronic illnesses, including leprosy, cholera, tuberculosis, and yellow fever. Complicating their postwar life, Spanish War Veterans had few medical records documenting their service-related disease exposure. As a result, these men applied for non-service-related pensions.[6]

Because many volunteers ended their war in US training camps, these men required an organization such as the USWV to lobby the government for benefits; their service at home, rather than overseas, precluded membership in the VFW. In 1912, the USWV commander in chief testified before a congressional subcommittee on pensions. He highlighted conditions at Chickamauga, Tennessee, training camp, where about half the men in his unit had suffered from typhoid fever, and, of the five men in his hospital tent, only he had survived. Afterward, he tried to return to school, but "the effect of the maladies contracted during the war put me back again and again into bed." Meanwhile, "those who had stayed behind had completed their courses." Although the school made allowances for those who had joined the military, he complained, "I lost that whole period, that formative educational period . . . and the other fellows who had stayed home had the best of me." The men and women who stayed home failed to understand that in this war, Tennessee training camps were more deadly than Cuban battlefields. That same year, a San Francisco newspaper headline documented a "Spanish War Veteran [who] suffers from Leprosy." He had a wife and four children. The paper assured its readers that the local congressional representative would introduce a special pension bill for this man. He needed legislation because the leprosy had appeared years after the individual's exposure.[7]

After enduring so much, Spanish War veterans rejected the idea that their service deserved such ignominy. Instead, USWV members asserted that, as the last fully volunteer US Army, they deserved special recognition. In 1920, the commander in chief of the USWV boasted, "We as an organization possess something that no other organization in the world has ever or ever will possess, and that is [that] the man who is privileged to wear the bronze emblem of our organization wears the emblem of the only organization composed exclusively of volunteers." The USWV commander rejected the idea that Spanish War veterans should be made to feel embarrassed because of their limited time in uniform. Noting the harsh conditions under which they served, he implored the assembled body, "Be not ashamed of your service, no matter whether it was rendered in the fever-stricken camps of America, in the trenches of Cuba, in the swamps of the Philippines or aboard ship. 'You did your duty, and you did it voluntarily.'"[8] From this perspective, Spanish War veterans weren't forgettable; they were exceptional.

Nevertheless, other veteran cohorts, including former World War I soldiers, minimized Spanish War vets' sacrifices. In 1921, comrade M. P. LaFleur, an American Legion representative, visited the national USWV meeting held in Minneapolis. LaFleur exclaimed that he "was surprised this morning to find a convention of this size. . . . I had not considered that your organizations was such a strong one." He changed his mind when he realized that "some of you have been in the late war [WWI], and possibly some belong to the Grand Army of the Republic." Only an association with these other wars made it "strong." Despite his barely veiled disdain, LaFleur understood the value of the USWV to its members. "I do know that your organization and the work that you do is a great help and the only salvation for your members," he said, acknowledging that a subset of men who needed help belonged to the USWV because other veterans' organizations refused to admit these men. Compared to those of most visitors to veterans' meetings, LaFleur's remarks were unusual: veterans usually competed with one another to heap praise on their host. Veterans of other wars visiting the USWV seemed less effusive.[9]

This disdain appeared to be mutual. Later, at the same meeting, USWV officials proposed a resolution that directly challenged the valor of World War I men: "Inasmuch as many of the World War men were drafted and are now drawing compensation in large amounts on the strength of disability that occurred in the line of duty, that Congress be petitioned to make provision whereby all veterans of the Spanish-American War now suffering with any disability can enter the [government] hospitals for treatment on an equal footing" with World War I veterans. Some members tried to remove the comment "drafted" but failed, and the measure passed as written.[10]

Oregonians in the USWV may have been responding to these poor relations when they appointed an official liaison to the American Legion in 1925, who, in turn, selected a liaison for their group. The American Legion wielded much more power, and the USWV needed their group's political influence. The mediator from the USWV hoped that the American Legion might help them address their marginalized status: "We haven't acquired in the past the things we should have. We don't have the standing in regard to pensions that some of the other veterans have." In his reply, the American Legion liaison, Wilbur Henderson, thanked the USWV for their assistance in obtaining a veterans' hospital for the area—so far, a very typical speech asserting veterans' need to work together in their common interests.[11]

Henderson's next set of remarks must have stunned his audience. He explained that he spoke as an individual and not as a representative of the American Legion, and proceeded to eviscerate these men. "You as an organization have been remiss in your duty to your comrades of '98," he scolded the older men. "The pension benefit of the Spanish American War Veteran was less than those of the Civil War or the World War." Did Spanish War vets believe that "the discrimination was due to lack of appreciation from the Government for your services?" Henderson did not wait for a reply, answering his own question with cynicism and no little bitterness: "If you did[,] you were fooling yourself and closing your eyes to the real answer to this apparent discrimination. . . . Officials are not moved to act by any such motives. . . . There is one force they appreciate[;] . . . every bit of beneficial legislation for ex-servicemen since the beginning of time has been the result of political force." In Henderson's mind, power came from electing veterans to office. Spanish War veterans failed because their only comrade-president, Theodore Roosevelt, rose to this position by accident. As a result, he professed "no sympathy for the fact that the pension benefits are not as satisfactory[,] as you have slept on your rights and neglected your opportunities. You are reaping the benefits of your inactivity." There were no thanks to the speaker, no more remarks, and the transcript continues at a new section. Ironically, World War I veterans would later encounter similar attitudes following World War II, as a new generation of veterans replaced them in the American pantheon.[12]

While an astonishing slap in the face, the speaker was correct. Less than a decade later, newly elected president Franklin D. Roosevelt proposed making veterans the bill payer for his New Deal programs that increased the budget deficit. When Roosevelt assumed office in 1933, he faced a national crisis—the Great Depression. In response, Roosevelt increased spending on relief measures to address this crisis that, in his mind, required offsetting budget cuts. To be fair, veterans' payments represented one-quarter of the federal budget. Just as significant, Roosevelt rejected their claim to any special consideration. In his message to Congress vetoing an early payout of the World War I bonus in 1935, Roosevelt cited a veteran who "came through in fine shape as most of them did . . . ; he is today 38 years old and in full possession of his faculties and health." FDR vetoed the bonus because he believed that this "able-bodied citizen should be accorded no treatment different from that accorded to other citizens who did not wear a uniform during the World War." While Congress overturned Roosevelt's veto of veterans' payments in 1935, Congress, prompted by the urgency of the economic crisis in 1933, passed the Economy Act cutting veterans benefits. This bill passed in days; veterans groups failed to mobilize quickly enough to block its passage.[13]

The impetus for this act appears to have been the lobbying efforts of the US Chamber of Commerce and the National Economy League. Both organizations had been working with the Hoover administration to slash benefits. In February 1932, the Chamber of Congress formed a select committee that recommended cutting part of the over one billion dollars spent on veterans and their families because these payments were the "most important factor in the government cost problem," representing "about twenty-four percent of all federal expenditures for" fiscal year 1931. The report acknowledged that those "disabled in the defense of the country" should receive full benefits; their target was those who "incurred no disability in the line of duty" or, in pension terms, those who received payments for non-service-connected disabilities.[14]

The Chamber of Commerce did not support FDR, but he (or his administration) agreed with these views. Almost immediately on his inauguration, Roosevelt proposed the Economy Act, which drastically cut benefits for veterans and their families. It was not only the amount of the cut that was shocking—it was its scope. The act reduced benefits for Civil War and World War I veterans, Spanish-American and Philippine-American War veterans, Boxer Rebellion and peacetime veterans, and their widows and orphans by four hundred million dollars, or almost eight billion in 2019 dollars. It cut pensions; it barred admission into soldiers' homes and veterans' hospitals. Virtually all of the veterans that served during and after the Civil War were affected. Unlike the soldiers' bonus controversy, in which veterans demanded an early bonus payout, the Economy Act drastically reduced already authorized payments.[15]

The administrator of Veterans Affairs, Brigadier General Frank T. Hines, provided Congress with a summary of the estimated cuts in benefits. He did so in part because the chairman of the US Senate Committee on Finance, Pat Harrison (D-MS), admitted that he had not read the bill. According to the table provided by Hines, pensions would be reduced for Spanish War veterans by ninety-five million dollars because the government could disallow payments it did not consider service-related. No other measure cited a specific war (except for the two million dollars saved eliminating payments to Civil War and Indian War widows who remarried). Officials characterized the other measures as "eliminat[ing] disability claims" or "eliminating furnishing of clothing at veterans' facilities." Hines's table suggested that the benefit reductions specifically targeted Spanish War veterans, which no doubt was more acceptable given their marginalized status.[16]

While many veterans lost some benefits, the Economy Act of 1933 affected Spanish War veterans more than any other group because these men had fewer documented, service-related disabilities. In the past, because of poor record keeping, the government accepted pension applications from Spanish War veterans under the rubric of non-service-connected disabilities because they knew that proving service-connected disabilities for their chronic illnesses was impossible. The 1933 law gave the president and, by extension, his appointees the authority to decide if a service or non-service disability proved legitimate and implicitly rejected the special status that had allowed Spanish War veterans to receive pensions. The law went one step further and disallowed non-service-connected pensions unless the person qualified as totally disabled. Officials were given vast latitude over who received benefits and how much they were given, an extraordinary extension of executive branch power in an arena where Congress had jealously guarded its prerogative.[17]

Confidential Senate hearings held on this legislation demonstrated that senators understood that they left non-service-related, disabled Spanish War veterans at the mercy of the bureaucracy. There were two hearings on this law, on March 10 and March 11, 1933. These hearings had nothing to do with carefully examining this bill; in both hearings, senators admitted that they had not even read the proposal. It is not surprising that the officials deemed the Senate hearing confidential; the attitudes toward veterans and their representatives evinced in these hearings likely made a poor impression in their home states. Because the committee chair had not read the bill, the director of the budget summarized each section for the committee. When he did so, he described the reductions that affected Spanish War veterans as "so-called non-service connected cases." Congressmen Clifton A. Woodrum (D-VA), who supported the bill, echoed the director's disdain when he asked questions about "so-called disability allowance. That is, the non-service connected cases." After the director of the Veterans Administration, General Hines, explained the changes in non-service-connected disabilities, senator Alben W. Barkley (D-KY) articulated his understanding of the bill: "Nearly all the Spanish War veterans would go off the pension roll." General Hines did not deny this possibility but explained that the president controlled the ultimate outcome. Since FDR delegated these decisions to the VA, however, it was more likely at General Hines's discretion.[18]

If there is a "smoking gun" in these hearings, it may be found in the typed transcript of an unpublished executive session hearing on March 11, 1933. Representatives of veterans' organizations, including the USWV, testified at this hearing, but senators allowed them a limited amount of time to make their statements. Most of their comments were two to three typed pages, so the limit must have been about five minutes. Veteran witnesses largely disagreed with aspects of the bill and rejected drastic cuts with such limited study. According to the VFW witness, the cognizant House committee reported this bill after three minutes of consideration. In his limited time, the USWV witness reiterated his members' problems with demonstrating service-connected disabilities: "The Surgeon General's reports will show you that there are no records. It was physically impossible for us to prove service connection."[19]

Senator Thomas P. Gore (D-OK) appeared particularly hostile to Spanish War veterans and grilled their witness, Rice W. Means, a former senator from Colorado, about Spanish War veterans' service: "Senator Means, do you remember how many men were killed in the Spanish-American War?" Means immediately reminded the senator that the Spanish War included the Philippines War and the Boxer Rebellion. Gore interrupted his reply and asked, "No, I mean in Cuba." Means had no answer. Senator Bennett Clark entered the discussion by reminding Gore that "the man that died in camp is just as dead as if he were killed in action." But Gore refused to be dissuaded: "I have heard the statement that 305 were killed and some thousands wounded."

After a confusing exchange in which Gore seemed unable to tell the difference between old-age pensions and non-service-connected disabilities, Means lost his temper: "Let me say this to you about the Spanish War: there were over 5,000 dead. In the Philippines alone we had over 688 engagements in which there were casualties." Validating Spanish War veterans' continued need for pension relief, Means explained there was "a greater percentage of sickness during that conflict than any war you ever had." Gore finally concluded by telling Means, "You are talking about one thing and I about another" and then continued his rant against pensions. At the end of this exchange, Gore revealed the origin of his hostility. He had been "assailed in 1914 in my race for reelection because I was not for" an expansion to Civil War pensions. With these remarks, the committee chair called the meeting to an end. The bill passed both houses of Congress and was enacted on March 20, 1933.[20]

By July 1933, almost 500,000 veterans lost their benefits, including 74,000 Spanish War veterans. The 124,000 Spanish War veterans still on the rolls had their payments reduced; veterans over the age of sixty-two had their pension cut in half, and those over seventy-five by 75 percent; both groups received fifteen dollars unless they were totally disabled, and then they received thirty dollars. While the target seems to have been Spanish War veterans, other veterans suffered. In what must have been a surprise to many, 387,000 World War I veterans lost their benefits. Tellingly, the headline of the article announcing these cuts made no mention of Spanish War veterans, referring only to the 387,000 World War I–era "ex-servicemen" affected by the legislation. In fact, the Associated Press article seemed pleased with these measures because the "the pension rolls" were "lightened."[21]

Ironically, it was the individual stories of the effect of these cuts—namely, veterans' suicides—that outraged Americans and prompted Congress to reexamine its decision. Immediately after the bill passed, Andrew J. Bess, described as a "Spanish War veteran," put a bullet in his head because of "failing health and worry over possible loss of [his] pension." The *Herald Press* (Saint Joseph, MI) reported on its front page that Spanish-American war veteran Joseph Schwab had placed a tube in his mouth attached to a stove's gas burners. According to the report, Schwab had been "despondent because of a year's unemployment and the reduction of his pension." The subheadline invoked the poignancy of Schwab's last action: "Last Seen Sunday at Cemetery Decorating

Graves of His Comrades." Police discovered Schwab's body on Memorial Day 1933. Thomas E. Smith, "a seventy-year-old Spanish War veteran," hung himself in Flagstaff, Arizona, because of his reduced pension. Newspapers across the nation reported that a veteran murdered a doctor at the National Soldiers Home in Dayton. James D. Shadbolt, a "disgruntled Spanish-American War veteran, who was cut off pension and disability rolls," killed the doctor after he was told he could no longer receive care at this facility. Newspaper syndicates reported Smith's death and Shadbolt's crime, suggesting that Americans across the country understood the Economy Act's effect on veterans.[22]

World War I veterans also ended their lives because of these reductions. The Associated Press reported that "a few hours after he received notice of the discontinuance of his adjusted service compensation . . . a disabled World War veteran, Steven Rider . . . slashed his throat. His widow and one child survive." Rider had given up his federal job, assuming he would receive this payment. In Wyoming, shell-shocked veteran Frank Maurin drank poison after he discovered that he had lost his disability payment. One former captain left an open letter to FDR criticizing his attitude toward veteran's compensation before he gassed himself. Another veteran failed to kill himself when an American Legion official "knocked a bottle of acid from his hand." He had left a note to FDR "declaring that he was taking his own life as 'the most forcible manner of calling [the] attention of yourself and the nation to the injustices being done to wounded veterans.'" By June 1933, Massachusetts-based American Legion officials attributed at least a dozen suicides in their state to this law.[23]

Almost immediately, Congress turned against the measure, partly because of these suicides. Responding to individual constituent's pleas, and organized opposition from veterans' groups, Congress decided to mitigate the impact of the law. In June 1933, Congress established independent review boards for veterans to challenge their reductions and limited disabled veterans' cuts to 25 percent. By 1934, another measure to reauthorize these boards passed both houses and overturned most of the Economy Act's economies. While Roosevelt vetoed this bill, Congress overrode his veto. It was not the influence of the USWV; instead, it was the VFW and its allies that successfully opposed this measure. The plight of Spanish War veterans, particularly those who never served overseas, made little impact on the American public. Only the inclusion of veterans of other foreign wars, particularly those of

World War I, mitigated the worst effects on the first generation of modern American veterans.[24]

As a result of this wholesale attack on veterans' benefits, antipathy dissipated between the cohorts of veterans. Veterans' groups understood that they needed a united front to protect their rights. The first indicator of this new solidarity was that the tenor of the comments of visitors to each other's meetings improved. The commander of the Disabled American Veterans of the World War visited the 1933 USWV national meeting and "pledge[d] to you this year, my comrades, the undying loyalty of the Disabled Veterans of the World War. We feel your problem is our problem. The day has now arrived when every man who has honorably worn the uniform of the United States—I care not what war it might have been—shall stand shoulder to shoulder and fight a common foe." The department commander of the California American Legion urged USWV members to "plead with the American public and to plead with the veterans themselves the case of all veterans, irrespective of the time they may have served." With an unusual amount of honesty, he admitted that this was not always the case: "The sooner we learn to eliminate all from our caucuses in State and National Legislative bodies the little private fights of our own, and thereby partially cut the throat of another group of comrades, the sooner we are going to regain that which our disabled men and our older men rightfully deserve." The lesson of the fight against the Economy Act seemed clear: if veterans wanted to regain in peace what they had lost in war—employment opportunities and their physical and mental well-being—they needed cross-generational unity. This belief in the political power of intergenerational veteranhood eventually prompted the American Legion, born in World War I, to welcome World War II veterans into their organization.[25]

As the twentieth century passed, the ranks of American veterans grew, as did their suffering. New generations of veterans always have some unmentionable, unspeakable, untreatable disease after war—untreated typhoid fever, undiagnosed PTSD, unrecognized Gulf War syndrome, untraceable Agent Orange. Two of my colleagues have lost their fathers to Agent Orange–related cancers—men who died in the service of their nation decades after their war's end. Another friend lost a husband to Agent Orange exposure and a son to lingering congenital disabilities from the herbicide. The veterans of the twenty-first century forever wars will age in a nation with fewer and fewer veterans for political support as twentieth-century veterans pass into memory. Who will stand with them when someone proposes the Economy Act of 2033?

NOTES

1. For more on the Spanish-American War see, G. J. A. O'Toole, *The Spanish War: An American Epic, 1898* (New York: Norton, 1984) and David F. Trask, *The War with Spain in 1898* (Lincoln: University of Nebraska, 1996). For more on the Philippine-American War, see Brian McAllister Linn, *The Philippine War, 1899–1902* (Lawrence: University Press of Kansas, 2000) and David Silbey, *A War for Frontier and Empire: The Philippine American War, 1899–1902* (New York: Hill and Wang, 2007).

2. US Department of Defense, Defense Casualty Analysis System, "Principal Wars in Which the United States Participated: U.S. Military Personnel Serving and Casualties, 1775–1991," accessed January 26, 2020, https://dcas.dmdc.osd.mil/dcas/pages /report_principal_wars.xhtml. The tables on this site capture Spanish-American War casualties and not those of the Philippine-American War (1899–1902). For the figures for the Philippine-American War, see Allan R. Millet, Peter Maslowski, and William B. Feis, *For the Common Defense: A Military History of the United States, 1607 to 2012* (New York: Free Press, 2012), 681.

3. Barbara A. Gannon, "'They Call Themselves Veterans': Civil War and Spanish War Veterans and the Complexities of Veteranhood," *Journal of the Civil War Era* 5, no. 4 (Dec. 2015): 528–50; Rodney G. Minott, *Peerless Patriots: Organized Veterans and the Spirit of Americanism* (Washington, DC: Public Affairs Press, 1962), 17; Stephen R. Ortiz, "The New Deal for Veterans: The Economy Act, the Veterans of Foreign Wars and the Origins of New Deal Dissent," *Journal of Military History* 70, no. 2 (Apr. 2006): 415–38. See also Stephen R. Ortiz, *Beyond the Bonus March and GI Bill: How Veteran Politics Shaped the New Deal Era* (New York: New York University Press, 2012). Tellingly, several lengthy encyclopedias focused on the Spanish Wars failed to include articles about veterans' organization. See Jerry Keenan, *Encyclopedia of the Spanish American and Philippine American Wars* (Santa Barbara, CA: ABC-Clio, 2001); and Spencer C. Tucker, James Arnold, and Roberta Wiener, ed., *The Encyclopedia of the Spanish-American and Philippine-American Wars: A Political, Social, and Military History*, 3 vols. (Santa Barbara, CA: ABC-Clio, 2009).

4. United Spanish War Veterans (USWV), *Seventh National Encampment*, 1910, 7, 98. (The USWV met yearly at national "encampments" or meetings. Various printers published transcripts for these proceedings, which I will cite according to their number and year. Many are easily available online.) Operations in the Philippines began with the declaration of war in 1898 and officially ended on July 4, 1902. After this date, American troops continued to fight a low-level insurgency on the islands. Linn, *Philippine War,* ix, 11. Theodore Roosevelt's books on his experience played a key role in focusing the cultural memory of the Spanish-American War on the charge at San Juan Heights in Cuba. See Theodore Roosevelt, *The Rough Riders* (1899; repr., Mineola, NY: Dover, 2006).

5. Mr. George Huddleston, "Spanish War Pensions," *Congressional Record* 77 (June 10, 1933), 5667, text from *Congressional Record Permanent Digital Collection*; William D.

Barnard, "George Huddleston, Sr. and the Political Tradition in Birmingham," *Alabama Review* 36 (October 1983): 243–58.

6.   Vincent J. Cirillo, "Fever and Reform: The Typhoid Epidemic in the Spanish-American War," *Journal of the History of Medicine and Allied Sciences* 55, no. 4 (Oct. 2000): 363–97; William Osier, *The Principles and Practice of Medicine. Designed for the Use of Practitioners and Students of Medicine,* 3rd ed. (Edinburgh: Young J. Pentland, 1892), 33–36; Walter Reed, Victor C. Vaughn, and Edward O. Shakespeare, *Report on the Origin and Spread of Typhoid Fever in US Military Camps during the Spanish War of 1898* (Washington, DC: Government Printing Office, 1904), 674; Charles C. Bass, "Malaria," in *Practice of Medicine,* ed. Frederick Tice, MD (Hagerstown, MD: W. F. Prior, 1924), 611–12. Margaret Humphreys (MD/PhD, Duke University) confirmed my understanding of the sources, explaining that there was no real treatment for typhoid fever until World War II. For a contemporary admission of no treatment, see D. D. Stewart, MD, *Treatment of Typhoid Fever* (Detroit, MI: George S. Davis, 1893), 49. For more on the abject failure of military medicine in the Spanish Wars, see Vincent J. Cirillo, *Bullets and Bacilli: The Spanish American War and Military Medicine* (New Brunswick, NJ: Rutgers University Press, 1999); Bobby A. Wintermute, *Public Health and the US Military: A History of the Army Medical Department, 1818–1917* (New York: Routledge, 2011).

7.   USWV, *Twenty-Second National Encampment,* 1920, 75, and *Twelfth National Encampment,* 1915, 64; "Spanish War Veteran Suffers from Leprosy," *San Francisco Call,* March 7, 1912. For more on leprosy and Spanish-American War veterans see, US Army Medical Department, Office of Medical History, *Preventive Medicine in World War II: Communicable Diseases,* vol. 15, accessed January 25, 2020, http://history. amedd.army.mil/booksdocs/wwii/communicablediseasesV5/chapter4.htm.

8.   United Spanish War Veterans (USWV), *Proceedings of the Twenty-Third National Encampment,* 1921, (n.p.), 11, 23.

9.   USWV, *Twenty-Third National Encampment,* 1921, 90.

10. Ibid., 104.

11. USWV and Ladies Auxiliary, Department of Oregon, *Seventeenth Annual Encampment* (Salem, OR; State Printing Department), 18.

12. Ibid., 19.

13. Ortiz, "New Deal for Veterans"; Franklin D. Roosevelt, "Message to Congress: Vetoing the Soldiers Bonus Bill," May 22, 1935, https://www.columbia.edu/cu/lweb/digital /collections/rbml/lehman/pdfs/0784/ldpd_leh_0784_0097.pdf; Eric Rauchway, *The Money Makers: How Roosevelt and Keynes Ended the Depression, Defeated Fascism, and Secured a Prosperous Peace* (New York: Basic Books, 2015), 59.

14. Ortiz, "New Deal for Veterans," 419; "Advocates Change in Pension Policy," *New York Times,* February 1, 1932.

15. "President Urges Cuts: Ask Courageous Action of New Pension System Directed by Him," *New York Times,* March 11, 1933; "Measure Little Altered," *New York Times,* March 16, 1933; US Federal Reserve, Federal Reserve Bank of Minneapolis, "Inflation Calculator: What's a Dollar Worth?" accessed January 9, 2020, https://www.minneapolis fed.org/about-us/monetary-policy/inflation-calculator.

16. US Senate, Committee on Finance, Executive Session—Confidential, "To Maintain the Credit of the United States Government," March 10, 1933 (Washington, DC: Government Printing Office, 1933), 8, 40.

17. US House of Representatives, 73rd Cong., 1st Sess., *Congressional Record*, March 16, 1933, 549.

18. Ortiz, "New Deal for Veterans," 424; Paul Dickson and Thomas B. Allen, *The Bonus Army: An American Epic* (New York: Walker, 2006), 208–9, 220; US Senate, Committee of Finance, "Executive Session," 7, 8, 10; James E. Sargent, "Clifton A. Woodrum of Virginia: A Southern Progressive in Congress, 1923–1945," *Virginia Magazine of History and Biography* 89, no. 3 (July 1981): 353. The House Committee with jurisdiction over this measure reported the bill favorably on that Saturday, March 11, only days after it had been introduced, suggesting that there had been little consideration of the bill in the other legislative chamber. US House of Representatives, 73rd Cong., 1st Sess., Committee on Economy, "Maintenance of Credit of the United States, Report to Accompany H. R. 2820," *Congressional Record*, March 11, 1933.

19. US Senate, Committee of Finance, "Executive Session," March 11, 1933, 52.

20. Ibid., 56–57; US Congress, Statutes at Law, "An Act to Maintain the Credit of the United States Government," 1st Sess., March 17, 20, 1933, 8–16. Resistance to war veterans' pensions is not just a phenomenon of the 1930s. Scholars have placed veterans benefits into a larger context of government spending and social policy since the mid-nineteenth century. See Theda Skocpol, *Protecting Soldiers and Mother: Political Origins of Social Policy in the United States* (Cambridge, MA: Belknap Press of Harvard University Press, 1992); Beth Linker, *War's Waste: Rehabilitation in World War I America* (Chicago, IL: University of Chicago Press, 2011).

21. "Approximately 387,000 Ex-Service-Men Receiving Disability Allowances Not Connected Directly with Duty Are Dropped," *San Francisco Examiner*, July 1, 1933.

22. "Veteran Takes Life," *Orlando Sentinel*, March 15, 1933; "Benton Harbor Man's Body Is Found in Home," *Herald-Press* (Saint Joseph, MI), May 31, 1933; *Petaluma Argus-Courier* (Petaluna, CA), June 12, 1933; "Vet's Hospital Physician Slain," *Morning Call* (Allentown, PA) July 1, 1933. The *San Francisco Examiner* reported this slaying right under its report on the effect of the Economy Act cuts.

23. "Helena Veteran Commits Suicide," *Billings (MT) Gazette*, June 22, 1933; "Casper Veteran Commits Suicide," *Billings (MT) Gazette*, May 4, 1933; "Veterans Suicides, Leaving Letter to President Roosevelt," *Greenwood (MI) Commonwealth*, June 30, 1933; "Veteran, Frustrated in Suicide Starts Fast," *Nashville Banner*, June 2, 1933; "Claims Cuts Drove 12 Vets to Suicide," *Boston Globe*, June 6, 1933.

24. Ortiz, "New Deal for Veterans," 435–36. For more on the efforts to repeal these cuts, see Jessica Adler, *Burdens of War: Creating the United States Veterans Health System* (Baltimore, MD: Johns Hopkins University Press, 2017).

25. USWV, *Thirty-Fifth National Encampment*, 1933, 75–76.

New Frontiers for the New Negro

Revisiting the World War Memoir and the Postwar Veteran Politics of Jesse L. Fraser in the 1920s

ROBERT F. JEFFERSON

In 1919, World War I, embittered postwar experiences of African Americans, and inchoate ideas about the New Negro movement converged in the life histories of many known and lesser-known Black ex-GIs. Among the thousands of Black vets in the latter category was Jesse Lee Fraser, a former serviceman from Charleston, South Carolina. In many ways, Fraser's story mirrors much that we associate with the African American experience in the early twentieth century. Having grown up in a working-class household, he dropped out of school and moved to Chicago, Illinois, where he managed to land meaningful work as a coal teamster. After being drafted into the army, he was assigned to the 365th Infantry Regiment on October 29, 1917. While in Brest and in the Meuse–Argonne, Fraser, like so many other African American soldiers, observed not only examples of institutionalized racism, horrendous work conditions, and rank brutality but also burgeoning transnational consciousness and universal democracy for the first time in his life.

But what sets Fraser apart from his contemporaries (and deserves the attention of scholars) was the degree to which the transplanted Chicagoan used memoir and first-person narrative to highlight both the trajectory of his marginality as a Black World War veteran and his evolving political consciousness. With remarkable candor, *The World War Memoirs of Jesse L. Fraser* conveys the immediacy of this veteran's wartime and postwar experiences with a distinctiveness one can find only in writing of this genre.[1] Although Fraser was not singled out for heroic duty in France, his copious ruminations about his service with Company C of the 365th Infantry Regiment—as he and other members of the unit tried to establish their reputation amid the fire and gas of the Champagne sector—and about his interactions with French troops and civilians provides a useful backdrop for understanding the myriad foundations of the New Negro among African Americans during the war.[2] Not only that, but Fraser's wartime reflections unwittingly reveal apocryphal visions of postwar Black life that were articulated through experience and memory.

This chapter explores how the social process of memoir writing captured and rearticulated the experience, immediacy, and memory of war in the context of one of the most consequential conscious-raising moments in African American history—the New Negro movement.[3] Using Fraser's life as a case study, the piece traces the social, political, and ideological mapping of the emerging New Negro consciousness and identity among Black World War veterans in the 1920s. More than tropes, the wartime first-person testimonies rendered by returning Black veterans such as Jesse Fraser provided flesh-and-bone identity and ideas about the transformative nature of self that were forever etched in Claude McKay's celebrated poem of July 1919 "If We Must Die."[4]

The fusion of autobiography and first-person narrative in the life story of Jesse Fraser and his developing understandings of the New Negro emerged sometime between the conclusion of World War I and the American return to peacetime status. After the guns of war fell silent with the armistice on November 11, 1918, the French Army paid tribute to the gallantry of the 365th Infantry Regiment in the October and November offensive by awarding the Croix de Guerre to each man in the unit. Composed of soldiers hailing from all across the United States, the 365th was a part of the famed 92nd Infantry "Buffalo Soldier" Division of the US Army. Serving with the American Expeditionary Forces, the unit saw extensive combat in France during the war, engaging enemy forces during the Meuse–Argonne offensive and earning grudging recognition from their German adversaries and French allies throughout the region. In the days following the Bois Fréhaut action, the survivors of the fighting received an emotional farewell from town officials and the people in the French villages as they marched towards Le Mans, before moving on to Brest, where they eventually found themselves on board the SS *Olympic* bound for home.

Fighting and living in war-torn Europe had reshaped the consciousness of Jesse Fraser and his fellow soldiers in profound ways. After staying in Pont-à-Mousson for a month, Fraser passed through La Pas, where he described with humor the welcome the 365th Infantry received from villagers: "They came over to our lines and we shook hands with them. They felt our hair and rubbed our skin to see if the black would come off. They also looked in our mouths to see if our tongues are black. All-in-all, we were happy to see our new friends."[5]

The glimmers of racial democracy that Fraser and other Black soldiers experienced while interacting with the French people were often punctuated with bouts of racism within their own ranks. While undergoing delousing and reequipping in Brest, the men anxiously awaited embarkation for home. But they quickly discovered that as one battle had ended, a much larger war had just begun. Almost immediately on their arrival in the port city, general John J. Pershing's Expeditionary headquarters issued a secret directive, advising French commanders on how to handle the growing numbers of Black soldiers in their midst. On January 5, 1918, the general headquarters of the 92nd Division issued orders to military police to arrest Black soldiers who conversed with French women or who were seen entering or exiting the homes of French inhabitants. During their time in Brest, Harry Haywood and his comrades in the 370th Infantry Regiment were informed by senior officers of the extent to which the American staff headquarters planned to enforce racial segregation abroad: "The American command of General Pershing was not satisfied just to separate us; they tried to extend the long arm of Jim Crow to the French." And to compound the indignities that Black soldiers endured, physical and verbal assaults by racist white MPs were commonplace, and LeMans and Brest were declared off-limits to Black troops.[6]

In late January 1919, Fraser and the men with the 365th Infantry were well on their way, unsure of what they would find on returning home. Of course, they sought the comforts of family, friends, and the familiar surroundings of hearth, community, and neighborhood. But they also knew that despite president Woodrow Wilson's call to make the world "safe for democracy," the harsh realities of American racism, poverty, and class oppression still existed. Such thoughts dotted the writings of Jesse Fraser at the time. Fraser notes, "Thank God for his protection through all the dangers I have been in[,] and I offer the Almighty my sincere thanks for allowing me to go through it all without a scratch. We are all happy and glad the war is over. But while we have assurance that we're all going home, we don't know what home has to offer us." Other soldiers also expressed such misgivings about the voyage home and reentering American society. For example, William A. Hewlett, a soldier returning home from France, expressed his concerns in the following manner: "There is an air of liberty; equality; and fraternity here which does not blow in the black man's face—in liberty loving, democratic America. If that is the White American idea of true democracy—then why did we fight Germany; why did we frown on her autocracy? Was it to make democracy safe for white people in America with the black race left out; if we have fought to make safe democracy for the white races, we will soon fight to make it safe for ourselves and our posterity." Around the same time, a columnist for the Black news weekly the *New York Age* posed a similar question: "Today['] s newspapers tell stories of an entire Negro regiment, cited for gallantry in the great offensive in Champagne in September and October 1918 and being granted the Croix de Guerre as a result of the French army order. While France is thus honoring American soldiers shall America deny to their fellows at home right of employment in industry and supervision?" W. E. B. Du Bois, who perhaps more than any other contemporary observer recognized the growing maturity and race consciousness that Europe had fostered among Black World War GIs, theorized about the transformation in their thinking: "A new, radical Negro spirit has been born in France, which leaves us old radicals far behind. Thousands of young black men have offered their lives for the Lilies of France and they return ready to offer them again for the Sun-flowers of Afro-America."[7]

In many ways, Du Bois's observations accurately describe the returning experiences of Fraser and most returning Black veterans. Between March and June 1919, more than 380,000 African Americans were discharged from the armed forces. But for the thousands of soldiers who were released from military duty and who began to make the trek to points south, the transition to civilian life proved to be quite difficult, and they were hardly prepared for the backlash that followed their return from overseas service. Many white Americans perceived Black veterans' reappearance in Southern cities and towns while wearing the nation's uniform as a dire threat to the entire Jim Crow apparatus. And, all too often, recently returned Black vets found themselves becoming moving targets of physical harassment and possible death throughout the region. Perhaps their first nights home were similar to that of Lee Conley Bradley—namely, a brusque reintroduction to the unwritten rules, customs, and etiquette of Jim Crow followed up with a harsh reminder of what they might encounter anywhere else in American society. Better known by his stage name "Big Bill Broonzy," Conley served as a member in the American Expeditionary Force and was assigned to the Services of Supply during the war. Like many Black GIs, he experienced both military racism and semblances of racial democracy in France, forever altering his consciousness of the world around him. But no sooner had Broonzy reappeared in his home state of Arkansas than Jim Crow made its reemergence with tremendous force. As Broonzy remembered years later, "I got off the train. . . . I met a white fellow that I was knowin' before I went to the Army. So he told me 'Listen boy, now you been in the Army? I told him 'Yeah.' He says, 'How'd you like it?' I said, 'It's O.K.' He says, 'Well . . . you ain't in the Army now.' 'And those clothes you got there . . . take 'em home and get out of 'em and get you some overalls. Because there's no nigger gonna walk around here with no Uncle Sam's uniform on up and down the streets." Needless to say, Broonzy promptly decided to permanently bid farewell to the Deep South forever, eventually ending up in Chicago, where he became a legendary blues musician.[8]

For Jesse Fraser, Chicago proved to be in many respects as vexing as Broonzy's Arkansas. After arriving at Camp Grant in March 1919, he received his final pay voucher and was mustered out of the army, whereupon he boarded an outbound train heading for the Windy City. On his first day home, the ex-sergeant and other Chicago soldiers with the 365th marched from the Coliseum to the Union Depot in the breezy late winter weather to the hearty cheers of an increasingly swelling crowd. Afterward, flanked by a squad of mounted policemen, they passed a reviewing stand before finally being reintroduced to a long line of relatives, sweethearts, and well-wishers who waited anxiously for them at the end of the parade procession. For Fraser, his first night home carried bittersweet tidings. He was met by his longtime girlfriend Ollie Bell, who promptly bestowed the veteran with heart-felt hugs and kisses before the couple retired to her parent's home located outside of the city. Fraser eventually married Bell with the hope of making a seamless transition to civilian life. But he, like so many ex-GIs, faced an uphill battle. After moving to a small bungalow located just below Chicago's South Side,

Fraser spent the rest of the spring and well into July working feverishly to land employment—but to no avail.[9]

As he renewed old acquaintances, the battle-tested veteran quickly discovered that new challenges awaited him. As thousands of African American ex-GIs were discharged and made their reentry into the industrial workforce, they encountered racial backlash from organized labor and native-born white workers at almost every turn. Despite the stockyard organizing efforts made by local affiliates, the American Federation of Labor barred Black workers from their ranks. Throughout the spring of 1919, violence against Black newcomers in the city rose sharply. Often, the most extreme instances of interracial violence hinged on the virulent strife between labor and management in the city. When the Corn Products Company attempted to hire six hundred workers during a labor dispute in Argo, Illinois, that spring, white strikers, led by the International Union of United Brewers, Flour, Cereal, and Soft Drink Workers, beat them without compunction. On other occasions, countless Black war veterans saw a ray of hope when they gained union membership during labor disputes, only to have their aspirations dashed when they were discharged once the strikes ended. Indeed, the economic situation that African American city dwellers faced was such that by the late summer of 1919, Black unemployment had reached nearly ten thousand. But despite being barred from the skilled trades, the newly wedded World War veteran elected to use his veteran's preference to take the civil service examination and was eventually hired as a substitute clerk in the Chicago main post office in June of that year.[10]

Although Fraser did not realize it at the time, the city post office provided him with not only countless episodes of white supremacy, craft conservatism, and racial discrimination but also stark examples of racial consciousness, Black veteran solidarity, and grassroots civil rights militancy. As recent historiography suggests, Chicago's New Negro movement took on many appearances, held many personas, and stood on many corners. Indeed, historian Chad Williams effectively reminds us that the "activism and racial militancy of black veterans fundamentally shaped the historical development and ideological diversity of the New Negro movement." But the presence of and the role played by African American veterans in New Negro conscious-raising decade of the 1920s will remain tentative if we don't consider the principal sites at which their identities were forged. This was no less true for those who pushed through the double doors of the mammoth twelve-story building that overlooked the corner of Van Buren and Canal Streets at the time. For Black veterans such as Jesse Lee Fraser, the post office represented such a place. To enter the post office of the 1920s was to enter a world composed largely of men, a male-dominated world that was steeped in class antagonisms that were mitigated by centuries of racism. Within moments of their arrival, post office clerks and mail sorters quickly realized that they had entered into a world that closely resembled the military one they thought they had left behind. More likely than not, they donned blue uniforms and badges that made them indistinguishable from each other and marked them as "government issued" entities of the US Postal Service.[11]

When Fraser first reported to work at the Chicago post office that summer, he was given an assignment in the processing section of the building. In that position, he saw many of his fellow GIs, with whom he was able to reminisce about old acquaintances and compare impressions about working conditions in the building. But quite often their conversations revolved around important ideas in New Negro ideology: a heightened sense of civic consciousness, manliness, and a shared expectation of citizenship rights. Between January and June, New Negro ideas animated the thoughts and actions of many of Chicago's Black veterans. In February, some Black World War ex-GIs affiliated with the Bureau for Returning Soldiers and Sailors had begun to translate their personal frustration into collective action by marching from the South Side to the city center. Formed by the US Employment Service prior to World War I, the bureau worked diligently to match employers with returning ex-GIs in need of work after the war. In the Windy City, Black bureau personnel and their allies organized former soldiers and worked tirelessly to create job opportunities for African American veterans by dispatching thousands of circular letters to Chicago employers, urging them to find places for the recently discharged men. In the months following demobilization, A. L. Jackson, director of the Wabash Avenue YMCA, met with Chicago industrialists, imploring them to hire Black veterans. "These boys are all good Americans," Jackson asserted. "There are no slackers, no hyphens among them." Likewise, other Black leaders in the city, such as the Reverend Archibald Carey, an African Methodist Episcopal Church pastor, the editors of the *Chicago Defender* and the *Broad Ax,* and Ida Wells-Barnett, noted journalist, and chair and spokeswoman for the local Protective Association, initiated efforts to provide subsistence for ex-soldiers. Even though Fraser himself never joined these efforts, he was clearly impressed by the self-organizing efforts of these political figures and support organizations, and was deeply enamored of these moments of Black military-related militancy. Among the pages of his memoirs, he reflected at the time, "I never knew that there is such a struggle going on at home. I realize that I'm a part of the hopes, dreams, and fears and maybe something good is happening here after all."[12]

Between January and June, a combination of events captivated the attention of Fraser and his World War contemporaries in ways that resulted in a convergence of their past lives and present circumstances, greatly facilitating the crystallization of New Negro sentiment and veteran organization. Between June and August, Chicago was a cockpit of racial strife. For the unabated influx of Black newcomers, the squalid, overcrowded living conditions on the South Side and the resultant housing shortages increased racial tensions in adjacent districts. In addition, realtors and white property owners' associations redoubled their efforts to banish Blacks from their neighborhoods, often resorting to legal strategies that ranged from zoning legislation, restrictive covenants, and redlining to extralegal measures such as intimidation and violence. Throughout the summer of 1919, twenty-six Black homes in predominately white neighborhoods were bombed.

For Fraser and his fellow postal employees, the situation worsened by the day. In his memoirs, he records the overriding concerns he and other clerks and letter carriers expressed regarding the possibility that the racial strife would interrupt their ability to do their jobs. Indeed, the situation was such that in the weeks preceding the riot, Fraser noted that he and his fellow postal employees expressed little faith in the police and had discussed arming themselves that summer. "If we need to protect our ourselves, we shall do it without a thought," Fraser exclaimed. So, when racial tensions boiled over in the city in late July, he and his comrades stood poised for action.[13]

On July 27, a racial confrontation between white and Black swimmers on a South Side Chicago beach and the uprising that ensued afterward produced one of the most gut-wrenching and tension-filled moments for Fraser and dozens of Black male postal workers. During a five-day period, African American letter carriers and chauffeurs were kicked and beaten by white mobs as they attempted to carry mail throughout the Black community. Violence spread from the beach in the North and West Sides and the Loop as roaming mobs gathered, shooting, beating, and stabbing Black victims, and white gunmen in automobiles and Black sharpshooters exchanged fire with menacing force. On July 29, racial antagonism took on a particular demeaning tone for Fraser and his fellow rank-and-file employees. On July 29, the war veteran had just arrived to begin his day of work at the post office only to learn that he had been reassigned to a substation that was located miles away from his place of residence. As if this weren't enough, the rebuff was followed up by the stinging rejoinder of racism. After watching white clerks enter the building without incident, Fraser attempted to pass through its double doors. However, department officials thwarted his progress, telling him, "We can't afford any trouble from your kind here, Bub." The encounter was seared in his memory in profound ways. After recounting the incident to his nephew fifteen years later, he remarked, "What a loathsome moment. I thought that I left this sort of thing in Europe. But it now looked to me like a new war was to be fought by Negroes on another front." Fraser's response is revealing, for the incident affronted not only his identity as a war veteran but also his New Negro sensibilities as a Black man.[14]

In many ways, Fraser's embittered interpretation of the events surrounding the riot stemmed directly from his heightened sense of citizenship and manhood. But it is also important to remember that his frame of reference was enveloped in the collective feelings that Black ex-GIs expressed as marginalized veterans returning home from the War to End All Wars. In the weeks following the violence, Stanley B. Norvell, a former war veteran and Chicago native, wrote a letter to newspaper editor Victor Lawson, explaining how a new race consciousness had arisen from the ashes of the global conflict: "The five hundred thousand Negroes who were sent overseas to serve their country were brought into contacts that widened both their perceptions and their perspectives, broadened them, gave them new angles on life, on government, and on what both mean. They are now new men and world men, if you please." For other war veterans and postal workers, the Chicago violence provided a different frame of reference. Harry Haywood, another former World War veteran and noted Black revolutionary, witnessed the horrific violence, but he was also enamored of the idea of Black self-defense and organization during the fighting itself. Haywood returned from Europe around the same time as Fraser and had entered the Chicago post office on the heels of the racial strife in the Windy City. As the race rioting unfolded, he recalled on several occasions, groups of whites had driven a truck at breakneck speed up South State Street, in the heart of the Black ghetto, with six or seven men in the back firing indiscriminately at the people on the sidewalks. At the same time, he praised the careful preparations carried out by a group of Black ex-GIs to protect their neighborhoods. As he later noted in his autobiography, veterans took positions at Thirty-Fifth and State, waiting to ambush white rioters. The bloodshed that Norvell, Haywood, and other war veterans witnessed was quelled only after six regiments of state militiamen were dispatched into the riot district. The harvest of disorder carried deadly results. When the episodes of racial hatred ended, twenty-three Black and fifteen white Chicago city dwellers were left dead and more than five hundred injured.[15]

Between 1920 and 1929, Black World War veterans such as Jessie Fraser launched a new campaign to restore the reputation of the 365th Infantry in historical memory. Prior to the unit's deployment in 1918, *Chicago Defender* publisher Robert Abbott presented the men of the unit with a special flag and colors. But once the troops and their unit flag arrived in Brest, they were confronted with white racism and slanderous rumors at the hands of the US Armed Forces at almost every turn. The men with the unit had never forgotten the indignity of being the only regiment committed to battle against the German enemy in Vosges and in the Forest of Argonne without its unit flag. The painful memories of unit neglect and nonrecognition festered into humiliation and outrage when the ex-soldiers returned home in late February 1919. As they trudged through the streets of New York in the harsh winter weather, they were made painfully aware of the fact that theirs was the only unit that participated in the victory parade without its unit colors. In his memoir, Fraser remembered that as he and other soldiers passed the reviewing stand, he heard shouting from the crowd, "Where is that regimental flag?" "I winced because it was so embarrassing," he wrote. Native Chicagoans found the action so egregious that they flooded the offices of their state politicians, US representative Martin Madden and senator J. Hamilton Lewis, with petitions and letters, demanding that an investigation be launched into the treatment of World War African American soldiers, particularly those in the 365th.

For their part, 365th veterans, along with other prominent Chicago residents, formed a group committed to drawing public attention to the flag issue and to championing the memory of the unit. In an editorial to the Associated Press on February 1919, they stated, "And now we ask you AMERICANS, white and black alike: what are you going to do about it? In the name of our wounded brave who spilled their blood in its defense, we demand a congressional investigation of the loss of our flag and colors and a vindication of our honor." Among the group's prominent members were former soldiers, sergeants Moses Boone and Kingdon Brown, and officers William J. Powell and C. H. Payne, to name a few. The battle to salvage the unit flag raged on throughout the 1930s and 1940s. Over the decades, the group continued to make its case for rehabilitating the unit's reputation, holding memorials and parading through the streets of Chicago while raising money for the diminishing ranks of their fellow veterans. And among those who actively participated in these gatherings was Jesse Fraser.[16]

Fraser did not live long enough to see the return of the unit flag. He died on May 16, 1964. In many ways, his life and death were typical. On a damp, rainy Friday morning, friends, family, former 365th Infantry veterans, and postal employees crowded into the sanctuary of a chapel at Vincennes Avenue and onto its steps to pay their respects. One by one, they told stories of the sense of family and community that Fraser brought to the Chicago post office and to the city's South Side. They paid tribute to his memory as each attendee formed a procession to file by his open casket. As they viewed his remains, one can only imagine what was on their minds. Of course, they talked about the old times, revisited previous hardships, and renewed old ties. But little did they realize that the strands of memory that contained the intrinsic meaning of his life, the collective and personal battles he experienced and witnessed during the war, and his lessons of peace and death were now in the possession of his most cherished legacy. In his eulogy, Reuben Fraser, his nephew, unwittingly gave voice to his uncle's written legacy penned years ago by stating, "For my uncle, he always talked about how we had a future waiting for us if only we reached for it and proceeded to build it for ourselves. And in many ways, I lived out his words by serving in the army, getting married, and having a family of my own. No man could have given me more, folks." In Reuben Fraser's benedictory words, we find the New Negro sentiments as reflected in his uncle's life and postwar politics. Thus, in Jesse Fraser's correspondence and postwar politics, we are given a vivid window onto the World War battles he fought, the peacetime world that he sought to build, and the feelings of marginality that he wished to bring to the attention of successive generations.[17]

NOTES

Many sincere thanks to John Kinder, Jason Higgins, and the anonymous reviewers for their valuable comments, questions, and feedback. This piece is dedicated to Queen Esther Williams Douglas, whose life and example inspired me to realize the impossible and to discover and appreciate history where it might be found.

1. As of 2021, *The World War Memoirs of Jesse L. Fraser* remains unpublished. The author has a copy in his possession.

2. Especially see recent works by Jeffrey T. Sammons and John H. Morrow, Jr., *Harlem's Rattlers and the Great War: The Undaunted 369th Regiment and the African American Quest for Equality* (Lawrence: University Press of Kansas, 2014); Chad L. Williams, *Torchbearers of Democracy: African American Soldiers in the World War I Era* (Chapel Hill: University of North Carolina Press, 2010); Adrian Lentz-Smith, *Freedom Struggles: African Americans and World War I* (Cambridge, MA: Harvard University Press, 2009); Richard Slotkin, *Lost Battalions: The Great War and the Crisis of American Nationality* (New York: Henry Holt, 2005).

3. Several valuable pieces come readily to mind. See Chad L. Williams, "Vanguards of the New Negro: African American Veterans and Post–World War I Racial Militancy," *Journal of African American History* 92, no. 3 (2007): 347–70; Steven A. Reich, "Soldiers of Democracy: Black Texans and the Fight for Citizenship, 1917–1921," *Journal of American History* 82, no. 4 (March 1996): 1478–504. For a foundational work on the subject, see W. E. B. Du Bois, "Returning Soldiers," *Crisis* 18, May 1919, 13.

4. Claude McKay, "If We Must Die," *Liberator* 2, no. 7 (July 1919): 21.

5. *World War Memoirs of Jesse L. Fraser*.

6. This account of anti-Black racism in the immediate aftermath of the war draws on the following sources: "Secret Information Concerning Black American Troops," *Crisis* 17 (May 1919): 16–17; *Blount, Reminiscences of Samuel E. Blount, Corporal and Company Clerk, Company D, 367th Infantry, 92nd Division, U.S. National Army, in the Service from October 30th, 1917 to March 10th, 1919*, Schomburg Center for Research in Black Culture (New York: New York Public Library, 1934); Harry Haywood, *A Black Communist in the Freedom Struggle: The Life of Harry Haywood*, ed. Gwendolyn Midlo Hall (Minneapolis: University of Minnesota Press, 2012), 48.

7. "Negro Troops Win War Cross; French Croix de Guerre Awarded to the Entire 365th Regiment," *Columbian Evening Missourian*, January 2, 1919, 1; *World War Memoirs of Jesse L. Fraser*; "Ask Explanation of Railroad Order to Limit Employment," *New York Age*, December 7, 1918, 1; letter, William A. Hewlett to W. E. B. Du Bois, August 26, 1919, in *The Correspondence of W. E. B. Du Bois*, vol. 1, *Selections, 1877–1934*, ed. Herbert Aptheker (Amherst: University of Massachusetts Press, 1973), 233; W. E. B. DuBois,

"An Essay Toward a History of the Black Man in the Great War," in *The Seventh Son: The Thought and Writings of W. E. B. DuBois*, ed. Julius Lester (New York: Random House, 1971), 2:130–31.

8. Bill Broonzy, *Big Bill Blues: William Broonzy's Story as Told to Tannick Bruynoghe* (New York: Oak, 1964); Kevin D. Greene, *The Invention and Reinvention of Big Bill Broonzy* (Chapel Hill: University of North Carolina Press, 2018), 25–29.

9. Jesse Lee Fraser Career 201 File, Final Payment Roll, National Personnel Records Center, Saint Louis, Missouri; *World War Memoirs of Jesse Fraser*; "365th Infantry Coming Home Monday, Planned Fete," *Chicago Broad Ax*, March 8, 1919; "How Chicago Welcomed Her "Buffalo Boys" of the 365th Infantry," *Chicago Daily Tribune*, March 11, 1919, 3.

10. Paul C. Young, "Race, Class, and Radicalism in Chicago, 1914–1936," (PhD diss., University of Iowa, 2001); James R. Barrett, *Work and Community in the Jungle: Chicago's Packinghouse Workers, 1894–1922* (Urbana: University of Illinois Press, 1987), 172–73; William M. Tuttle, "Labor Conflict and Racial Violence: The Black Worker in Chicago, 1894–1919," *Labor History* 10, no. 3 (Summer 1969): 408–32.

11. See Davarian L. Baldwin, *Chicago's New Negroes: Modernity, the Great Migration, and Black Urban Life* (Chapel Hill: University of North Carolina Press, 2007); Williams, "Vanguards of the New Negro." For a stimulating historical discussion of African American employment in the post office and the issues connected to politics, civil rights, and labor, see Philip F. Rubio, "There's Always Work at the Post Office: African Americans Fight for Jobs, Justice, and Equality at the United States Post Office, 1940–1971," PhD diss, Duke University, 2006.

12. Jonathan S. Coit, "'Our Changed Attitude': Armed Defense and the New Negro in the 1919 Chicago Race Riot," *Journal of the Gilded Age and Progressive Era* 11, no. 2 (April 2012): 225–56; "Chicago to Rout Blues of These Negro Fighters," *Chicago Daily Tribune*, February 26, 1919, 5; William M. Tuttle, Jr., *Race Riot: Chicago in the Red Summer of 1919* (1970; repr., Urbana: University of Illinois Press, 1996); Ida B. Wells, *Crusade for Justice: The Autobiography of Ida B. Wells*, ed. Alfreda M. Duster (Chicago, IL: University of Chicago Press, 1970); *World War Memoirs of Jesse L. Fraser*.

13. William M. Tuttle, Jr., "Contested Neighborhoods and Racial Violence: Prelude to the Chicago Riot of 1919," *Journal of Negro History* 55, no. 4 (October 1970): 266–88; "U.S. Troops May Be Put around Post Office," *Chicago Tribune*, July 31, 1919; *World War Memoirs of Jesse L. Fraser*.

14. Tuttle, Jr., *Race Riot*; "A Night of Flaming Terror in Chicago; Twenty Dead in Chicago Riots," *Centralia (IL) Sentinel*, July 29, 1919, 1; Reuben E. Fraser, Jr., interview by Robert F. Jefferson, May 5, 1993, Apple Valley, Minnesota, recording in possession of the author.

15. Stanley B. Norvell and William M. Tuttle, Jr., "Views of a Negro during 'The Red Summer' of 1919," *Journal of Negro History* 51, no. 3 (July 1966): 216; Harry Haywood, *Black Bolshevik: Autobiography of an Afro-American Communist* (Chicago, IL: Liberator Press, 1978), 82; "Order Is Forced in Riot Zones about Chicago," *Centralia (IL) Sentinel*, August 4, 1919, 1. As scholars have noted, the violence of the summer of 1919 marked a pivotal moment in the relationship between Black Chicago residents and the police department. The racial violence also unveiled a psychic revolution in Black political consciousness. For a thoughtful reading of the significance of the Chicago uprising, see Simon Balto, *Occupied Territory: Policing Black Chicago from Red Summer to Black Power* (Chapel Hill: University of North Carolina Press, 2019).

16. "365th Infantry Lands at New York: White Officers Junk Regimental Flag; Soldiers Ashamed," *Chicago Defender*, March 1, 1919, 1; *World War Memoirs of Jesse L. Fraser*; "Expose 'Junker' of 365th Infantry Flag," *Chicago Defender*, August 9, 1919, 11; William J. Powell, "Soldier Gives Facts on Slur to 365th Flag," *Chicago Defender*, July 14, 1923, 2; "The Flag That Never Came Back," *Chicago Defender*, May 3, 1930, 7; "The Flag That Never Returned," *Chicago Defender*, November 23, 1935, 4; Jesse Lee Fraser clipping file, in the possession of the author.

17. "Obituary, Jesse Fraser," *Chicago Tribune*, May 20, 1964, 45; funeral service program, Jesse L. Fraser and Reuben E. Fraser, Jr., clipping files, in the possession of the author; Fraser interview.

The Unseen Army

Neuropsychiatry, Patient Agency, and World War I

EVAN P. SULLIVAN

In a statement to the US House of Representatives Commerce Committee in January 1921, Dr. Thomas Salmon argued that the inadequate state of psychiatric care for shell-shocked veterans necessitated more funds for new facilities. The Rockefeller Foundation adviser on mental diseases claimed that due to the lack of appropriations and facilities, veterans were committed to nonveteran government institutions for criminals and drug addicts, or were sent to asylums, almshouses, and sanitariums in poor condition, which generated profit for those who ran the institutions. "Many a mother has told me," Salmon explained, "that she would rather see her son under a cross in France than to have him adjudged to a State institution." As a result of the abysmal prospects of care, some men were "lurking at home, afraid to come forward, getting worse all the time." This "unseen army," Salmon argued, would not volunteer for treatment until the government provided adequate institutions for their care.[1]

Insufficient treatment of the "unseen" army of neuropsychiatric patients— American survivors of the World War I—predated Salmon's appeal to con-solidate the many agencies responsible for dispensing veteran care. Indeed, it took place within a military medical culture that stigmatized all forms of mental illness or distress.[2] Under this and other pressures, hospitals tried to avoid an asylum atmosphere. US Medical Corps officers who worked in psy-chiatry even tried to change their titles, as many found that "neuropsychiatry" was too closely associated with individuals diagnosed as insane, "and [that] as soon as a patient is admitted to a hospital for treatment he is immediately classed by the outsider as a 'nut.'" Through the early 1920s, psychiatrists were sometimes singled out from other doctors and known simply as "N.P.s", or "nut pickers." "This spirit," wrote one officer, "pervades all of the activities of the Veterans' Bureau along these lines with the result that there is continual internecine joking among the patients of the hospital which oftimes [*sic*] creates marked and unnecessary depression among those whose cases are frequently designated as 'N.P.'"[3]

The stigma of neuropsychiatric wounds pervaded wartime culture, even in publications that fostered generous attitudes toward veterans' care. A cartoon in the *Red Cross Magazine* from 1919, for example, depicts a disabled veteran sitting at his work desk with his crutch next to him against the wall. A man sits before him, presumably a boss or a manager, questioning how well he is getting along, and whether he is better now than before the war. The man responds, "Why! Of course I'm better off than before the war. You see it wasn't my bean that was amputated."[4] Cultural and social tropes such as this positioned neurological wounds as inferior to physical ones. Moreover, they reinforced ideas about the inadequate masculinity of those who continued to suffer the long-term effects of wartime trauma. If a man could not carry on after the war, the thinking went, he could not fulfill the productive and familial duties expected of him by society and the state.[5] Not surprisingly, American service members diagnosed with neuropsychiatric conditions faced disproportionately inadequate care in hospital ships, US Army General Hospitals, and civilian hospitals as compared with other disabled veterans, such as amputees or blinded veterans.

This chapter examines the lived experiences of American neuropsychiatric patients in the aftermath of World War I. Frequently faced with stigma and condescension, such patients engaged in complex and often frustrating negotiations about power over their own bodies, voicing their concerns through written protests and physical violence. Because neuropsychiatric wounds were socially uncomfortable and difficult to treat with conventional medicine, physicians tended to overlook veterans' attempts to assert control over their narratives. The overwhelming societal focus on other war wounds, as well as the "unseen army's" lack of political capital within the curative rehabilitation establishment, further served to marginalize neuropsychiatric vets' efforts at autonomy. But fragments of their lives remain in the archives and in the surveys of psychiatrists who recorded their postwar fates. These fragments show a continuous struggle to be heard within a system that singularly defined what it meant to be cured. Indeed, their experiences reveal the deficiencies of rehabilitation, particularly in a society so willing to ignore the social costs of war's wounds.

SHELL SHOCK REALITIES: 1918–20

The Great War left nearly seventy thousand American soldiers with psychiatric wounds—so many, in fact, that the surgeon general ruled that the term "shell shock" was not a sufficient diagnosis to describe the men left mentally traumatized ("neurotic," "psychoneurotic," "insane") at the war's end. Symptoms included nervous tics, trauma-induced blindness or deafness, anxiety, depression, vomiting, and confusion.[6] Because "curative discourse uniquely framed . . . American medical policy," most patients encountered a medical-policy atmosphere more hospitable than that of Europe.[7] That said, the lasting complexities of psychiatric wounds challenged the usefulness of "curative" treatment, despite guidelines that outlined neurosis as something that could be fixed.[8] In addition, military personnel's lack of understanding often led to mistreatment, as soldier-patients and veterans with neurosis regularly confronted not only hostile ideas about mental health but also prolonged stays in wards.

The poor treatment of neuropsychiatric casualties began long before they returned stateside. Patients of the American Expeditionary Forces endured slow and uncomfortable journeys to their respective hospitals in the United States. Medical officers struggled to segregate patients who had vaguely defined symptoms, and the US Army Medical Department responded with a classification system that singled out "mental cases" and their care requirements in special compartments on transport ships. Passenger lists were divided into two sections, with disturbed or suicidal men requiring constant supervision in one group, and all other cases in another. But medical transport ships did not always follow the classification system, and no amount of planning could erase the contingencies of demobilization or societal stigma to mental illness. Neuropsychiatric patients who arrived at US Army General Hospital No. 1 in New York City, for example, showed signs of neglect, allegedly due to a rush caused by the need to transport other wounded patients. Patients were regularly cared for in uncomfortable parts of the ship, and suffered in close confinement under armed guard. To make matters worse, the rough ocean experience aggravated symptoms of combat trauma and had "a permanent effect" on many of the cases. On one ship, conditions were so bad that a group of twelve officer-patients signed a protest letter about the "unbeliev-able conditions on the MANCHURIA," where they claimed to have faced degrading treatment.[9]

But the ocean transport was not the last stop in patients' multihospital odysseys. Soldiers with neuropsychiatric conditions were repeatedly shuffled from one hospital to another in attempts to adhere to official classification systems, as commanding officers of various hospitals preferred certain classes of patients to others. Such medical efforts at diagnostic specificity mirrored similar currents in civilian medicine around the turn of the century.[10] Some transfers were justified, as with the case of patients at Fort McHenry who were transferred to the army hospital in Dansville, New York, which was better equipped for neuropsychiatry because it had more specialized equipment and personnel.[11] General Hospital No. 1 in New York also transferred patients to Dansville. However, Dansville's administrators sought to control what kinds of neuropsychiatric patients were sent there. While the hospital actively accepted "neurasthenics, shell shock cases and the milder psychosis," it limited or excluded "violent cases" so as not to create an "asylum atmosphere."[12] The hospital at Fort Porter in Buffalo, meanwhile, wanted to swiftly discharge all epileptics to make room for "insane patients."[13] Ironically, the systems meant to streamline care further reinforced neuropsychiatric patients' maltreatment and marginalization within the military medical bureaucracy.

Patients sent to Dansville found respite from their experiences in transit. Eugene Bondurant, the relatively forward-thinking commanding officer there, wrote of his colleagues' general unwillingness to treat psychiatric patients with the same respect as other soldiers. To remedy this culture, he argued they should be treated in wards within general hospitals just as any other sick or wounded man, a practice that could potentially decrease the "stigma of mental disease." Bondurant also opposed the use of bars on windows, seclusion, and bodily restraints. But even the best of circumstances did not make up for a lack of physicians trained in treating war neuroses. Indeed, Bondurant hoped that some of the Dansville hospital personnel would be transferred elsewhere.

For example, he said, the older chief nurse at Dansville was "entirely destitute of experience in psychopathic hospitals . . . and entirely out of sympathy with my non restraint methods." She had little interest in "this class of patients" and "was ordered here under misapprehension of the nature of this hospital."[14]

Not every hospital had as progressive a commanding officer as Dansville. Nor were they prepared for the influx of neurological patients returning from overseas. Plagued by deficient hospital infrastructure, medical officers at Fort Des Moines, for example, sometimes resorted to using "mechanical restraints" on patients. In order to save costs, however, they largely avoided guarding and restraining individual suicidal or runaway patients. Instead, they attempted to install heavy locked doors and barred windows, and built a permanent enclosure surrounded by a nine-foot fence to prevent escape.[15] Thus, while American views on neuropsychiatric trauma were more accepting than those of their European counterparts, realities on the ground made life difficult for soldier-patients hoping to recover from mental injury.

Against this backdrop, neuropsychiatric patients negotiated their hospital existence in several ways. Some reacted specifically to their lack of autonomy. Men at Dansville, for example, wrote frequently to family members and advised them to visit and aid in their discharge. Over time, family members learned from correspondence that the ultimate decision about their release hinged on a certain Captain Patterson, so they focused their efforts on him specifically.[16] In this way, patients used their knowledge of hospital administration to negotiate their own release.

Autonomy worked in other more direct ways as well. For example, David Repp, an epileptic patient at US Army General Hospital No. 30 at Plattsburgh, was given a pass to visit the town. He did not return until two in the morning, and refused to obey orders to turn in his civilian clothing. When the military police were called in to take him to the guardhouse, "he had an Epileptic seizure." The police took his clothing under lock "for an indefinite period," thus confining him to the hospital and to "only such clothing as will permit him to visit the General Mess."[17] In this context, Repp's seizure provided temporary, though involuntary, deflection from the external restrictions of his bodily movement. Perhaps another important point about Repp's treatment is that his behavior—staying out all night—might have prompted administrators to restrict his freedoms, but they used his seizure as the main justification for those restrictions.

Still, recovering patients often paid a high price if their bodies and minds thwarted the control of military caregivers. In some cases, patients with epilepsy, hysteria, or "constitutional psychopathic states" at Plattsburgh were court-martialed, and courts recommended confinement with hard labor, a fairly regular sentence for soldiers more broadly. This happened so frequently that three months after Repp's seizure and confinement, the chief of neuropsychiatry, Aaron Rosanoff, issued a statement arguing that confinement and labor were detrimental to the health of the patients. Instead, Rosanoff recommended that an examination board consisting of at least three psychiatrists look at court-martials before sentencing and adjust punishment according to the patient's health.[18]

"LOCKED US IN A PEN": WRITING RESISTANCE

In addition to attempting to avoid confinement, a number of American patients with neuropsychiatric conditions turned to a different sort of protest: collective writing. Historian Ana Carden-Coyne argues that many narratives of wounds in war are characterized by silence. During World War I, the social and cultural environments of military hospitals "encouraged the suppression of pain." According to Carden-Coyne, soldiers were taught to refrain from voicing their physical and mental suffering in order to maintain masculine dignity.[19] In an atmosphere in which medical staff encouraged stoicism, soldier writing "provided a *counter narrative* to the medical case report, and the staff report, over which they had no control." Writing allowed otherwise marginalized patients to achieve "the affect of resistance."[20]

Two particular examples demonstrate how hospitalized neuropsychiatric patients used their pens to claim a sense of control over their lives. In December 1918, two soldiers who transferred from Fort Porter to Dansville—part of the extensive shuffling of shell-shocked individuals from one hospital to the next—composed a poem called "Nut Ward." The poem explored how it felt to experience trauma in combat, compounded by the insufficient postwar medical care patients received. According to the poem, they went to France to defend the country only to come back shell-shocked: "We shook as with shaking palsy, we jumped at the slightest sound." Having been treated well, "like men," at hospitals in France, they encountered different circumstances once in the United States: "Here they stripped us of our clothing, and locked us in a pen. They sent us to 'Fort Porter', In a class with the insane; Imagine yourself in a 'Nut Ward', Would it not give you pain? . . . For the boys are brace and human, With the heroes battle scars; They fought to keep their freedom, Then are locked behind the bars. We ask you people for whom we fought, While we give you a little light, If you had to live in a 'Nut Ward', Tell us—would you think it right?"[21] The patients penned this poem to appeal to public sympathy, establish their freedom from confinement, and distance themselves from "insane" veterans. Yet it appeared in no newspaper. It was published in no book or journal. It stayed hidden from view.

Eight months later, in August 1919, at the Plattsburgh hospital—a woefully understaffed institution with over one thousand cases—patients claimed they were being treated like "useless junk," underfed, and congested in their rooms.[22] Over two hundred patients wrote to military authorities to protest their treatment and demand to be demobilized. Their joint statement accused the military of holding them against their will "beyond the period of the emergency called for." They also charged that their "further tenure of service is due entirely to the mal-administration of affairs and not to any cause of circumstances." The men argued that they had fulfilled their contract and should be honorably discharged.[23] Much like the Dansville poem, the Plattsburgh statement was silenced and relegated to the archives. Read today, however, it highlights neuropsychiatric patients' attempts to negotiate power and autonomy within the military-medical framework of World War I–era army hospitals.

After the war, some soldiers were sent to psychiatric wards; others were discharged in a rudimentary fashion. In the physical examinations prior to release, most medical officers gave little more than a passing glance at the thousands of men they had to inspect. At Camp Sherman, Ohio, for example, a handful of physicians examined around 1,900 men per day looking for everything from cardiovascular symptoms to signs of tuberculosis. Camp Grant's physicians saved time by examining men in groups of fifteen. At word of command, "they [would] go through certain movements used as tests for nervous and mental defects, for example: Rise! Stand erect! Close eyes! Open eyes! Tongues out!" The examiner marched around, observed, and passed on to the point that "the military element" of medicine "appeared to out-balance the scientific value of demonstration." In camp after camp, reports noted the superficiality of discharge exams, particularly in neuropsychiatric sections. And inspectors labeled most neuropsychiatric exams in camp hospitals as "questionable" or "superficial."[24] Within this context, psychiatric wounds went easily unseen into the postwar years.

ANXIETY NEUROSIS AND VETERAN VOICES IN THE FENTON SURVEY

In 1919, Norman Fenton and the National Committee of Mental Hygiene conducted a follow-up survey of "war neurotics" whom Fenton and other psychiatric staff had treated at Base Hospital 117 in France during the war. In his questionnaires and correspondence with ex-patients, Fenton sought to study the postwar realities of shell shock and to determine how well former patients "readjusted" to civilian life. The initial survey resulted in almost nine hundred replies. Some men who lived near New York City visited Fenton in person at his office. Others met him when he took trips to Boston, Philadelphia, and Washington, DC. Fenton also wrote to the American Red Cross and enlisted their support to find and communicate with former patients.[25] Fenton repeated his study five years later, in 1924, comparing the data to his previous figures.

Like patients' own writing, Fenton's studies shed light on the realities of invisible wounds within the limited framework of curative rehabilitation. More than that, though, they describe a military-medical culture that relied on vague definitions and social stigma when determining patient treatment and expectations. While Fenton found that veterans wounded by "sudden emotional or physical shock" were indeed marginalized in their postwar care, his study also drew attention to a lesser-known but perhaps more numerous category of patients.[26] Grouped under the diagnosis "anxiety neurosis," these men exemplify the experiences of the unseen army, who often struggled daily with their symptoms despite being labeled as cured. Soldiers who suffered from anxiety neuroses showed such varied symptoms as general nervousness, irritability, excitability, depression, headaches, dizziness, and heart palpitations. Other vaguely defined diagnoses, such as "anticipation neurosis" or "effort syndrome," were marked by similar symptoms.[27] Anxious veterans existed within a complex rehabilitative culture governed by an aversion to mental illness and a drive to pressure patients to make good by returning to economic stability.

Although anxiety was one of the largest and overlooked characteristics of the "unseen army," pinpointing anxiety neurosis was a challenge due in part to the ubiquitous nature of the symptoms. After all, plenty of veterans with other physical illnesses dealt with nervous symptoms and depression. Veterans suffering the effects of heart disease proved to be especially susceptible. For example, one veteran, "Mr. P," enlisted in 1917 and saw active service in Europe. He contracted rheumatic fever and experienced a heart murmur. After four years of vocational training, the Veterans' Bureau reduced his compensation. He then labored "under constant strain and anxiety," and expressed to physicians at the US Naval Hospital in Philadelphia symptoms of weakness, palpitations, and dizziness. Another veteran who developed cardiac symptoms overseas felt general nervousness despite no physical evidence of cardiac irregularities. Doctors at that hospital estimated that 30 to 40 percent of heart symptoms had nervous symptoms as well.[28]

The numbers in Fenton's survey reflect the disparity between the large numbers of "anxious" patients and the prevailing belief that "neurosis" is only temporary and thus need not be given due consideration in treatment. According to Fenton's discharge numbers from Base Hospital 117, neurosis accounted for almost 39 percent of his patients, second only to "normal" men.[29] Despite their higher numbers, however, medical personnel did not find it imperative to do further study and address their needs but instead sought to discharge them as "cured." One physician in a *Naval Medical Bulletin* editorial from 1922 charted the categorization system of neuropsychiatric disabilities that physicians used in military hospitals during the war. According to the report, the group of patients with anxiety was extensive, "but for hospitalization" it should be extremely small."[30]

To better understand patients' postwar readjustment challenges, Fenton charted institutional problems of aftercare. One such problem was the inadequate stream of information between the state and the veterans. Many former patients were scattered throughout the country and did not necessarily live close to cities, where agencies for veterans' benefits were located. Several were also discharged without full knowledge of their benefits. Men therefore went to physicians without their benefits and accrued large medical bills. Agencies such as the American Red Cross helped give veterans information about their entitlements but did not fully succeed. In his latter survey in 1924, Fenton found that the newly formed Veterans' Bureau was overburdened, and he helped refer over two hundred men in need of services to the Red Cross, over four hundred to the American Legion, over one hundred to neuropsychiatric clinics, and over a dozen to the Veterans' Bureau directly.[31]

Social stigma added to the challenges of veterans with anxiety neurosis. Fenton explained that medical officers were "generally averse to treating . . . neurotic individuals." Some men were discharged after a brief hospitalization or, if their symptoms showed up years after the war, they were not hospitalized at all. Compensation claims proved difficult for some when the medical boards relied solely on a man's own account of his war experiences rather than any medical documentation from the army. Other men were simply eager to be out of the military. One who had punctured eardrums and a nervous disorder did not receive any compensation. According to Fenton, "He claimed to have been so badly treated in the course of his experience on the transport, and later in America, that he wanted nothing further from the Government than his discharge."[32]

The most important aspect of Fenton's study, however, is what it suggests about how World War I–era rehabilitation defined "cure." Rehabilitation rested on the assumption that economic adjustment meant successful readjustment to society, which ignored the lasting, acute, and often debilitating nervous symptoms that veterans experienced. Much of what Fenton and others considered "success" translated into economic terms, as in holding a steady job. In this regard, Fenton's surveys sent a mixed message. As he argued near the end of his survey from 1919, of all of the patient groups trying to "carry on" after the war, the most successful were those with anxiety neurosis, with over 75 percent succeeding. "Anticipation neurosis" and gas neurosis, both nervous disorders, ranked high as well, with success ratings of 75 and 73 percent, respectively. Among the least successful were those diagnosed with "hysteria," or the more severe forms of psychiatric distress, of which about 50 percent were successfully "carrying on."[33] In other words, veterans who left the war with invisible but permanent psychiatric wounds faced a precarious economic existence.

Despite the relative positivity surrounding these numbers, Fenton's survey paints a picture of widespread suffering and marginalization among neuropsychiatric veterans. As the measure of rehabilitative success was primarily one of economic results, so too was much of Fenton's analysis. Many of his returned questionnaires show that men who worked still became angry, were easily excited, or dealt with nervousness, restlessness, headaches, or dizziness. One man replied that his health was excellent, except that loud noises such as a factory whistle or a passing train "will set my nerves aquiver. . . . [I] am trying to gradually get control of myself and I think I will."[34]

Even those who had to readjust to more intrusive wounds continued to suffer. Although these men were sometimes assigned to lighter work in their former places of employment, many were sensitive about their reduced status. Over time, some men were able to work fairly well but were often unhappy because of neurotic troubles such as tremors, tics, speech difficulties, weakness, jumpiness, the inability to concentrate, or other "spells."[35] In the 1924 survey, Fenton concluded that while four-fifths of the respondents were "carrying on" in civilian life, many were either still very nervous or were not being adequately cared for by the Veterans' Bureau.[36]

While most complaints focused on veterans' social and familial lives, employment was a particularly difficult problem. One man fainted in a railroad station when a train puffed suddenly. Another claimed, "I make mistakes I ordinarily would not make." A respondent who returned to work as a chauffeur found that when he got into a crowded part of a city with many other vehicles, he "loses his head," and had had two accidents. Another, after returning to work as a printer, had frequent dizzy spells that interfered with the quality of his product. The last spell led to a serious injury to one of his fingers. Men reported many injuries and serious accidents from their nervous conditions. "I used to work a pneumatic drill," one respondent writes, "but I cannot any longer; the constancy of action is so much like a machine-gun. I tried my best but could not stick it out. I had a semibreakdown."[37]

Fenton's survey is a remarkable source for a variety of reasons. The men's testimonies were shared as part of surveys intended primarily for education, rather than disability claims intended to justify higher benefits, lending them an air of legitimacy. Respondents had little to gain by sharing stories of suffering in the context of the survey, but they shared them nonetheless. And while not necessarily forms of protest, Fenton's surveys give voice to the many men of the unseen army who, despite the curative employment-based standards of rehabilitation, continued to suffer from anxious neurological symptoms.

Most prominently among those Fenton diagnosed with "anxiety neurosis," shell-shocked veterans of Base Hospital 117 relayed their troubles with family, social interactions, and work. Many who were classified as "cured" were far from it and continued living with significant symptoms from their war wounds in a society seeking to move forward from the war years.

Critically examining postwar contexts surrounding mental illness and war wounds highlights important trends. For veterans of World War I, rehabilitation as a mechanism of state postwar readjustment dictated veteran healing and coping potentials. The assumption of a "cure" rested almost exclusively on masking visible physical trauma and becoming a productive economic unit in society. As a result, many who had "rehabilitated" on paper, including numerous men with neuropsychiatric injuries, still had permanent symptoms that interfered with their lives.

At the same time, the culture that surrounded mental illness, shown in the treatment patterns of neuropsychiatric wards in US Army General Hospitals and then carried into the hospitals of the Veterans' Bureau, positioned mental wounds in a negative light. Many accounts relied primarily on medical texts. Patient protests from US Army hospitals and survey responses to Norman Fenton bring the veterans' voices to the forefront of the discussion. They highlight that in the immediate aftermath of war, veterans were not passive victims of military medicine and the rehabilitation ethos. They voiced their discontent with being treated like "useless junk." But the negative stigma surrounding neurological wounds persisted, and veterans returned to postwar life "readjusted" but still struggling. They often had few outlets for support, as the curative discourse of rehabilitation precipitated the outsourcing of hospitals to state and private oversight.

In contrast to American veterans of the World War I, soldiers of the twenty-first century with posttraumatic distress were not entirely "unseen." As historian David Kieran so convincingly argues, psychological injuries have become a defining feature of America's wars in Iraq and Afghanistan. Yet, army researchers in some cases continue to view psychological distress as temporary, and veterans continue to suffer in silence despite the cultural salience of such wounds and their ability to provoke critical questions about what state-sponsored violence does to human bodies.[38] While the context of war trauma between 1918 and 2018 may be different, the social and medical marginalization of such veterans remains unnervingly constant. Understanding the limits of postwar psychiatric treatment in America's first truly modern war could very well help us to better understand the limits of treatment in the wars of the twenty-first century and to question our own standards of care. Perhaps, then, we may enable veterans of Iraq and Afghanistan to avoid going unseen, and for American society to think more critically about the costs of war.

NOTES

Thank you to *Nursing Clio* editors Drs. Sarah Handley-Cousins and Cassia Roth for their generous comments and suggestions on an abbreviated version of this chapter exploring the war years. Evan P. Sullivan, "Neuro-Psychiatry and Patient Protest in First World War American Hospitals," *Nursing Clio,* November 7, 2018, https://nursingclio.org/2018/11/07/neuro-psychiatry-and-patient-protest-in-first-world-war-american-hospitals/.

1. "Declares Soldier Insane Neglected: Dr. Salmon Urges Hospitals Be Built for Them: Rogers and Sherburne Heard on Consolidation of Bureaus," *Boston Globe,* January 8, 1921, 3.
2. See Gerald Grob, *The Mad among Us: A History of the Care of America's Mentally Ill* (New York: The Free Press, 1994).
3. G. Franklin Shiels to the Surgeon General, "Change in Nomenclature," July 14, 1925, RG 112, series NM 29, box 429, folder 730: Neuro-Psychiatry, US National Archives, College Park, Maryland (hereafter UNA).
4. Samuel Hopkins Adams, "You and Our Maimed Soldiers," *Red Cross Magazine* 14, no. 6 (1919): 65.
5. For a discussion of rehabilitation in American society during World War I, see Beth Linker, *War's Waste: Rehabilitation in World War I America* (Chicago, IL: University of Chicago Press, 2011).
6. Fiona Reid, "War Psychiatry and Shell Shock," *1914–1918 International Encyclopedia of the First World War,* December 11, 2019, https://encyclopedia.1914-1918-online.net/article/war_psychiatry_and_shell_shock.
7. Annessa C. Stagner, "Defining the Soldier's Wounds: U.S. Shell Shock in International Perspective" (PhD diss., University of California, Irvine, 2014), 1–3.
8. Stagner, "Defining the Soldier's Wounds," 10.
9. "Memorandum: Care of Insane Soldiers during Their Ocean Transportation from the A.E.F.," June 1919, RG 112, series NM 29, box 429, folder 730: Neuro-Psychiatry, UNA.
10. Allan V. Horwitz and Gerald N. Grob, "Mental Health and Mental Health Policy: The Troubled History of Psychiatry's Quest for Specificity," *Journal of Health Politics, Policy and Law* 41, no. 4 (August 2016): 522–23.
11. The Commanding Officer of General Hospital No. 2 to the Surgeon General, "Transfer of Patients Suffering from Psychoneuroses," April 18, 1918, RG 112, series 31-J (K), box 232, folder 702.3: General Hospital #13 (K), UNA.
12. Major Eugene D. Bondurant, "Memorandum for Major Williams," September 25, 1918, RG 112, series NM 29, box 231, folder 323.7–5: Gen. Hospital #13, UNA.

13.   The Surgeon General to the Commanding Officer, "Administration of Psychiatric Department," November 27, 1918, RG 112, series UD 8, box 876, folder: Disposition of Insane, UNA.

14.   Eugene Bondurant to Pearce Bailey, January 15, 1919, RG 112, series 31-J (K), box 231, folder 323.7–5: Gen. Hospital #13 (K), UNA.

15.   E. Stanley Abbot to the C.O. of U.S. General Hospital No. 26, "Means to Prevent Escape of Insane Patients," July 12, 1918, and July 16, 1918, RG 112, series UD 8, box 16, folder 710: Neurologist & Psychiatrist (INSANE), UNA.

16.   Donald L. Ross, Chief of Neuro-psychiatric Service to the C.O. of U.S. General Hospital No. 13, "In Regard to the Difficulties of Visitors to Patients Consulting Officers Other Than Those Directly Responsible for the Care of the Patient Visited," February 17, 1919, RG 112, series UD 8, box 969, folder: 705.1: Admission of Patients, UNA.

17.   D. S. Spellman to the Commanding Officer, "Discipline of Patients," November 16, 1918, RG 112, series UD 8, box 1109, folder 250: Morals & Conduct, UNA.

18.   Chief of Neuro-Psychiatric Service at U.S. General Hospital No. 30 to the Commanding Officer, February 24, 1919, RG 112, series UD 8, box 1109, folder 250: Morals & Conduct, UNA.

19.   Ana Carden-Coyne, "Men in Pain: Silence, Stories and Soldiers' Bodies," in *Bodies in Conflict: Corporeality, Materiality and Transformation*, ed. Paul Cornish and Nicholas J. Saunders (New York: Routledge, 2014), 54–57.

20.   Carden-Coyne, "Men in Pain," 58–63.

21.   "Fort Porter" December 19, 1918, RG 112, series 31 (K), box 231, folder: 333—U.S.A. Gen. Hosp. #13, Dansville, NY (K), UNA.

22.   General Hospital 30 to the Surgeon General, July 2, 1919, RG 112, series 31-J (K), box 276, folder 210.711–1: General Hospital #30, UNA; "Transfers of Our Wounded Soldiers" RG 112, series UD 8, box 1107, folder: 201.23: Complaints, UNA.

23.   Men of U.S. General Hospital No. 30 to the Secretary of War, RG 112, series UD 8, box 1107, folder: 201.23: Complaints, UNA.

24.   W. S. Shields, "Quotations from Reports of Sanitary Inspections Made during the World War, Vol. II," 90–92, RG 112, Series NM20–29A, Box 417, UNA.

25.   Norman Fenton, *Shell Shock and Its Aftermath* (St. Louis: C. V. Mosby, 1926), 73–84.

26.   Ibid, 100.

27.   Ibid., 90–100.

28.   D. Ferguson, "Some Clinical Types of Functional Heart Disease," *United States Naval Medical Bulletin* 28, no. 1 (Jan. 1930): 95.

29.   Fenton, *Shell Shock and Its Aftermath*, 97.

30.   "Editorial on Neuro-psychiatric Disabilities," *United States Naval Medical Bulletin* 17, no. 2 (Aug. 1922): 282–84.

31.   Fenton, *Shell Shock and Its Aftermath*, 82–123.

32.   Ibid., 79–82.

33.   Ibid., 104.

34.   Ibid., 91.

35.   Ibid., 91.

36.   Ibid., 123.

37.   Ibid., 92.

38.   David Kieran, *Signature Wounds: The Untold Story of the Military's Mental Health Crisis* (New York: New York University Press, 2019), 1–9.

II.

MARGINALIZED VETERANS IN THE AMERICAN CENTURY

Unsuitable for Service

Bedwetting Veterans since World War II

JOHN M. KINDER

It is thus not lack of cleanliness or health that causes abjection but what disturbs identity, system, order. What does not respect borders, positions, rules. The in-between, the ambiguous, the composite.
—Julia Kristeva, *Powers of Horror: An Essay on Abjection*

There is a tendency to consider anything in human behavior that is unusual, not well known, or not well understood, as neurotic, psychopathic, immature, perverse, or the expression of some other sort of psychological disturbance.
—Alfred C. Kinsey, *Sexual Behavior in the Human Female*

About four-fifths of the way through his memoir *Helmet for My Pillow* (1957), former marine and World War II veteran Robert Leckie offers a remarkable admission. Describing the dreary weather conditions on the South Pacific island of New Britain, Leckie recalls, "I would be wet not only from the rain—for sometimes it stopped, and at other times it did not fall so fast that a jungle hammock could not repel it—but because of an affliction which had begun the moment I left Australia was now active again. It had begun during the discomforts of Guadalcanal, had disappeared in the civilized living of Melbourne, and had reappeared on Goodenough, New Guinea and now on New Britain. I learned later from doctors to call it enuresis. When asleep, the bladder empties—and that is that."[1]

Leckie was not alone. During World War II, hundreds of thousands of US troops woke to the sight of yellow sheets and the ammoniac tang of fresh urine. If discovered, enuretic GIs could face harsh treatment or administrative discharge. The US Army alone dismissed some 356,000 enlistees for bedwetting, "inaptness," or inadaptability (the three were often conflated).[2] In subsequent decades, the armed forces continued to stigmatize nocturnal enuresis and other forms of urinary incontinence. To this day, veterans discharged for bedwetting—or those who develop enuresis subsequent to military service—remain largely invisible figures, marginalized by both the US military and the ethos of masculine toughness that continues to dominate veteran culture.

Why was the military so concerned about US troops yellowing their sheets? And what happened to enuretic veterans in the years after leaving service?

This chapter seeks to answer such questions by sketching a rough history of enuresis and American veterans since World War II. In the minds of military administrators, enuresis was more than an impediment to military service; it was a sign of mental unfitness and social "unsuitability." Drawing on everything from military textbooks to anonymous Web chats, I attempt to show what happened to victims of antienuresis policies—men and women stigmatized both before and after discharge.

It's a project fraught with complications. After all, the armed forces discharged, at the minimum, tens of thousands of enuretic troops in World War II alone. What's more, few outside of the world of military medicine would have recognized "enuretic veterans" as a distinct population of ex-soldiers. Indeed, any discussion of enuresis among US vets invariably collapses three seemingly distinct groups: men and women discharged not long after enlistment, those who (like Leckie) developed symptoms of enuresis during their active military service, and veterans who experienced enuresis in later age (often in the aftermath of surgery). In this chapter, my use of the term "enuretic veteran" (or "enuretic vet") is meant to describe a constellation of ex-military personnel who struggle with some degree of urinary incontinence. That said, the bulk of my discussion focuses on men who experienced enuresis while still in uniform, either in training camp or in the aftermath of some kind of trauma. As we shall see, these groups faced hostility throughout their military careers, from their time in service to their lives as veterans.

Nevertheless, even an abbreviated account of enuretic vets offers important insights into the sociology of veteran marginalization. No matter the cause, a diagnosis of enuresis might result in a number of outcomes—from immediate dismissal to decades of social isolation and shame. This chapter shows us how ideas about "unsuitability" intersected with notions of gender and bodily control. At a time when men were expected to "bottle up" their emotions and practice rigid self-will, enuresis was considered a sign of immaturity—a yellow stain of unmanly failure. Further, it points to a stigma-laden hierarchy of bodily fluids, in which urine came to be viewed as more unsettling than blood. Out of place, beyond conscious control, "unhygienic," and hinting of deeper pathologies, enuresis threatened military culture's fiction of invulnerability. In the end, I hope that the story of men like Leckie will prompt future scholars to ask tough questions about the logic that turned wetting the bed into a rationale for social precarity.

THE MILITARY STIGMAS OF BEDWETTING

> *The truth is we were kids. It shoulda been called The War of Children.*
> *We had colonels, for crying out loud, who still wet the bed.*
> —Vietnam War veteran quoted in 1979

At first glance, it is difficult to grasp why enuresis (bedwetting) would prove to be such a concern for the wartime military. After all, what did the occasional piss-yellowed blanket matter in a conflict that would see thousands of gallons of blood, sweat, and other noxious fluids spilled on the battlefield? Depending on the circumstances, a World War II–era soldier might spend weeks or more without a shower, his skin caked with dirt, his feet pickled by body odor, fungus, and the peaty smell of rotting socks. Surely, given the war's inevitable punishment of soldiers' bodies, the military would be willing to set aside its official squeamishness about ill-timed urination? Not so.

In fact, since the early twentieth century, the military has pursued a relentless campaign against enuresis, even if it meant sacrificing much-needed manpower and resources in the process. Antibedwetting policies reflected a number of concerns. First, there was the matter of *hygiene*. Though imbued with a gloss of science, hygiene was more than a matter of "cleanliness" (or, put another way, the absence of dangerous germs). Since the Progressive Era, social reformers had transformed hygiene into a kind of secular ideal, a fusion of scientific discipline and middle-class moralism to be sought in all realms of civic life.[3] By the World War II era, the dictates of "hygiene" would be evoked to justify all kinds of social practices, from campaigns against venereal disease to policies against nocturnal leakage. Bedwetting "cannot be tolerated aboard ship because of hygienic reasons," wrote one naval officer in 1949, "in addition to the fact that the fault cannot be concealed and will be subject to much public comment."[4] In the eyes of wartime observers, hygiene was as much a matter of social propriety as a condition of good health. For this reason alone, concluded William Bisher, a major in the Army Medical Corps, bedwetting had no place in military life. The "natural reaction" to involuntary urination "is one of deep disgust," he declared. The enuretic man represented a "disturbance in morale" and an "outcast in the military scene," a menace that needed to be eliminated as soon as possible.[5]

Enuresis posed other threats. As Robert Leckie freely admitted, bedwetting was considered a "common dodge of fakers and malingerers" eager to escape service, an association that lingers to this day.[6] More worrisome still, nocturnal enuresis (or incontinence of any sort) threatened the military's ethos of *bodily control*—individual self-control and collective control of troops' bodies en masse.[7] According to generations of drill sergeants, the military's near total control of recruits' bodies (when they ate, when they slept, when they showered, when they shat) was essential to wartime effectiveness. Hence, the dangers posed by urinary leakage. Recruits could have their heads shaved, their waists slimmed, their movements honed to robotic precision, but disciplining bladders sometimes proved impossible.

Even so, the most common rationale for the military's fixation on bedwetting stemmed from *psychology*. Schooled in Freudian psychoanalysis and eugenics, World War II–era psychologists believed that aberrant psychological traits manifested themselves physically. A skilled psychologist (or even a not-so-skilled base physician) could be taught to spot the signs of latent deviancy before it was too late. Throughout the war years, military physicians diagnosed enuresis as "symptom of [an] underlying mental or physical condition" such as psychopathy, mental deficiency, or psychosis.[8] Nocturnal bedwetting was associated with one trait in particular: childishness, or, in military parlance, "inadequate maturation."[9] This association was more than a reference to the ubiquity of bedwetting in early life. As Adrienne Asch and Michelle Fine observe, "Having a disability [is often] seen as synonymous with being dependent, childlike and helpless—an image fundamentally challenging all that is embodied in the ideal male: virility, autonomy and independence."[10] Within this context, adult enuresis took on heightened urgency. If a new recruit couldn't learn to hold his urine, how could he be expected to keep cool under gunfire? The military needed *men* or, at the very least, teenagers who had progressed beyond the rubber-sheet phase of childhood development.

To be clear: World War II–era physicians did not consider bedwetting, temper-tantrums, and other "infantile traits" terribly important *in and of themselves*.[11] In a war that would take the lives of hundreds of thousands of US troops, medical experts had far bigger issues to worry about, including keeping GIs' urinary tracts free from the burning effects of venereal disease. Still, military doctors claimed that weeding out enuretic recruits—whose psychological collapse was considered all but inevitable—would lower the number of "actual casualties" down the road.[12] In the eyes of medical officials, enuretic troops represented a problem population—dangerous to themselves and even more dangerous to those around them. Indeed, they belonged to an amorphous category of unwanted enlistees (the "psychiatric unfit") whose members displayed all the telltale signs of future trouble: "abnormal negativistic attitude," "silly inappropriate laughter," "recognized queerness," "homosexual proclivities," and a "history of nocturnal incontinence."[13]

The military spared little effort when it came to weeding out past and future bedwetters. At induction, enlistees were grilled about their history of enuresis followed by a one-to-three-night observation period to "rule out the possibility of deceitfulness." If discovered, particularly in training camp, bedwetting troops might be turned over to a proverbially tough sergeant who sought to cure the men's afflictions through a regimen of ridicule and harsh discipline. Enuretic GIs were forbidden to drink liquids after midafternoon, were awakened at night, and were forced to purchase "specially designed rubber bag[s]" at their own expense.[14] Over time, some military physicians adopted novel approaches to the problem, including exiling confirmed bedwetters to specially designated enuresis tents to spend the night. Yet such tactics proved little match for bladders in need of emptying.[15] During a six-month period in 1942, a naval neuropsychiatric unit at Camp Allen (Virginia) discharged 225 out of 668 referred patients—more than a quarter for persistent enuresis.[16]

Despite such measures, large numbers of enuretics managed to evade early detection. Recall the case of Robert Leckie. After his enuresis worsened, Leckie was sent to a navy hospital "Nut Ward" on Banika (Solomon Islands), where he was promptly told to undress and hand over his belt and razor blades—instruments, presumably, of potential suicide. The ward psychiatrist (a "Freudian," according to Leckie) attempted to discover the "abnormality" underlying the patient's symptoms. However, all attempts at "curing" Leckie ended in failure, and he was returned to his unit only to be knocked out of combat by a blast concussion.[17]

Leckie's experience illustrates two key points. The first is that military physicians were (and still are) all too willing to overlook enuresis in times of military necessity. Much like homosexuality, also categorized as incompatible with military life, bedwetting was grounds for immediate dismissal—except when it wasn't.[18] To this day, the military has a long tradition of setting aside idealized versions of the warrior body when its ranks are running low. Bedwetting soldiers might not be "suitable" for decades-long military careers or entitlements, the logic goes, but they can take a bullet as well as the next man, at least until they are no longer needed. For this reason alone, we should be skeptical about accepting military "standards" (about bodies, minds, and so forth) at face value.

More important still, cases such as Leckie's forced military psychiatrists to rethink their earlier assumptions about the etiology of bedwetting. As the war dragged on, more and more troops appeared to develop persistent enuresis in the aftermath of trauma (or as a consequence of rattled "nerves").[19] For a short while, beginning in January 1943, military physicians came to view enuresis as a "disability" comparable to an injury or disease incurred in service. In the run-up to separation, troops were given full physical and mental examinations—all in an effort to determine the "cause" of the malady. However, not all physicians accepted the new diagnosis. Even if a particular bout of bedwetting was sparked by battlefield trauma, they figured, its potential had been lurking inside the patient all along, just waiting to be released. It did not matter if a GI wet the bed on the first night of training camp or after watching his best friend get blown to pieces: an enuretic was an enuretic, and thus unfit for wartime duty. Consequently, military officials soon abandoned the disability framework, instead recategorizing enuretic patients—when they had passed their time of usefulness—as "not adaptable for military service."[20]

Such distinctions had major consequences for veterans. For starters, there was the matter of government support. Those dismissed for service-connected "disability" were entitled to a range of state-sponsored veterans programs, including the newly created GI Bill. Organizations such as the Disabled American Veterans and the American Legion waged fierce campaigns on behalf of the nation's war-injured heroes, celebrating disabled vets as icons of patriotism and manly virtue. Those labeled as "unadaptable," however, had few such allies. While technically entitled to "veteran" status, men and women discharged for enuresis would have been marginalized from the burgeoning veterans state, the complex of institutions, programs, and legislation developed on veterans' behalf.[21]

Doubly burdensome was the shame and stigma associated with less-than-honorable exits from wartime service. The most unfortunate vets received "blue discharges," so named for the blue form on which they were printed. Introduced in 1916, blue discharges were originally meant to be neither "honorable" nor "dishonorable"—a legal no-man's-land that identified little more than a past (and often temporary) affiliation with the US Armed Forces. Very quickly, however, potential employers came to view blue discharges with suspicion. As one critic testified before Congress in 1949, a blue discharge "gives the impression that there is something radically wrong with the man in question, something so mysterious that it cannot be talked about or written down, but must be left to the imagination."[22] Writing in the *Pittsburgh Courier*, a prominent African American newspaper, John H. Young III argues that the blue discharge was less an administrative designation than a "weapon to settle personal differences" and a means of "punishing Negro soldiers who do not like specifically, unbearable conditions growing out of the Army's doctrine of white supremacy." All told, according to Young, blue discharges tarnished the "future of over two hundred thousand helpless Negro and white" veterans, some for little more than wetting their sheets.[23]

Against the backdrop of the Cold War, military regulations toward enuresis remained as strict as ever. Between 1948 and the early 1970s, thousands of enuretics were discharged from the military for reasons of "unsuitability," a broad administrative category that covered everything from "homosexual tendencies" to "group inaptitude" and "financial irresponsibility."[24] "Unsuitable" service personnel typically received a mandatory general discharge that, while less socially disabling than a "blue discharge" (discontinued in 1947), still conveyed an air of suspicion. Meanwhile, American society at large continued to characterize bedwetting as a symptom of more ominous maladies. The publication of J. M. MacDonald's paper "The Threat to Kill" (1963) popularized the notion that the combination of animal cruelty, fire setting, and bedwetting was predictive of future violence.[25]

Only after the launch of the US war in Vietnam did military attitudes toward enuresis begin to change. During the first half decade of the conflict, military psychiatrists largely downplayed the phenomenon of war-related bedwetting. Indeed, the American Psychiatric Association's highly politicized *Diagnostic and Statistical Manual of Mental Disorders (DSM) II,* released at the height of the conflict in 1968, was generally hostile to the concept of mental trauma, excluding many forms of combat-induced stress disorders.[26] By the war's end, however, bedwetting had lost some of its earlier stigmas. Writing in 1975, military psychiatrists Franklin Del Jones and Arnold W. Johnson Jr. described enuresis—along with sleepwalking and nightmares—as an expected symptom of the "culture shock" experienced by American troops arriving in Vietnam. "A firm stand by the medical officer, perhaps coupled with the issuing of a rubber sheet or ordering of night duty, usually took care of these problems," they counseled reassuringly.[27] In 1976, the Department of Defense discarded enuresis as a category of "unsuitability" (redefining it, instead, as a "nonvolitional medical problem").[28] Most significant of all, a growing number of military physicians accepted a trauma-induced model of adult enuresis, recognizing bedwetting as a symptom of post-traumatic stress disorder (PTSD). The Vietnam veteran-turned-psychologist Charles Figley epitomized this change of thinking. Profiled in *People* magazine in 1988, Figley made headlines after visiting Moscow to work with psychologically damaged Afgantsy, Soviet veterans of the decade-long invasion of Afghanistan. "The key is to get the vets not to blame themselves for their trauma," he told his Soviet colleagues. "Even though they may experience symptoms that are at odds with their macho image—nightmares, bed-wetting, self-mutilation—it doesn't mean they are losers."[29]

In spite of such changes, contemporary military policy continues to frame bedwetting as a disqualifying impediment to military service. As of the 2010s, enuresis—along with sleepwalking, fear of flying, phobia of submarines, wool allergies, and "pseudofolliculitis barbae of the face/and or neck" (razor bumps)—remained on a long list of "conditions" considered worthy of "separation by reason of convenience of the government."[30]

ENURETIC VETERANS: INVISIBLE AND FORGOTTEN

What happened to the tens of thousands of American veterans discharged as unsuitably enuretic? And what about the countless more who developed symptoms of enuresis in the years following military service?

The short answer is, we don't really know. To some degree, this gap in knowledge represents a lack of interest. Despite a growing body of scholarship on the relationship between disability and military service, historians have made few attempts to grapple with banal, even abject, aspects of embodied existence. The bulk of historical scholarship addresses veterans with culturally salient health issues (lost limbs, post-traumatic stress, Gulf War syndrome, and, more recently, traumatic brain injury), the kinds of service-connected traumas that are sometimes dubbed "signature wounds."[31] Men and women discharged for "physical and mental conditions" not rising to the level of disability, in contrast, have attracted little attention from scholars and activists alike.

But scholarly indifference is only partly to blame. There's also the matter of sources (or lack thereof). Many enuretic vets, particularly those quickly separated from service, would have had minimal contact with the Veterans Administration (VA) and the record-keeping systems (case files, pension records, medical forms, etc.) on which historians so often rely.[32] More striking still is the virtual invisibility of bedwetting in war-themed popular culture. Leckie's account notwithstanding, one would be hard-pressed to name a single memoir, novel, or film that addresses the topic of military enuresis in depth—let alone the adversities of veterans, including victims of Agent Orange–related prostate cancer, who developed urinary issues later in life. Above all else, bedwetting continues to be stigmatized as evidence of delinquency, mental unfitness, and, in adults, cowardice. To wet the bed, we're taught, is a mark of shame, something to be hidden or denied. It's no surprise, then, that veterans have been loath to acknowledge their experiences with enuresis.

We can nevertheless draw some inferences about the struggles facing military personnel discharged for bedwetting. One of enuretic veterans' greatest obstacles, for example, would have been the "separation program number" (or SPN) they received on their discharge papers. A SPN was a three-letter code meant to identify why a person was exiting the armed forces. Between the late

1940s and the early 1970s, the military used more than five hundred different SPN codes, including 46C (apathy/obesity), 257 (unfitness, homosexual acts), and 263 (bedwetter).[33] Although the numbers' meanings were supposed to be secret, critics charged that they served as a kind of "coded blacklist." According to an article in the *Gay Liberator* in 1974, "most major employers and agencies" used SPN numbers as an easy way to weed out "undesirables."[34] The personnel department at sales giant Marshall Field's told the *New York Times*, "The code number is the first thing we look at when we are hiring a veteran," despite government prohibitions against that very practice.[35] Future NYC mayor Ed Koch specifically used enuresis to illustrate how "trivial" codes can haunt the lives of discharged soldiers.[36] "It's a lot like putting a brand on cattle," one veterans' group charged, a sign of disgrace that would follow enuretic veterans for the rest of their lives.[37]

We also know that enuretic veterans faced hostility within the VA, which tended to lump bedwetters in with other "problem" populations of disgruntled vets. Digitized records of the Board of Veterans' Appeals Court tell stories of enuretic veterans caught in a maze of bureaucracy and indifference—sometimes for decades—all in an effort to gain official recognition of their conditions.[38] One unnamed vet, who served from April 30 to June 29, 1973, accused the military of discharging him for enuresis instead of for a strained back, which would have qualified him for VA benefits. (His claim was denied.[39]) Another argued that the military had repeatedly ignored the service connection to her bedwetting. At a time when few African American women joined the US military, she had entered the armed forces on August 25, 1961, only to be discharged for "unsuitability" within a few months. She argued that her bedwetting was a symptom of service-related stressors, including "being a black woman subject to a racist atmosphere, being mistreated by superiors because she wore a blond wig when off duty, and being mistreated by a psychiatrist." The VA countered—first in 1962 and then multiple times over the next four decades—that her enuresis, and its accompanying PTSD, was a product of civilian sources. When in uniform, she had displayed an "immature reaction with a symptomatic habit reaction of enuresis." Her appeal for service connection was once again denied.[40]

The tragic story of one marine illustrates the decades-long trauma that sometimes accompanied military dismissals on account of enuresis-related "unsuitability." Only nineteen when he enlisted in July 1953, this young man soon began to experience signs of emotional distress. According to early evaluations, the new recruit raised several red flags: he was "immature, shy, and somewhat withdrawn" and "more interested in books than in making friends." Within a few months, he was sent to the psychiatric unit for "emotional immaturity and inadequacy manifested by severe enuresis," and by September's end, he had been discharged. Although the VA claimed that he had been enuretic since childhood, the ex-marine told a different story, recounting (in a report in 1990) that his bedwetting and mental impairment resulted from his terror of a particularly brutal drill sergeant. What followed was a half century of marginalization and misery. Denied a service connection for "anxiety reaction" in 1954, he struggled to find a permanent job. By the 1970s, he was an alcoholic, unemployed and living on the street. On top of the persistent enuresis, he was diagnosed with paranoid schizophrenia. He continued to apply to the VA with little luck. As the 1990s drew to a close, he hallucinated regularly, his affect "vacillating between tears and anxiousness." Finally, in March 2002, roughly fifty years after he was initially booted out of uniform, his service connection was granted.[41]

Of course, we shouldn't assume that all enuretic veterans endured decades of relentless suffering. Many men and women would have tried their best to put the experience behind them—to hide, as much as possible, any evidence of their "unsuitability." Moreover, we can't dismiss the possibility that unhappy troops might turn to enuresis as a form of resistance, a deliberate effort to push back (physically, sensorially) against the tucked-and-tidy world of military discipline. Plus, let's face it: sometimes wetting the bed is little more than wetting the bed—the one-time product of too much drinking and too little concern about the urinary consequences.

Still, the results of veterans' appeals courts suggest a few broad patterns. First is the fact that enuresis was rarely, if ever, discharged troops' sole disqualifying attribute. Very often, enuretic troops were diagnosed with a host of "problems"—some genuine, many others exaggerated—to justify their immediate separation from service. Indeed, at times it seems as if bedwetting was little more than a convenient excuse to get rid of anyone who threatened the racial or gender status quo. The weaponization of enuresis diagnoses proved especially damning when it came to African American troops, already the object of vicious, systemic racism. The case of one Black marine, who served from August to October 1952, is telling. During basic training, he endured racist abuse on a daily basis. At one point, he was forced to dig a hole ("which he assumed was going to be his grave") and assaulted with the butt of a rifle. The experience left him so terrified that he sweated through his sheets, at which point he was accused of enuresis. Despite the stigma, he decided to accept the lie so that he might try to report his brutal treatment. It worked: when he was "taken for psychiatric consultation and he described the abuse, he was discharged."[42]

In addition, it's clear that—for some veterans, at least—the battle against bedwetting lasted a lifetime. One marine, for example, served for four years (January 1958 to January 1962), all the while trying to hide his enuresis from others. His "strong fear of embarrassment and criticism . . . followed him into civilian life," and four decades later, the self-described "loner" continued to suffer from "social impairment," occupational difficulties, and "urinary leakage."[43] For an untold number of enuretic veterans, the military was not a source of identity or lifelong pride; rather, it was just one of a series of institutions (schools, jobs, hospitals, the government) that reinforced their marginalized status as not-quite-disabled, all-but-unmentionable subjects.

ENURETIC VETERANS IN THE DIGITAL AGE

And yet, things *are* getting better. While the military's "no bedwetters wanted" policy remains firmly in place, growing numbers of vets have sought to destigmatize enuresis in all its forms. Younger vets in particular have turned to the Internet to "out" themselves as past (and present) bedwetters and share tips for managing their condition. This development is hardly surprising. Since the development of the social web in the late 1990s, veterans' groups both large and small have gone online to build community and foment activism.[44] Discussions once held at local veterans' halls or in the offices of VA examiners are now shared on the Web—often behind a veil of anonymity. Plus, unlike the veteran "green zones" (safe spaces) established on some college campuses, websites and social media offer users the chance to seek *specific* communities within the broader veteran population.[45]

Sheltered by these online communities, enuretics and their allies attempt to break down long-held beliefs about bedwetting. Take, for example, a remarkable series of messages on Leatherneck.com from September 2008. One notable discussion centered on the story of a young marine who "wet his rack every night during training." In other circumstances, this would qualify him for a psychiatric evaluation, if not immediate discharge. Yet, according to the post, he successfully completed basic training, thanks in no small part to the men around him. (His company commander forbade him from hydrating after 16:00.) In the eyes of his comrades, the recruit's battle against bedwetting represented an opportunity to demonstrate his willingness to give it his all, whatever the circumstances. "He made it, he's my brother in arms and a fellow marine," explained one online contributor. "He had heart, and that's all that matters."[46]

Similar community-based resources flourish across the online veteran-sphere.[47] In April 2017, the website My PTSD Forum featured a series of posts about bedwetting before, during, and after military service. It opened with a "worried girlfriend" telling the story of her boyfriend, a veteran of nine months in Afghanistan. Since his discharge, the twenty-three-year-old had stopped taking his antidepressants and had become plagued by nightmares and bedwetting ("mostly when he's drunk"). What should she do? Responses varied. One participant admitted to wetting the bed during nightmares: "It['] s . . . actually very normal for a trauma victim." Others suggested therapy or a visit to the urologist. The final contributor described an elaborate bedding system (complete with a mattress protector) that he used to deal with nightmare-induced sweating.[48]

The following year, a vet writing under the handle "Paul1134" published a remarkably candid post about urinary incontinence as a consequence of "Agent Orange related cancer surgery." His condition is far from unique. Following surgery, many patients can no longer control the sphincter function of their urethra (i.e., the process of opening and sealing the urinary tract). Some choose to wear incontinence pads ("adult diapers") beneath their clothing, while others require a silicone pump implanted in the scrotum.[49] Embarrassed, Paul1134 initially tried to hide his condition. That is, until he was "bitch slapped" by another disabled veteran who asked him to think about the struggles of newly injured amputees: "Ever see another veteran [in hospital] who is using a walker or crutches because s/he lost a leg or other limb?" Casual misogyny aside, the message was clear: if amputees aren't ashamed of their medical devices, Paul1134 shouldn't be embarrassed about wearing adult diapers to bed.[50]

Make no mistake: the proliferation of online discussions does not lead to policy change. In a 2013 forum on "Diaper Talk," one participant confessed, "I know my roommate found out I wet the bed occasionally and quite frequently when drunk. He was pretty understanding and sometimes poked fun at me when we were alone but I shudder to think what would have happened if he were less understanding." Another described how, even after he was caught, he continued to live in fear: "All I had was a gentleman's agreement and not all that knew of my predicament were gentlemen." Still, scattered evidence suggests that attitudes are evolving, at least in some quarters. Although "no branch will take an active bedwetter," one medically retired vet disclosed that he wore "diapers episodically under my uniforms many times during the last couple years, without any hassles from anyone."[51]

CONCLUSIONS

On April 4, 2010, HBO aired the fourth episode of *The Pacific*, a docudrama-style miniseries based on the experiences of three marines fighting in World War II. Released as a companion to 2001's *Band of Brothers*, *The Pacific* shared its predecessor's tendency to blend "Greatest Generation" nostalgia with heightened scenes of cinematic bloodshed. Much of episode four traces the story of a thinly fictionalized "Robert Leckie" struggling with nocturnal enuresis after fighting in New Britain. Like the book, the television show offers a broadly sympathetic portrait of wartime bedwetting. Although his commanding officer mocks Leckie's condition ("What fucking kind of marine pisses himself?"), everyone else treats him with compassion. According to his friendly psychiatrist, Leckie is just "tired"—a diagnosis that pans out when he's allowed to leave the hospital (presumably enuresis-free) at the episode's end. *The Pacific*'s empathetic take on trauma-induced bedwetting deserves recognition, if only because the producers could have easily excised the bed-wetting episode from the show's narrative. As a historical reconstruction, however, it leaves much to be desired. Gone is any mention of the link between enuresis and psychological "abnormality." Instead, it substitutes a far more reassuring (and decidedly more recent) interpretation of enuresis as a product of psychological distress.[52]

For all of its gaps, this chapter's history of enuretic veterans suggests some important takeaways for future scholars. The first involves the need to get creative, particularly when it comes to sources. If we can't find marginalized vets in familiar spaces (e.g., physical archives, libraries, oral history collections, the *Congressional Record*), we need to look elsewhere, including YouTube, Facebook, Twitter, and online forums, where the latest generation of veteran-advocates are developing new tools for raising awareness and cultivating support.

Second, it's important to look critically at the military's use of exclusionary (and often antiquated) understandings of physical and mental impairment, including those seemingly rooted in "common sense." Since the early 1940s, military policy makers have increasingly defined *two classes* of enuretic troops: those who enter the armed forces with enuresis and those who develop it during or in connection to military service. These, of course, are not neutral categories. They are hierarchical. In one, bedwetting is a marker of "unsuitability," a sign of deviance that requires immediate attention. In the other, enuresis is an embarrassing, albeit honorable, reminder of war's toll on those who fight—one more in the seemingly endless catalog of disorders, injuries, conditions, and pathologies left in war's wake. The VA has decided—rightly, some might argue—that only the second of these categories deserves recognition. Enuresis prior to enlistment is reason for dismissal; enuresis after trauma is a legitimate product of war. For all that, historians need not accept such distinctions without question. At the very least, we should be cautious about reinforcing the very stigmas we seek to debunk.

Finally, and most importantly, it's crucial to remember that veterans policies have always been weighted toward populations whose bodies (and bodily functions) adhere to specific social, cultural, and biophysical norms. Throughout US history, a wide range of people—women, people of color, gays and lesbians, transgender Americans—have been deemed morally "unfit" or constitutionally "unsuitable" for military service. If bedwetting is indeed a sign of pathology, it is more a product of social context than biophysical impairment.

Put another way: there is nothing inherently wrong—nothing inherently "unsuitable"—about emptying a few ounces of urine on a bed sheet. Only in a culture rooted in ableism—a culture that frets about clamping American orifices while seeking novel ways of opening holes in the bodies of others—would pissing the bed be a reason for dismissal.

NOTES

My sincerest thanks to my hosts at the US Naval War College's conference "Veterans: Enduring, Surviving and Remembering War" (2019), where I delivered an early draft of this chapter.

1. Robert Leckie, *Helmet for My Pillow* (1957; repr., Random House, 2018), 202–3.

2. Medical Department, US Army, *Physical Standards in World War II* (Washington, DC: Office of the Surgeon General, 1967), 45.

3. See Nancy K. Bristow, *Making Men Moral: Social Engineering during the Great War* (New York: New York University Press, 1996).

4. Bureau of Medicine and Surgery, *Physical and Psychobiological Standards and Examinations*, Title VIII Military-Medical Courses, NAVPERS 10818 (Bureau of Naval Personnel, March 1949), 36.

5. William Bisher, "Enuresis in the Adult," *Military Surgeon* 96, no. 3 (March 1945): 244.

6. Leckie, *Helmet for My Pillow*, 222. When I presented an early draft of this paper at the Naval War College, a top administrator, on learning of the topic, jokingly explained how naval cadets continue to see bedwetting as an easy way to get out of service.

7. On enuresis and the significance of self-control in Western society, see Emily A. Elstad et al., "Beyond Incontinence: The Stigma of Other Urinary Symptoms," *Journal of Advanced Nursing* 66, no. 11 (Nov. 2010): 2460–70.

8. Medical Department, US Army, *Physical Standards in World War II*, 104.

9. Bureau of Medicine and Surgery, *Physical and Psychobiological Standards*, 36. On the links between enuresis and childhood, see Deborah Blythe Doroshow, "An Alarming Solution: Bedwetting, Medicine, and Behavioral Conditioning in Mid-Twentieth-Century America," *ISIS*, 101, no. 2 (June 2010): 312–37.

10. Adrienne Asch and Michelle Fine, "Introduction: Beyond Pedestals," in *Women with Disabilities: Essays in Psychology, Culture, and Politics*, ed. Michelle Fine and Adrienne Asch (Philadelphia, PA: Temple University Press, 1988), 3.

11. Bureau of Medicine and Surgery, *Physical and Psychobiological Standards*, 18.

12. Ibid., 37.

13. Medical Department, US Army, *Physical Standards in World War II*, 195.

14. William C. Menninger, *Psychiatry in a Troubled World: Yesterday's War and Today's Challenge* (New York: Macmillan, 1948), 181, 183.

15. William Menninger, a neuropsychiatrist during World War II, argued that the notion that physical development could cure enuresis was an "erroneous belief." Menninger, *Psychiatry in a Troubled World*, 181.

16. Bureau of Medicine and Surgery, *Physical and Psychobiological Standards*, 40.

17. Leckie, *Helmet for My Pillow*, 218, 221, 244.

18.   On the "incompatibility" of homosexuality in the armed forces, see Margot Canaday, *The Straight State: Sexuality and Citizenship in Twentieth-Century America* (Princeton, NJ: Princeton University Press, 2009).

19.   Psychiatrist Kyril B. Conger, for example, recorded that "occasional enuresis are seen under combat and emotional stress"—a condition sometimes known as "buzz-bomb bladder." "Functional Urinary Frequency in the Soldier," *Bulletin of U.S. Army Medical Department* 7, no. 441–44 (May 1947): 212.

20.   Medical Department, US Army, *Physical Standards in World War II*, 103, 104.

21.   According to Title 38 of the US Code (Jan. 1, 1959), section 101(2): "The term 'veteran' means a person who served in the active military, naval, or air service, and who was discharged or released therefrom under conditions other than dishonorable." Quoted in Harry V. Lerner, "Effect of Character of Discharge and Length of Service on Eligibility to Veterans Benefits," *Military Law Review,* no. 13 (July 1961): 122.

22.   *Investigations of the National War Effort Blue Discharges: Hearings Before US Congress. House, Committee on Veterans' Affairs,* H. Rept. No. 1510, 79th Cong., 2nd Sess. (1949a), 210.

23.   John H. Young III, "Veteran Benefits Denied Holders," *Pittsburgh Courier,* October 20, 1945. Margarita Aragon draws explicit parallels between the stigmatization of enuresis and "blackness" in World War II: "Like enuresis, on the surface of things, the black soldier's color itself . . . did not interfere with duty but underneath that surface roiled conflicts and maladjustments." Margarita Aragon, "'Deep-Seated Abnormality': Military Psychiatry, Segregation, and Discourses of Black 'Unfitness' in World War II, *Men and Masculinities* 22, no. 2 (2019): 230. Furthermore, Emily A. Elstad et al. argue that people of color are more likely than white people to be stigmatized for enuresis. Elstad et al., "Beyond Incontinence," 3.

24.   Michael Ettlinger and David F. Addlestone, *Military Discharge and Upgrading and Introduction to Veterans Administration Law* (Washington, DC: National Veterans Legal Services Project, 1982/1990), available for download at https://ctveteranslegal .org/resources/. According to AR 615–369 (Oct. 27, 1948), an "Unsuitability" discharge applies to a person who "does not possess the required degree of adaptability for military service" due to "lack of general fitness, want of readiness or skill, or unhandiness" (Ettlinger and Addlestone 5.2.3.2).

25.   John M. Macdonald, "The Threat to Kill," *American Journal of Psychiatry* 120, no. 2 (Aug. 1963): 125–30. The "MacDonald Triad" remains a fixture in serial killer–themed popular culture; indeed, television shows such as Netflix's *Mindhunter* (2017–) continue to use enuresis as shorthand for blossoming sociopathy. Nevertheless, scholars have become increasingly skeptical of MacDonald's original analysis, especially its inclusion of enuresis. Karen Franklin, "Homicidal Triad: Predictor of Violence or Urban Myth?" *Psychology Today,* May 2, 2012, https://www.psychologytoday.com /us/blog/witness/201205/homicidal-triad-predictor-violence-or-urban-myth.

26.   Gerald Nicosia, *Home to War: A History of the Vietnam Veterans' Movement* (New York: Three Rivers Press, 2001), 202–8.

27.   Franklin Del Jones and Arnold W. Johnson, Jr., "Medical and Psychiatric Treatment Policy and Practice in Vietnam," *Journal of Social Issues* 31, no. 4 (1975): 56. See also Bruce Boman, "The Vietnam Veteran Ten Years On," *Australian and New Zealand Journal of Psychiatry* 16, no. 3 (1982): 107–27.

28.   Ettlinger and Addlestone, *Military Discharge,* 16/9.

29.   Quoted in David Grogan, Kanta Stanchina, and Toni Schlesinger, "A Tale of Two Wars: Vietnam Vet Charles Figley Helps to Heal Russia's Traumatized Afgantsy," *People*, October 24, 1988, https://people.com/archive/a-tale-of-two-wars-vietnam-vet-charles-figley-helps-to-heal-russias-traumatized-afgantsy-vol-30-no-17/. See also Michael Granberry, "Lessons of Vietnam for Soviets: U.S. Rehabilitation Team to Meet Afghan Returnees," *Los Angeles Times*, August 23, 1988, https://www.latimes.com/archives/la-xpm-1988-08-23-mn-845-story.html; Robert Gilman, "The Tracks of War: An Interview with Charles Figley," *In Context: A Quarterly of Human Sustainable Culture* 20 (Winter 1989): 30–37.

30.   Milpersman 1910–1920, "Separation by Reason of Convenience of the Government— Physical or Mental Conditions, " CH-35, April 25, 2011, https://pdf4pro.com/view /milpersman-1910-120-separation-by-reason-of-580648.html; see also Kathleen Gilberd, "Military Psychiatric Policies and Discharges—An Introduction for Attorneys and Counselors," *Military Law Task Force of The National Lawyers Guild*, April 2017, https://nlgmltf.org/programs-and-services/military-law-library/memos/military -psychiatric-policies/.

31.   For a critique of the concept of "signature wounds," see John M. Kinder, "The Embodiment of War: Bodies for, in, and after War," *At War: Militarism and U.S. Culture in the Twentieth Century and Beyond*, ed. David Kieran and Ed Martini (New Brunswick, NJ: Rutgers University Press, 2018), 226–27.

32.   The name of the Veterans Administration was changed to the Department of Veterans Affairs in 1989. In this chapter, I refer to both institutions as the VA.

33.   Lists of the various versions of military SPN codes are widely available online. See, for example, "Military Separation Codes," accessed July 14, 2020, https://www.utvet .com/SPNnumeric.html.

34.   "SPN: Pentagon Blacklists Vets," *Gay Liberator*, no. 36 (Apr. 1974): 2.

35.   Quoted in Dana Adams Schmidt, "Pentagon Studying Coded Data Filed, on Misdeeds of Veterans," *New York Times*, March 12, 1972.

36.   Edward I. Koch, ". . . And Catch 126," *New York Times,* October 8, 1973.

37.   Vietnam Veterans Against the War, "Secret Discharge Codes," *Winter Soldier: A Publication of Vietnam Veterans against the War/Winter Soldier Organization* 4, no. 4 (Apr. 1974): 7.

38.   The US Department of Veterans Affairs has digitized the results of the Board of Veterans' Appeals decisions from 1992 to the present. Though the results are very detailed, the appellants are anonymous. All of the following court records were found at https://www.index.va.gov/search/va/bva.jsp.

39.   The court countered by arguing that the appellant's "history of bedwetting was a habitual response to even minor emotional stress" and was "symptomatic of his immaturity." Citation Nr: 0014662, Decision Date: 06/05/00, Docket no. 96–04 090, on Appeal from the Department of Veterans Affairs Regional Office in Providence, RI.

40.   Citation Nr: 0121379, Decision Date: 08/23/01 Archive Date: 08/29/01, DOCKET NO. 00–00 490, on Appeal from the Department of Veterans Affairs (VA) Regional Office (RO) in St. Paul, Minnesota.

41.   H. N. Schwartz, Member, Board of Veterans' Appeals, Citation Nr: 0202412, Decision Date: 03/14/02 Archive Date: 03/25/02, DOCKET NO. 01–06 153A. According to the veteran's physician, the man's "paranoia and suspiciousness began while on duty with the U.S. Marine Corps and came in large part because he did not understand what was happening to him."

42. Wayne M. Braeuer, Citation Nr: 1527836, Decision Date: 06/29/15, Archive Date: 07/09/15, DOCKET NO. 10–48 988.

43. Nathan Kroes, Citation Nr: 1758334, Decision Date: 12/15/17 Archive Date: 12/28/17, DOCKET NO. 15–20 393.

44. For an early analysis of the how the Web is transforming social relations, see S. Craig Watkins, *The Young and the Digital: What the Migration to Social-Network Sites, Games, and Anytime, Anywhere Media Means for Our Future* (Boston, MA: Beacon Press, 2009).

45. Ironically, many campus "green zones" aren't physical spaces but training programs designed to educate volunteers (faculty and staff) about how to create a more "veteran-friendly" environment. See Ann Nichols-Casebolt, "The Green Zone: A Program to Support Military Students on Campus," *About Campus* 17, no. 1 (Mar.–Apr. 2012): 26–29.

46. "Bed-Wetting," Leatherneck.com, September 5, 2008, https://www.leatherneck.com/forums/showthread.php?70522-Bed-Wetting&s=443ea01d0481b4a48bc5162e1de2533.

47. "Veteran-sphere" (or "veteran sphere") is an amorphous term frequently used to describe publicly active (and activist) elements of veterans' culture. See, for example, Luke Ryan, "How to Become a Writer in the Veteran-Sphere," *Sandboxx*, April 6, 2020, https://www.sandboxx.us/blog/how-to-become-a-writer-in-the-veteran-sphere/.

48. "Ex Military Boyfriend, Served Afghanistan. Bed Wetting," My PTSD Forum, April 23, 2017, https://www.myptsd.com/threads/ex-military-boyfriend-served-afghanistan-bed-wetting.72439/.

49. Such was the case of Leslie "Roc" Whitted, an African American veteran of the Vietnam War who developed incontinence after a series of Agent Orange–related cancer surgeries in the early mid-2000s. As he recounted in an interview with Jason Higgins, after Whitted received a urinary pump, "life was much better. Prior to that I was skeptical of going any place or if I did, I had a small contingency of pads and underwear, but if you're out at somebody's house, you can change in the bathroom, but what do you do with the wet what-you-call-it. I escaped all that by getting this pump installed, and so far, it has a shelf life of seven years. I probably have about two years left before I begin to see signs of them needing to replace it again." Leslie R. Whitted, interview by Jason A. Higgins, May 31, 2019, Incarcerated Veterans Project (author's collection).

50. Pauli134, "I Wear Adult Diapers! So What?" Daily Kos Community, March 25, 2018, https://www.dailykos.com/stories/2018/3/25/1752082/-I-Wear-Adult-Diapers-So-what.

51. "Military Dealings with Bedwetters," ADISC.org, September 5–16, 2013, https://www.adisc.org/forum/threads/military-dealings-with-bedwetters.78345/.

52. "Part Four" of *The Pacific* aired on HBO on April 4, 2010. A possible allusion to enuresis occurs at another point in the episode when Lebec, a Canadian replacement officer, is stripping off his clothes in the rain. As Leckie looks on, Lebec hangs his undershorts on a clothesline, then, staggering and unsettled, sniffs his hand. A moment later, he puts a gun in his mouth and commits suicide.

Uncle Sam's Generosity?

Chicano Veterans and the GI Bill, 1944–74

STEVEN ROSALES

I went and applied for it, and I was starting to go to school . . . but under the G.I. Bill, they paid you not very often. Sometimes it was three, four months before you got your check . . . and a lot of fellas dropped out of school.

—John Sótelo, 2003

For a lot of blacks and Chicanos and Latinos, it's what has made them getting training and an education, affordable.

—Jesus Barragan, 2011

INTRODUCTION

Perhaps it was inevitable that the GI Bill would provoke a variety of opinions, and recent scholarship has indeed turned its attention to the many limitations, outright exclusions, and declining benefits associated with the bill's capacity to promote socioeconomic mobility for discharged veterans. In particular, the original version signed into law in 1944 has come under intense scrutiny with regard to race, gender, and sexual orientation.[1] For example, although technically color-blind, the localized nature of the bill's implementation forced Black veterans to deal with existing discriminatory practices as an everyday reality, despite their dedicated service during the war. Moreover, the specific focus on returning soldiers, both wounded and able-bodied, rather than on a larger community that encompassed defense workers or the public at large, ensured a heterosexual norm that filtered benefits to male heads of house-holds to the overwhelming exclusion of women. Furthermore, the Veterans

Administration's (VA) view of homosexuality left veterans who had been discharged "undesirably," an ambiguous administrative term, without benefits.

All of these biases operated in tandem with logistical issues common to any bureaucracy as vast as the VA, as well as the state and local agencies sub-contracted by the VA, to produce an outcome that "orchestrated much less social engineering than it promised and has been given credit for."[2] Likewise, the nuanced outcomes associated with the 1944 GI Bill must also be extended to subsequent versions that provided benefits to veterans that served in Korea and Vietnam (and beyond). It is important to remember that the GI Bill has evolved since the original version, and in the case of the latter two conflicts, declining benefits were a tragic reality, producing a supplementary stipend in the pursuit of various educational and other training endeavors. This new reality differed sharply from the livable wage that supported veterans and their dependents as occurred after World War II.[3]

Utilizing twenty-five oral histories of Mexican American veterans from the American Southwest and the Great Lakes region, this chapter examines the legacy of the GI Bill across three generations, from 1944 to 1974.[4] Like other marginalized communities, Mexican Americans encountered a number of difficulties in their attempt to access the bill's entitlements; however, the effects of the bill were not always exclusionary.[5] For many, training received under the bill not only facilitated a degree of social mobility but also fostered activism in the pursuit of social and political equality. Indeed, the following individual vignettes illustrate Mexican Americans' achievements in a variety of occupations and professional endeavors, despite the decreased GI Bill benefits across the three cohorts.[6] Taken together, Mexican Americans' experiences suggest the need for a nuanced discussion of "marginalized veterans," one that does not erase histories of success in pursuit of evidence of systemic injustice.

This chapter joins a growing body of historical scholarship aimed at expanding our understanding of race beyond the Black-white binary that is central to US race rations. In drawing attention to Mexican Americans (and other Latina/o groups), historians have forced us to consider the complex, sometimes contradictory, ways race operates in federal policy and institutions, such as the armed forces. Oral history has emerged as a powerful method-ological tool in that effort, including the publication of compelling oral history collections.[7] Acquired through a "snowball" methodology in which each veteran provided contacted information that led to another, the twenty-five veterans featured in this chapter certainly cannot convey a complete picture of how Mexican Americans, much less all GIs, experienced the GI Bill. Coming from working-class backgrounds in the Southwest and Upper Midwest, these veterans experienced varying degrees of upward mobility (not always linear) from poverty to prosperity. Nevertheless, their narratives provide a deep understanding of individual experiences and suggest larger patterns in terms of Mexican American veterans and their service in World War II, Korea, and Vietnam. Furthermore, oral history allows us access to the more fluid and complex consequences of military service that are central to my analysis and that are often not readily available in archives and other forms of documentation.

WORLD WAR II AND THE RETURN TO CIVILIAN LIFE

The transformative potential of the 1944 GI Bill of Rights cannot be ignored. In terms of scale and generosity, no previous legislative effort to recruit and retain military personnel, or deal with disabled veterans and the widows of those killed in action, matched the sheer amount of resources disbursed by the federal government after World War II. Moreover, the focus on providing a benefits package to nondisabled veterans was without precedent.[8] In 1932, the so-called Bonus Army—a large group of World War I veterans who marched on Washington, DC, to secure early payment of promised bonuses—were forcibly removed by the US Army and publicly ridiculed.[9] Nevertheless, the social insurance programs of the New Deal, the lobbying efforts of the American Legion (the main veterans' organization), and fears of a possible recession on demobilization motivated new thinking that ultimately produced a stimulus package for individual servicemen. As described by historian Keith Olson, "The economy needed federal help; the veterans served as a convenient, traditional, and popular means to provide that assistance."[10] The result was a range of entitlements: low interest loans to enable returning servicemen to purchase homes, farms, and businesses; educational assistance at the collegiate and subcollege level; unemployment compensation for fifty-two weeks at twenty dollars a week, also known as the 52–20 Club; and job-placement services. All returning veterans, including an estimated 250,000 to 500,000

Mexican Americans, were entitled to receive these benefits if they had been released from active duty with a discharge other than dishonorable.

Of these various entitlements, particular attention has been placed on the education and training benefits that 7.8 million veterans would ultimately utilize. By far the largest subgroup—5.6 million—chose to attend vocational or business schools or participate in on-the-job and on-the-farm training. Among the beneficiaries of these programs, John López decided to become a carpenter's apprentice in 1948 after working multiple odd jobs following his discharge in December 1945. As he described it, "The GI Bill paid for it, tools . . . whatever I needed."[11] After acquiring a journeyman classification in 1951, López remained a carpenter for the next fifty years, finding steady employment through Los Angeles–based Local 235 of the United Carpenters of America, an affiliate of the American Federation of Labor. López was unstinting in his praise of the GI Bill: "I wouldn't have what I have now if it wasn't for the help [training and benefits] from the military."[12]

David Fuentes returned to Los Angeles in November 1946 to care for his ill mother and decide on a future. His initial desire was "to go to school." "I wanted to go to dentistry school, but there was a two year waiting list."[13] Fuentes would instead use the tailoring skills he had learned from his father: "I did a lot of sewing . . . 'cause my father showed me when I was a little boy, and so I went to tailoring school. I went to Glover's Institute and then I was a pattern maker for women's dresses and slacks."[14] For the next forty-four years, Fuentes remained in this occupation, which provided him with a comfortable middle-class lifestyle. Meanwhile, Raúl Medina returned to Fresno, California, to find that his wife had deserted him and sold the house they had been in the process of purchasing: "When I came home, I came home to nothing. I didn't have anything."[15] Medina credits the GI Bill with helping him to become a successful upholsterer: "I got the on-the-job training program . . . for upholstery, and that was always good to me because it's not a high-class, high-tech trade. You work with your hands and have a little bit of imagination. And I liked that."[16] Across the nation, in eastern Michigan, Guadalupe "Lupe" Ortega decided to further the haircutting skills he acquired as a soldier in the army and also become a homeowner after his discharge sometime in 1946. He said, "I went to [trade] school on the GI Bill . . . Greens Barber College. . . . It was only six months . . . in Detroit. . . . And I got a loan to buy a house here

[Saginaw, Michigan]."[17] Ortega successfully operated Lupe's Barber Shop in Saginaw for the next twenty-five years.

With the bill's generous financial provisions, the remaining 2.2 million veterans enrolled in a variety of public and private four-year universities as well as two-year junior colleges. As described by political scientist Suzanne Mettler in *Soldiers to Citizens: The G.I. Bill and the Making of the Greatest Generation,* "All tuition and fees were covered, up to a total of $500 per year—more than any university charged at that time—and veterans received monthly subsistence payments of $75 if single, $105 with one dependent, and $120 with two or more dependents."[18] For example, Jesse Ybarra enrolled at Trinity University in his hometown of San Antonio, Texas, after his discharge in December 1945, and he later recalled, "At that time, they [the GI Bill] would pay everything . . . schooling, books, everything you needed, they paid for."[19] Ybarra successfully acquired a bachelor's degree through the GI Bill, and a master's degree at his own expense, which he used to become a counselor at youth centers in Texas and California, where he worked with juvenile delinquents. Furthermore, the training he received as a medic in the US Army also proved to be quite helpful in this occupation. Ybarra described one such episode: "A guy got shot, and I had to use a tourniquet. . . . I had to apply the very thing [I learned in the army]."[20] Rolando Hinojosa also acquired a bachelor's degree after returning to the University of Texas in 1952. He gave a glowing account of the educational benefits that made this possible: "It was great! They paid for your tuition. . . . We got . . . free books. We got protractors, compasses, slide rules, pencils, ink, everything."[21] Hinojosa believed that many fellow veterans from his hometown of Mercedes, Texas, similarly benefitted: "That little area produced a lot of college kids because of the GI Bill, either [through service in] World War II, or in my case, the Korean War."[22]

By comparison, William Sánchez returned to the United States a changed man following his ordeal as a Japanese-held prisoner of war (POW) from May 1942 until September 1945: "You come back, you're totally a different person, you are never the same."[23] After three weeks of rigorous physical and mental health examinations at Fort Lewis, Washington, Sánchez received his entire back pay in one lump sum, enabling him to purchase a home in Los Angeles. He soon attended Woodbury College on the GI Bill, acquiring a bachelor's degree in business administration with a focus in international trade and finance. Ultimately, the bill's entitlements and his POW status, which included a tax-exempt status on all private property, enabled Sánchez to become a successful businessman. He stated, "I'm very fortunate . . . because of my service . . . I don't have to worry [financially]."[24]

Another veteran, Francisco Vega, was discharged at Fort Sam Houston in San Antonio, Texas, in December 1945. Having recently married in May 1946, Vega decided to move to the Upper Midwest with his wife, a former resident of Illinois. "I was trying to get into the University of Michigan," he said. "But every state university was just getting a flood of veterans . . . and these states were giving preference to their residents who were born there. So I couldn't get into [the] U of M."[25] To establish residency, Vega decided to enroll at Aquinas College, a small liberal arts academy in Grand Rapids, Michigan. For Aquinas and other similar institutions, returning veterans represented "money. I mean tuition, money for food, money for housing."[26] After two years at Aquinas, Vega transferred to the University of Michigan, and he and his wife lived in a barracks in nearby Ypsilanti that formerly housed defense workers that built bombers during World War II. He and fellow veterans bussed to the university, where Vega was immediately shocked by the huge class sizes and the difficult curriculum. As frustration and poor grades mounted, Vega decided to transfer back to Aquinas after one year, eventually graduating in 1950 with a bachelor's degree in Spanish and a minor in business economics. These experiences at both institutions, paid for by the GI Bill, provided Vega and his wife with a crowded yet comfortable lifestyle. He recalled, "We had money for food, for rent, and so on."[27]

Meanwhile, Richard Domínguez returned to Los Angeles in March 1946 and became a member of the acclaimed 52–20 Club. He supplemented this income by renewing his membership in the Screen Actors Guild, resuming an occupation he had begun prior to World War II, and that allowed him to serve as an extra in a number of Hollywood films. After his discharge, this income provided a bare level of subsistence, yet he remained in no hurry to pursue a career. As he described it, "I wanted to celebrate . . . and then I started school and finally got down to business. It took me a couple of years to do that."[28] Using the GI Bill's education benefits, Domínguez eventually acquired an associate degree from East Los Angeles Junior College.

All in all, while participation in the GI Bill was not widespread, training received under the bill, and one's status as a veteran, did facilitate a degree of social mobility for some while also promoting activism in the pursuit of social equality for the Mexican American community.[29] Moreover, this complicated reality associated with the original bill sets the stage for a similar examination of GI Bill entitlements encountered by veterans of the wars in Korea and Vietnam. In the case of Korea, lawmakers, veterans' organizations, and a majority of the public favored a continuation of benefits for able-bodied servicemen on their release from active duty after World War II. Yet cost concerns, in particular various abuses encountered in the administration of the first bill, dampened congressional activity on the matter. The outbreak of hostilities on the Korean peninsula at the height of the Cold War, however, provided the needed pressure for a new benefits package.

KOREA AND THE COLD WAR

Cold War tension with the Soviet Union and a stimulus package meant to help both the economy and returning veterans were important factors in the creation of a second GI Bill. Furthermore, as Melinda L. Pash expressed in her study *In the Shadow of the Greatest Generation: The Americans Who Fought the Korean War,* "81 percent of those who served overseas felt entitled to the same educational opportunities afforded earlier veterans, and another 78 percent believed the government should offer their generation low-cost home loans."[30] Signed into law on July 14, 1952, Public Law 500, also known as the Veterans' Readjustment Assistance Act, provided many of the same entitlements that veterans of World War II received, such as educational benefits, loan guarantees, assistance in securing employment, and unemployment compensation. Those who served after June 27, 1950, whether service was performed in the combat zone that encompassed Korea or in any other military location, and who separated from the military with ninety days of active service and with a discharge other than dishonorable, were eligible to receive these benefits.

Notable modifications included a maximum of thirty-six months of benefits, in contrast to the original bill's four years. Also, the 1952 act included no direct payment to colleges and training institutions for tuition, books, and fees. Rather, "the government directly paid this new wave of GI students' monthly stipends, making them responsible for covering both tuition and living expenses. Those returning to school full time received between $110 and $160 a month depending upon the number of their dependents."[31] While these and other modifications were meant to curb corruption and waste, they also made it difficult for many returning veterans to access their educational benefits. For example, individual payments hampered many veterans' ability to pay tuition and other registration costs prior to the commencement of the academic year, as required by most universities and training institutions. Most importantly, stipends did not keep pace with inflation and other living expenses, requiring most veterans to supplement their stipend with full- or part-time employment, a reality that also forced many to reduce their academic or training workload and become part-time students.

This point is evidenced in the testimony of Saginaw resident John López, who served in the US Air Force from 1948 to 1952 and subsequently enrolled at the DeVry Institute in Chicago to study electronics for one year: "They [the GI Bill] paid for your books and stuff like that, but you didn't have enough money left over to pay your rent. . . . It paid quite a bit, [but] I'm not saying it paid [for] everything."[32] Vincent Pardo, also from Saginaw, provided similar commentary on his experience at the same DeVry Institute following a three-year tour in the US Marine Corps from 1952 to 1955: "We [students] were getting only money once a month to pay for the classes. But they [VA] would not pay for sustaining yourself or [for] your [rent] where you were living. We would work five days a week [for] four hours in the morning in the places where they wanted to hire students. . . . And then we'd go to school from four o'clock in the afternoon till eight o'clock at night. And then we were also working extra, like Saturday or Sunday. . . . And that's what paid for my upkeep."[33] William J. Fisher, meanwhile, resumed his pursuit of a bachelor's degree at the University of Arizona after being demobilized from his status as a naval reservist in September 1951. However, family and other household responsibilities required an income much greater than the monthly stipend provided by the Korean War GI Bill. Fisher described his circumstances: "At one time, I was working for the [US] Post Office, going to school [part time], [I was] in the [USMC] reserves, and working at a liquor store at night. . . . My wife wasn't working and I had two kids. By being in the reserves, it was just . . . extra money. And then going to school was also extra money [from the GI Bill]."[34] After fourteen years as a part-time student attending evening and summer classes, Fisher received a bachelor's degree in elementary education in 1962.

Like Fisher, Ruben Moreno pursued a more gradual approach to his apprenticeship training as he struggled to support his family in the city of Tucson, Arizona: "I took an apprenticeship as a cabinet maker. . . . After four years of going to school at night and working at it, I was able to get my master's [certification]."[35] Eddie Trujillo took a similar approach in Los Angeles: "I started going to school at night [in a] machine shop. . . . I used it [GI Bill benefits] all."[36] Trujillo's veteran status also facilitated needed instruction in basic literacy skills. As he stated, "[Nearby administrators] had a school for Korean War veterans in LA [where] I was learning to read and write [and] arithmetic and all that."[37] Similarly, Gene García's path toward a better future in Los Angeles required patience and perseverance, more so given the rampant discrimination he encountered. Describing a pattern of racism and structural inequality encountered by Mexican Americans in all three cohorts, he detailed his ordeal: "I wanted to become a mechanic, I think, for the simple reason that my dad was a mechanic . . . so I went to . . . trade school in Los Angeles [to become an] automotive diesel mechanic. . . . I finished trade school [and received] my diploma. . . . [However], in those days they wouldn't hire Chicanos in the garages . . . and I looked and I looked . . . So continuing [the use of] my GI Bill, I went to body and fender school in Los Angeles."[38] However, García remained adamant that determination and hard work would provide promising results. This included returning to his GI Bill entitlements yet again after being laid off from work. He continued, "I went back to college, and this time I went . . . for general academic [training]. . . . [And] I got my [associates of arts] degree [at Riverside Community College]."[39] While on campus he encountered an old friend that provided a recommendation for employment in the missile defense industry, a career that ultimately spanned thirty-two years. He described his rapid advancement: "I was able to build all these valves and all this hardware that went on the missiles without any problem. . . . I started out as an assembler, from there I went to a test technician, and then . . . to a development technician."[40]

The examples of men like García notwithstanding, the Korean War–era GI Bill was neither as popular nor as successful as its antecedent. Although approximately 2.4 million Korean War veterans (or about 42 percent) claimed their educational, training, and other benefits, this level of participation represented a drop from the previous decade, when half of eligible GIs took advantage of the 1944 bill.[41] The less generous provisions of the Korean War GI Bill made it more difficult for returning veterans to pursue education and other forms of training. Under the later bill, vets often required supplementary forms of income and, because of a lack of funding, were forced to take a more gradual pursuit of educational goals and other forms of certification. Further, the financial disparity between the two bills established a precedent for subsequent legislation that would ultimately leave returning veterans from yet another US conflict with even fewer benefits from which to draw.

Table 1. Comparison of Training Participation Rates for the Three GI Bills

Program	Number Eligible	Number of Trainees	Percentage of Trainees
World War II (1944–1956)	15,614,000	7,800,000	49.9
Korean Conflict (1952–1965)	5,708,000	2,391,000	41.8
Vietnam Era (1966–June 20, 1972)	6,303,000	2,400,000	40.9*
Total	27,625,000	12,591,000	41.6

* Eligibility under the Veterans' Readjustment Benefits Act of 1966 continued for another ten years after separation from service.

Source: US Veterans Administration Information Service, pamphlet, G.I. Bill of Rights, 25th Anniversary, 1944–1969 (Washington, DC: Veterans Administration Main Office, 1969), 6–10.

THE VIETNAM WAR

With the termination of eligibility for the Korean War GI Bill in 1955, the idea for permanent financial assistance as a form of veteran readjustment increasingly gained public and congressional support. However, fears of an expanding federal government and financial considerations played a key role in establishing an opposition that delayed action on a permanent benefits program. An increased tempo of American involvement in Vietnam in the midsixties was needed to obtain results. Signed into law on March 3, 1966, Public Law 89–358, also known as the Veterans' Readjustment Benefits Act, retroactively provided a comprehensive benefits package to all peacetime and combat veterans that had served 180 days since January 31, 1955. Originally meant to last for eight years, an additional increase of two years ultimately extended this version of the GI Bill through the end of the calendar year 1976.

In addition to support for education and vocational training, the Vietnam-era GI Bill provided home loans, medical care, preference in civil service positions, and free counseling. The most prominent modification from the first two bills, however, was that eligible veterans were to receive one month of benefits for each one of active service (up to a maximum of thirty-six months), while the first two bills provided 1.5 months of assistance. This meant that a service member had to serve three years to be entitled to the equivalent of four academic years. Moreover, like its predecessor, the actual assistance took the form of a direct grant to the returning veteran with the following rates: single veterans enrolled full-time received a $100 allowance; veterans with one dependent, $125; and with two or more dependents, $150.[42]

These initial rates were noticeably lower than those provided to Korean War veterans, and consistent sentiment for a general increase led to a series of modifications from 1967 through the end of the program. More importantly, the prevailing perspective associated with this latest version was its supplemental nature rather than a subsistence wage meant to support veterans and their dependents. As J. Peter Matilda concluded in his 1978 study, "At its peak in 1949, monthly G.I. Bill benefits were 53.9 percent of monthly wages in manufacturing. . . . At its peak in 1975, Vietnam era enrollees received only 34.3 percent of average monthly wages in manufacturing."[43] It seemed, as historian Mark Boulton describes it, that "in some ways, the earlier bills had changed the equation of citizenship. Vietnam veterans might well have expected that when they returned home they would enjoy the same opportunities enjoyed by their predecessors. . . . [Yet] the Vietnam generation was being told that their service was not worth as much now that they were getting nothing more than a helping hand in their education."[44] Indeed, the following experiences clearly demonstrate that reduced GI Bill benefits made educational and other pursuits much more challenging, but not impossible, for Mexican American and other veterans of the Vietnam War.

George Mariscal returned from Vietnam in 1970. As he later recounted, "I came back and went right back to the city college I had flunked out of [prior to being drafted]. And there were a lot of vets there."[45] Expediting his return was the military's "early out" option that enabled service members who had served a tour in Vietnam to complete their contractual obligation early, by several months, if they could provide evidence that such a request would enable them to attend a college or vocational training. Mariscal's frugal endeavors on his return to Long Beach City College, which continued after his transfer to Cal State University Long Beach, capture the supplementary nature of the Vietnam-era GI Bill: "I used the whole thing. It was [approximately] $250 a month. . . . I came back to city college, which was cheap. In those days, it was like $10 to register, [so] I was saving a lot of that. . . . [Also], the first year or so, I lived at home. But then, in those days . . . an apartment [was] $95 a month. It was doable. Plus . . . I was going home and eating a lot."[46] Joe Rodríguez also used the military's early out option and returned to San Diego from Vietnam in 1966. "I was able to get out and go to school," he remembered. "In fact, you could get out early if you went to college."[47] Compared to Mariscal, Rodríguez offered a more glowing appraisal of the GI Bill and other military benefits: "[It was] good value. . . . I was able to finish my B.A. [at San Diego State]. . . . [And I] was able to go to school just on VA benefits and live comfortably."[48] Meanwhile, Raymond Buriel first enrolled at Riverside Community College, where he used his monthly stipend after completing his tour in the Marine Corps: "I went through junior college with that . . . I milked that thing. . . . It was very beneficial."[49] Another veteran, Leroy Quintana, left the army in 1969 and enrolled at the University of New Mexico, where he ultimately acquired a bachelor's degree. As he recalled, his monthly stipend was quite helpful: "It helped, [and I am] glad I got it. . . . I got married . . . a year after I came back. So that really helped in terms of finances . . . 'cause it allowed me to be free to go to school. . . . I did a lot of odd jobs, but not as many as I otherwise [would have had to]."[50]

In contrast, Daniel Cano offered a more pragmatic appraisal after he returned to Los Angeles following his discharge from the army in 1967: "It supplemented [my pursuit of a bachelor's] . . . but I had to still work."[51] His need for employment increased following his marriage and the birth of a child in 1971, which ultimately delayed the completion of his bachelor's coursework until 1978: "I started . . . at Santa Monica Community College [in 1969], and then I went to Cal State Domínguez Hills. . . . . In 1973, I got really serious about college, but then, by that time, I couldn't go to school full time because I had to work full time. So I went to school at night. That's why it took so long."[52] Alfredo Vea, however, decided to delay the use of his GI Bill benefits after he left the army in 1969 until he enrolled at law school at the University of California, Berkeley. As he later stated, his work ethic and willingness to perform outside jobs to make ends meet provided the necessary income to support himself and pay for his undergraduate degree: "I waited [because] I didn't know what I wanted to do. Plus, I always worked. I was a contractor when I was getting my B.A. . . . [I went] through nine years of [academic training] without owning a dime. I worked at night. I was just used to working."[53]

Across the nation, Raúl Mosqueda completed his four-year tour in the navy from 1968 to 1972 and returned to Saginaw, where he found himself recruited by a number of universities offering financial assistance for underprivileged students who had been part of the migrant labor workforce. Through funds provided by United Migrants for Opportunity Inc. in the fall of 1972 he decided to attend the University of Michigan, where he also used his GI Bill benefits. After acquiring a bachelor's degree in general studies in 1980, he enrolled in dental school at Indiana University, where he found his prior training as a dental technician quite helpful. In fact, Mosqueda offers the clearest example of a service member whose job in the military laterally transferred to the civilian sector with excellent results. He offered the following reminiscence: "That gave me the edge . . . [I had] some problems with the academic part, but all of the practical part . . . doing the extractions [and] doing the denture work . . . all of that I could whiz right through it. . . . Having the experience of [being] a dental tech gave me . . . confidence."[54] Gilbert Guevara also returned to Saginaw after a two-year tour in the army from 1967 to 1969, and he found his veteran status helpful in returning to his job at Saginaw Steering Gear. He recalled, "I still had a job there. They said to me, 'Because you were drafted, your job will be here when you come back.'"[55] Rather than return, he instead decided to enroll at Saginaw Valley State University. Unfortunately, family and community responsibilities prevented Guevara from completing his bachelor's degree: "I was married [and] then I got involved in the community, and one thing led to another, so that I just gradually was [attending less classes]. . . . [However, the GI Bill] paid for the classes that I took."[56]

CONCLUSION

The reminiscences of these Mexican American veterans are evidence of some veterans' ability to use the GI Bill to achieve various levels of occupational success. However, in the case of Korea and Vietnam, the supplementary nature of vets' monthly stipends failed to meet their needs. Moreover, quantitative data has illustrated that in the aftermath of the Vietnam War, Hispanic veterans had less formal education compared to non-Hispanic veterans. In particular, the VA's *Chart Book on Black and Hispanic Veterans* listed 843,700 male Hispanic veterans in the United States in 1980. Of this figure, approximately 10 percent had completed four or more years of college, whereas approximately 20 percent of the 26.5 million, or 5.2 million, non-Hispanic male veterans had done so.[57] Thus, despite the opportunities for socioeconomic advancement commonly associated with the GI Bill, the actual data—and the lived experiences of the men discussed in this chapter—suggest a more complicated story. The GI Bill provided financial and other forms of assistance for many Mexican American veterans that served from 1944 to 1974—just not as many as one might assume. The explanation can be tied to a variety of factors, including personal indifference, uneven implementation, social and educational discrimination, and the declining value of monthly stipends that left Korean and Vietnam War veterans with fewer benefits from which to draw. Nevertheless, to focus solely on failure or unfulfilled potential inadequately conveys the entirety of the GI Bill experience for Mexican American and other veterans. This is not an attempt to perpetuate a hagiography of military service, but rather an effort to champion the transformative potential of GI Bill benefits for socially marginalized groups, such as Mexican Americans. When combined with perseverance and hard work, promising results were still possible despite structural inequalities and decreased benefits over time.

With the termination of the Vietnam-era GI Bill in 1976, Congress enacted a new contributory program called the Veterans Educational Assistance Program that was subsequently replaced with the reinstatement of a new GI

Bill under Ronald Reagan in 1986. Sadly, the downward trend in benefits continued with both of these programs.[58] The latest version enacted in 2009, however, has come full circle, with generous entitlements that rival the first bill in 1944. Indeed, recent efforts to recruit within the growing Latina/o community have stressed the educational benefits and job security derived from a tour of duty. Faced with difficulties meeting annual recruitment goals since the involvement of US forces in Afghanistan in 2001 and in Iraq in 2003, the military has zeroed in on the Latina/o community with greater earnest. In this atmosphere, Spanish-language recruiting efforts send a two-sided message, emphasizing military service as an opportunity to lay claim to both a larger sense of national belonging and potentially life-changing material benefits.

NOTES

1. Accounts that analyze the bill's exclusions based on race and gender include David H. Onkst, "'First a Negro . . . Incidentally a Veteran': Black World War Two Veterans and the G.I. Bill of Rights in the Deep South, 1944–1948," *Journal of Social History*, 31 (1998): 517–44; Lizabeth Cohen, *A Consumer's Republic: The Politics of Mass Consumption in Postwar America* (New York: Knopf Doubleday, 2003); and Kathleen J. Frydl, *The GI Bill* (New York: Cambridge University Press, 2009). For accounts of homosexual exclusion, see Allan Bérubé, *Coming Out Under Fire: The History of Gay Men and Women in World War II* (New York: Free Press, 2000); and Margot Canaday, "Building a Straight State: Sexuality and Social Citizenship under the 1944 G.I. Bill," *Journal of American History* 90, no. 3 (2003): 935–57.

2. Cohen, *Consumer's Republic*, 156.

3. A partial listing of scholarship that generally supports a more positive depiction of the 1944 GI Bill and its transformative potential include David R. B. Ross, *Preparing for Ulysses: Politics and Veterans during World War II* (New York: Columbia University Press, 1969); Keith W. Olson, *The G.I. Bill, the Veterans, and the Colleges* (Lexington: University of Kentucky Press, 1974); Harold M. Hyman, *American Singularity: The 1787 Northwest Ordinance, the 1862 Homestead and Morrill Acts, and the 1944 GI Bill* (Athens: University of Georgia Press, 1986); Michael J. Bennet, *When Dreams Come True: The GI Bill and the Making of Modern America* (Washington, DC: Potomac Books, 1999); Glen C. Altschuler and Stuart M. Blumin, *The GI Bill: A New Deal for Veterans* (New York: Oxford University Press, 2009); and Suzanne Mettler, *Soldiers to Citizens: The G.I. Bill and the Making of the Greatest Generation* (New York: Oxford University Press, 2009).

4. This larger national story continues the process of decentering Mexican American studies away from the US-Mexico border. Indeed, as the Chicano/Latino population continues to grow at an exceptional rate—it currently comprises one-sixth of the US population—new geographic spaces, such as the Midwest and the American South, have become more central to the study of US Latinos/as.

5. Markers of identification for communities of Hispanic descent have become common-place. I employ "Mexican American" to describe individuals of Mexican ancestry having US citizenship through birth or naturalization. The term "Chicano" references the era of the Chicano movement and the Vietnam War, roughly 1965 through 1975. Lastly, I utilize the terms "Latino" and "Hispanic" as all-encompassing forms of identification.

6. Portions of this chapter first appeared in Steven Rosales, "Fighting the Peace at Home: Mexican American Veterans and the 1944 G.I. Bill of Rights," *Pacific Historical Review* 80, no. 4 (2011): 597–627; and Steven Rosales, *Soldados Razos at War: Chicano Politics, Identity, and Masculinity in the U.S. Military from World War II to Vietnam* (Tucson: University of Arizona Press, 2017).

7. Examples include Charley Trujillo, *Soldados: Chicanos in Viet Nam* (San Jose, CA; Chusma House, 1990); Lea Ybarra, *Vietnam Veteranos: Chicanos Recall the War* (Austin: University of Texas Press, 2004); Maggie Rivas-Rodríguez, *A Legacy Greater Than Words: Stories of U.S. Latinos and Latinas of the WWII Generation* (Austin: University of Texas Press, 2006); and Rosales, *Soldados Razos*.

8. Recent scholarship on the evolution of assistance provided to veterans prior to World War II include Frydl, *GI Bill*; and Altschuler and Blumin, *GI Bill*.

9. Additional information on the Bonus marchers can be found in Stephen Ortiz, *Beyond the Bonus March and GI Bill: How Veteran Politics Shaped the New Deal Era* (New York: New York University Press, 2009).

10. Olson, *G.I. Bill*, 24.

11. John López, interview by Steven Rosales, March 9, 2003, Riverside, CA, audio tape (in author's possession).

12. Ibid.

13. David Fuentes, interview by Steven Rosales, April 24, 2003, Los Angeles, CA, audio tape (in author's possession).

14. Ibid.

15. Raúl Medina, interview by Steven Rosales, February 18, 2003, Riverside, CA, audio tape (in author's possession).

16. Ibid.

17. Guadalupe Ortega, interview by Steven Rosales, May 29, 2010, Saginaw, MI, audio tape (in author's possession).

18. Mettler, *Soldiers to Citizens*, 7.

19. Jesse Ybarra, interview by Steven Rosales, January 14, 2003, Riverside, CA, audio tape (in author's possession).

20. Ibid.

21. Rolando Hinojosa, interview by Steven Rosales, March 26, 2005, Austin, TX, audio tape (in author's possession).

22. Ibid. Hinojosa initially served in the US Army from August 1946 until December 1947 but was recalled to active duty in November 1949, ultimately acquiring extensive combat experience during the Korean War. Due to his initial seventeen-month tour of duty, however, he was entitled to receive twenty-four months of benefits under the Servicemen's Readjustment Act of 1944 in addition to an unspecified amount from the Korean War version.

23. William Sánchez, interview by Steven Rosales, April 29, 2003, Los Angeles, CA, audio tape (in author's possession).

24. Ibid.

25. Francisco Vega, interview by Steven Rosales, September 15, 2009, Grand Rapids, MI, audio tape (in author's possession).

26. Ibid.

27. Ibid.

28. Richard Domínguez, interview by Steven Rosales, March 26, 2003, Whittier, CA, audio tape (in author's possession).

29. In the case of political activism, see Rosales, *Soldados Razos*.

30. Melinda L. Pash, *In the Shadow of the Greatest Generation: The Americans Who Fought the Korean War* (New York: New York University Press, 2012), 209–10.

31. Ibid., 211.

32. John López, interview by Steven Rosales, May 22, 2010, Saginaw, MI, audio tape (in author's possession).

33. Vincent Pardo, Jr., interview, by Steven Rosales, May 23, 2010, Saginaw, MI, audio tape (in author's possession).

34. William J. Fisher, interview by Steven Rosales, August 10, 2003, Tucson, AZ, audio tape (in author's possession).

35. Ruben Moreno, interview by Steven Rosales, August 9, 2003, Tucson, AZ, audio tape (in author's possession).

36. Eddie Trujillo, interview by Steven Rosales, April 19, 2003, Victorville, CA, audio tape (in author's possession).

37. Ibid.

38. Gene García, interview by Steven Rosales, March 2, 2003, Riverside, CA, audio tape (in author's possession).

39. Ibid.

40. Ibid.

41. US Veterans Administration Information Service, pamphlet, *G.I. Bill of Rights, 25th Anniversary, 1944–1969* (Washington, DC: Veterans Administration Main Office, 1969), 6–10.

42. See Sar A. Levitan and Joyce K. Zickler, *Swords into Plowshares: Our GI Bill* (Salt Lake City, UT: Olympus, 1973).

43. J. Peter Mattila, "G.I. Bill Benefits and Enrollments: How Did Vietnam Veterans Fare?" *Social Science Quarterly* 59, no. 3 (1978): 535–45.

44. Mark Boulton, *Failing Our Veterans: The G.I. Bill and the Vietnam Generation* (New York: New York University Press, 2014), 117.

45. George Mariscal, interview by Steven Rosales, December 11, 1997, San Diego, CA, audio tape (in author's possession).

46. Ibid.

47. Joe Rodríguez, interview by Steven Rosales, December 23, 1997, San Diego, CA, audio tape (in author's possession).

48. Ibid.

49. Raymond Buriel, interview by Steven Rosales, December 30, 2002, Riverside, CA, audio tape (in author's possession).

50. Leroy Quintana, interview by Steven Rosales, February 11, 1998, San Diego, CA, audio tape (in author's possession).

51. Daniel Cano, interview by Steven Rosales, November 26, 2002, Los Angeles, CA, audio tape (in author's possession).

52. Ibid.

53. Alfredo Vea, interview by Steven Rosales, December 14, 2002, Oakland, CA, audio tape (in author's possession).

54. Raúl Mosqueda, interview by Seven Rosales, June 13, 2010, Saginaw, MI, audio tape (in author's possession).

55. Gilbert Guevara, interview by Steven Rosales, June 14, 2010, Saginaw, MI, audio tape (in author's possession).

56. Ibid.

57. Stephen J. Dienstfrey and Robert H. Feitz, *Chart Book on Black and Hispanic Veterans: Data from the 1980 Census of Population and Housing* (Washington, DC: Office of Information Management and Statistics, Statistical Policy and Research Service, Research Division, 1985).

58. For more information on these two programs, see Bernard Rostker, *I Want You! The Evolution of the All-Volunteer Force* (Santa Monica, CA: Rand, 2006); Beth Bailey, *America's Army: Making the All-Volunteer Force* (Cambridge, MA: Harvard University Press, 2009); Jennifer Mittelstadt, *The Rise of the Military Welfare State* (Cambridge, MA: Harvard University Press, 2015).

Red, White, Lavender, and Blue

LGBT Soldiers and Veterans and the Fight for Military Recognition

HEATHER MARIE STUR

Private first class Marty Klausner confessed his homosexuality to an army psychiatrist at the army hospital station in Torrance, California, in early 1945. He thought the psychiatrist seemed kind and understanding, but Klausner eventually received a "blue" discharge from the army. A blue discharge was an undesirable discharge for homosexuality, at that time classified as a psychological illness, and it was nicknamed "blue" because of the color of the paper on which it was issued. Klausner's blue discharge prevented him from receiving GI Bill benefits and made it difficult for him to get a job when he returned home to Pittsburgh to live with his parents in June 1945.[1] Blue discharges affected gay veterans for their entire lives, having a longer and more profound impact on some than their military service did.

In the first half of the twentieth century, the military criminalized homosexuality by making sodomy illegal, as it was in the civilian world according to state laws throughout the United States. Article 125 of the Uniform Code of Military Justice bans "unnatural carnal copulation" with "another person of the same or opposite sex or with an animal." At the time, the military focused on behavior rather than identity. In theory, heterosexuals could also be discharged for committing sodomy. Yet, because the act was primarily associated with gay men, the policy's main effect was to ban all homosexual encounters and, by implication, outlaw homosexuality altogether.

During World War II, the military changed its thinking about homosexuality to conform with the prevailing belief in American society that homosexuality was a mental illness. This policy shift meant that gays and lesbians could be discharged for their identity, regardless of whether they engaged in criminalized behavior such as sodomy.

Even as US military policies reflected oppressive societal attitudes toward homosexuality, the experience of military service also fostered opportunities for activism and community at the dawn of the Cold War. Although the military made homosexuality a crime, historian John D'Emilio has shown how World War II created the conditions for the start of the gay rights movement of the late twentieth century. Wartime mobilization took young people from their small towns and away from the watchful eyes of parents, teachers, and neighbors, and concentrated them on military bases. Gay men and lesbians met and developed networks that grew after the war ended. Many gay and lesbian groups went underground in the 1950s as a result of the "lavender scare" of the McCarthy era. The FBI and other law enforcement agencies targeted homosexuals in the US Department of State and other government agencies as security risks due to the perceived mental disorder of homosexuality. This context contributed to the military's solidifying its policy of excluding gays and lesbians entirely. In the early 1980s, the military revised its policy again to assert that homosexuality was incompatible with military service and affirmed that gays and lesbians were to be discharged. Gay and lesbian service personnel challenged the military's stance through various court cases arguing that the military's approach to homosexuality violated equal protection rights.

Since the American Revolution, the US military had focused on prohibiting sexual acts between members of the same sex, not homosexuality per se. The criminalization of sodomy, rather than of gay people, followed the tradition of the British military in the North American colonies. Sodomy was punishable by prison time, whether the convicted soldier was homosexual or heterosexual. As psychologists became more influential in American society in the 1930s and 1940s, they developed screening techniques for classifying homosexuality as a mental illness that deemed gay men ill-equipped for military service. Shifting the emphasis from a particular act to the individual required the military to expand its screening and medical bureaucracy to include a surveillance and interrogation apparatus, and to revise its discharge and appeal processes.[2]

Prior to the peacetime draft Congress enacted in September 1940, the military had not concerned itself with the sexual orientation of recruits.

Mobilization changed that. More than sixteen million men between the ages of twenty-one and thirty-five registered a month after Congress enacted the peacetime draft. With so many young men at their disposal, military leaders instituted strict qualification standards and screening processes to exclude minorities, including African Americans, women, and gays and lesbians. Military authorities used the same reasoning for excluding all three groups: they would not be able to handle combat; they would threaten unit cohesion; and integrating them would sacrifice military readiness in order to turn the military into a social laboratory.[3]

During World War II, the military recognized homosexuality in three categories that had three different punishment schemes. One category was men who committed sodomy by force; they were subject to court-martial and, if convicted, a prison sentence and a dishonorable discharge. At the other end of the military's classification of homosexuality was the "casual homosexual" who had engaged in homosexual contact out of curiosity or drunkenness. A soldier in that category was to be treated and returned to duty, reflecting the belief that homosexuality was a medical, and thus "curable," disorder. In between these two ends of the spectrum was the "true pervert," a nebulous category that generally referred to a soldier who engaged in homosexual acts or had homosexual desires. A soldier classified in the middle category was to receive an undesirable or "blue" discharge. Some advocates of the undesirable discharge asserted that it was a kinder way to remove gays from the military, where they allegedly did not belong, than to court-martial them. But blue discharges were not subject to the same scrutiny and evidence requirements as courts-martial, and so they offered a method for the military to quickly discharge soldiers suspected of being gay. The army discharged about five thousand soldiers for homosexuality during World War II, and the navy about four thousand sailors.[4]

The military handed out undesirable discharges for various behaviors and incidents that indicated "moral turpitude," but only those related to homosexuality barred veterans from receiving GI Bill benefits. Veterans Administration (VA) officials made this decision, side-stepping a provision in the World War Veterans Act of 1924 that stated that a veteran had to be convicted of an offense in a civil or military court in order for the military to deny benefits. When local VA officials questioned the legality of withholding benefits from veterans with blue discharges for homosexuality based on the 1924 law, VA administrator Frank Hines placed homosexuality in a category separate from other reasons for blue discharges. Hines stated that VA offices were to consider discharges for homosexuality dishonorable for the purpose of conferring benefits. In 1946, the American Civil Liberties Union challenged Hines's directive as illegal under the 1924 veterans' law, but the VA headquarters reasserted its position on homosexuality discharges as egregious enough to justify denying benefits.[5]

In 1945, the Veterans Administration denied benefits to soldiers who had received undesirable discharges due to "homosexual acts or tendencies." It was the first piece of federal legislation that excluded gays and lesbians from receiving economic benefits from the government. Conferring and denying government benefits to veterans was part of a broader process that connected military service to citizenship. The idea of the citizen soldier had been central to American identity since the founding of the United States, and minority groups such as African Americans and immigrants have used military service to prove their worth as US citizens. In the wake of World War II, the American welfare state expanded as the GI Bill aimed to help returning veterans reintegrate into civilian life. Three years after the end of the war, the GI Bill represented 15 percent of the federal budget, and nearly half of college and university students across the United States were veterans. Two million veterans secured loans through the GI Bill. Financial support from the government was one of the citizenship rights that veterans received after World War II, and by using homosexuality to prohibit gay veterans from accessing federal economic benefits, the government blocked gay veterans from full citizenship.[6]

In the first few years after the war, Congress called the VA out on its policy of denying GI Bill benefits to veterans with blue discharges for homosexuality. The House Committee on Military Affairs criticized the ambiguous nature of the blue discharge, which, for some veterans, was worse than a straightforward dishonorable discharge. Blue discharges carried with them no record of court proceedings or evidence of wrongdoing that dishonorable discharges required, so the burden was always on the veteran to explain why they had not been discharged honorably, even if they had an exemplary record of service. Not only did blue discharges block veterans' access to benefits, they also made it difficult for veterans to gain employment or admission to college. Members of the Committee on Military Affairs agreed with military leaders that gays should be removed from the armed forces, but they argued that separation should occur with an honorable discharge that would allow gay veterans to get on with their lives without a blue discharge following them. From 1945 to 1947, the military complied with the congressional recommendation that discharges for homosexuality be classified as honorable, but eventually military authorities returned to their original classification of undesirable.[7]

Congress worried about the World War II–era blue discharges well into the 1950s, although congressional concerns focused on the stigma undesirable discharges carried because of their association with homosexuality, not on injustices done to gay veterans. In 1957, representative Clyde Doyle (D-CA), proposed a bill that would allow veterans with blue discharges to apply for an upgrade in discharge status if they could prove their "character, conduct, activities, and habits" had been virtuous in the three years since they were discharged from the military. Although blue discharges had been granted for various character traits and behaviors that military authorities had deemed incompatible with armed service, such as using illegal drugs, going AWOL, or reporting racism, the public mostly associated blue discharges with homosexuality. It was a dangerous stigma during 1950s McCarthyism, an era marked by the antigay crusade waged by senator Joseph McCarthy (R-WI). McCarthy's accusations led to the "lavender scare," which destroyed the lives of gays and lesbians by labeling them national security risks and enemies of traditional family values. Gay Americans faced ostracization, firing, and violence during the McCarthy era. Doyle and other legislators were not concerned with the fates of veterans holding blue discharges for homosexuality; they sought to protect those with blue discharges for other offenses from being labeled gay. In the 1950s, the emphasis on the nuclear family as the central ordering force in US society meant that one of the most convincing ways for a veteran to prove that he had lived a respectable life since receiving a blue discharge was to demonstrate that he was the head of a household that included his wife and children.[8] Congress and the military worked together to ensure that veterans discharged for homosexuality would remain classified as deviant, and that the performance of heterosexual nuclear family life was the ideal social behavior in 1950s America.

Movements for gender and sexual equality in the 1960s, as well as the counterculture's challenge to traditional social norms, converged with US military mobilization for the Vietnam War. With military personnel needs in mind, defense authorities gave officers the discretion to ignore homosexuality among their troops if the servicemen in question were good soldiers.[9] Throughout the decade, gay rights organizations held demonstrations in major cities such as Washington, DC, and Philadelphia, and the Stonewall uprising in New York City in 1969 garnered nationwide attention for the gay rights movement. The increasing visibility of gay activism in the civilian world emboldened some gay service members to challenge the military's discriminatory policies regarding homosexuality. In 1975, air force sergeant Leonard Matlovich came out as gay and filed a lawsuit against the US Department of Defense for its ban on gays in the military. Matlovich and his lawyers fought for five years, arguing that the military's ban on gays was a violation of due process and equal protection, as the limiting of African Americans' service opportunities had been. On hearing Matlovich's case, judge Gerhard A. Gesell declared, "No one . . . who has studied the civil rights movement and the striving of blacks for opportunity will ever fail to recognize that the Armed Forces, more than any branch of the government and far ahead of the private sector in this country, led to erasing the stigma of race discrimination. . . . Here, another opportunity is presented." Yet Gesell decided to leave the fate of gays in the military to Pentagon officials, and in 1980, Matlovich gave up his fight, accepting a settlement and an honorable discharge in 1980.[10] It was an example of how, despite the efforts of the gay rights movement to make the case for equality in the civilian world, the fight was long from finished. The 1980s saw a devastating stigma attached to gay men as the AIDS crisis raged, and the military affirmed its exclusion of gays and lesbians from the services.

A year after Matlovich left the air force, US Army staff sergeant Perry Watkins challenged the army's discrimination against homosexuals. Watkins had joined the military in 1967, at the height of US military escalation in Vietnam, when he was nineteen years old. He was openly gay and told an army psychiatrist about his sexuality when he was drafted, but he was inducted anyway. After Watkins's tour of duty ended in 1970, he reenlisted, still open about his sexuality, which did not prevent the army from reaccepting him. Watkins continued to serve with distinction for a decade, until the army revoked his security clearance in 1980 due to his homosexuality. In February 1981, Watkins went to court in Tacoma, Washington, where he was stationed, to appeal the army's removal of his clearance, and his case made its way through the courts for two years. A district court judge ruled that the army couldn't use Watkins's homosexuality against him after allowing him to serve for years while knowing he was gay. But judges of the US Court of Appeals for the Ninth Circuit overturned the lower court's decision, ruling that a court could not force the army to defy its own rules unless the court found the rules themselves unconstitutional.[11]

Watkins's experience illustrates the military's shifting attitude toward homosexuality depending on personnel needs. During the Vietnam War, the army accepted Watkins's enlistment and reenlistment despite knowing he was gay. This was in keeping with an unofficial Defense Department policy during the Vietnam War that allowed officers to ignore a serviceman's homosexuality if he performed well as a soldier.[12] The services needed manpower, and that need overpowered the idea that gay men were not equipped to be good soldiers. Yet in 1980, when the United States was no longer heavily committed to a ground war, the army rescinded Watkins's security clearance due to his homosexuality. The armed forces treated homosexuality similarly during World War II, the Korean War, and Operation Desert Storm. Personnel needs outweighed opposition to gay military service, and homosexual discharges decreased while the United States fought in those conflicts. On return to peacetime, the military returned to its homosexual purges.[13] The navy discharged 533 sailors for homosexuality in 1951, but more than twice that in 1953 when the war ended. The next time navy discharges for homosexuality dropped below 500 was in 1970, during the Vietnam War.[14]

That deployment felt less threatening than the civilian world for some gay servicemen reflected the fluidity of military views on homosexuality. Korean War veteran Ric Mendoza-Gleason didn't worry about homophobia when he was stationed in Korea as much as he did when he was stateside. Reflecting on his time in East Asia, Mendoza-Gleason stated, "The commanders looked the other way and you know, you'd be leaving somebody's tent, and they didn't say anything, they didn't care." He continued, "We had a couple of guys who used to do drag at the bar, [and] the company commander thought they were wonderful. He used to cheer them on, and he was a really great guy. He was Polish, and he was very, very straight."[15] As Watkins had experienced, Mendoza-Gleason got by as a gay serviceman because the army needed him to fight in Korea.

For some gay Vietnam veterans, coming to terms with their sexual identity developed in parallel to their understanding of their veteran identity. Michael Job volunteered for the army during the Vietnam War to prove that he conformed to traditional masculinity. At the time, Job didn't realize what he was doing, but he was hiding his true sexuality even though he had not yet fully discovered it at that point. After his tour of duty, Job returned home and joined the antiwar movement and criticized the notion that military service, especially in war, was the ultimate expression of manhood. Another army veteran, Bob Yeargan, didn't come out until after he had retired from a twenty-year career in the military in which he earned the rank of lieutenant colonel. He had served two tours in Vietnam and suppressed his war trauma for as long as he concealed his sexual orientation. When Tom Samora was a sergeant in Vietnam, he felt guilty when he had to police his men's sexuality while he remained closeted and struggling to understand his identity. It wasn't until the 1990s that Samora accepted his sexuality and made peace with the war.[16]

In 1982, the Defense Department issued a policy statement declaring that homosexuality was "incompatible with military service." Defense officials believed that gay and lesbian service members hindered "the ability of the Armed Forces to maintain discipline, good order, and morale" and "to foster mutual trust and confidence among the members." The language mirrored the wording in statements opposing the integration of African Americans and women into the services. The statement also mentioned privacy concerns, noting that personnel "frequently must live and work under close conditions affording minimal privacy." Reflecting a holdover from the McCarthy-era lavender scare, the Defense Department statement also asserted that gays and lesbians could constitute "breaches of security."[17] Although the statement did not elaborate on the ways gay soldiers posed security threats, the idea that homosexuals were weak-minded, susceptible to bribery, and untrustworthy remained part of an old and tired caricature of them, despite the decorated service of soldiers such as Matlovich and others.

In a case in 1991 regarding the discharge of sailor Joseph Steffan after he revealed his homosexuality, DC Circuit justice Oliver Gasch used the privacy rationale to deny Steffan's reinstatement. Gasch stated that "with no one present who has a homosexual orientation, men and women alike can undress, sleep, bathe, and use the bathroom without fear or embarrassment that they are being viewed as sexual objects."[18] Colin Powell, who as chairman of the Joint Chiefs of Staff opposed allowing gays and lesbians to serve openly in the military, declared in 1992 that "to introduce a group of individuals who—proud, brave, loyal, good Americans—but who favor a homosexual lifestyle, and put them in with heterosexuals who would prefer not to have somebody of the same sex find them sexually attractive, put them in close proximity, ask them to share the most private of their facilities together, the bedroom, the barracks, latrines, the showers, I think that's a very difficult problem to give the military."[19] During testimony before the Senate Armed Services Committee, major Kathleen Bergeron of the US Marine Corps said, "I have seen what happens when lesbian recruits and drill instructors prey on more vulnerable recruits, and take advantage of this exposed environment."[20] Casting gays and lesbians as predators developed as the medical community shifted away from diagnosing homosexuality as a mental illness. From 1952 to 1973, the American Psychiatric Association had classified homosexuality as a mental disorder, and the military followed suit. In order to justify its continued ban on gays, the military emphasized the right to privacy. Authorities argued that gays and lesbians would invade their heterosexual comrades' privacy and potentially assault them.

When then–Arkansas governor Bill Clinton ran for president in 1992, he declared that he would "do for gays what Harry Truman did for blacks in 1948—eliminate the military's discriminatory policies by executive order." Clinton attempted to follow through on his campaign promise shortly after his inauguration, and he ordered the Defense Department to draft a new inclusion policy eliminating discrimination based on sexual orientation. Facing considerable resistance in Congress and among military leadership, Clinton proposed "Don't Ask, Don't Tell" (DADT) as a compromise. It prohibited military officials from asking about a soldier's sexual orientation, but if service members revealed their homosexuality, the military could discharge them. "Don't Ask, Don't Tell" went into effect in 1993 as part of the National Defense Authorization Act for Fiscal Year 1994.

"Don't Ask, Don't Tell" differentiated between "homosexuality," which the military would no longer ban, and "homosexual conduct," which it could. Because of the thin line between the two, some critics of DADT argued that the policy did not constitute a departure from the military's previous stance on homosexuality. In the case of *Witt v. Department of the Air Force* in 2008, a district court ruled that the service of major Margaret Witt, a lesbian, did not harm unit cohesion or military preparedness, thus rejecting one of the arguments commonly used to justify the ban on open gay service in the armed forces. Witt had enlisted in the air force in 1987 and was outed in 2004. This led the air force to discharge her in 2006 on the grounds of her sexual orientation.[21] In 2011, after the repeal of DADT, the air force removed the less-than-honorable discharge from her record, allowing her to receive full veteran benefits in retirement. "Don't Ask, Don't Tell" remained the military's approach to homosexuality until president Barack Obama repealed it in 2010.

Before and after DADT, LGBT veterans faced unique health concerns related to their LGBT status. Sexual orientation has affected if and how gay and lesbian veterans have sought medical care from the Veterans Administration and what, if anything, they have revealed about their identity. Before the repeal of "Don't Ask, Don't Tell" in 2011, gay and lesbian veterans worried about the ramifications of coming out as gay to a healthcare provider because homosexuality was banned in the military. This resulted in a lack of information about gay and lesbian veterans' health needs on separating from the military. Veterans who served under DADT have discussed how serving while closeted contributed to their post-traumatic stress disorder. The constant fear of being discovered, the inability to speak freely about their lives, and the alienation that marked the LGBT military experience during DADT were forms of trauma that followed soldiers into their lives as veterans. Even some gay veterans in the post-DADT era have worried that they will lose their VA and other benefits because of their sexual orientation. Given the history of discrimination against LGBT military personnel, fears have lingered despite legal protections. Since the repeal of DADT, representatives for the US Department of Veterans Affairs have asserted that the VA "never had a policy prohibiting care for gay, lesbian, and bisexual veterans or transgender veterans, and it has a patient nondiscrimination policy that also includes sexual orientation, gender identity, and gender expression."[22]

In 2012, about a year after the repeal of DADT, the VA established an LGBT health initiative. The VA established an Office of Health Equity to address disparities in veterans' health care based on age, race, sexual orientation, and other factors. Cultural awareness programs trained VA staff to understand the specific healthcare needs of gay and lesbian veterans. The VA also codified a nondiscrimination policy regarding the care of gay, lesbian, and transgender veterans, including changing its language regarding families so that partners who were not legally married would be considered family members. In addition, VA policy prohibits VA employees from attempting to change a patient's sexual orientation. In order to increase its visibility in the LGBT community, the VA set up booths at gay pride and National Coming Out Day events, sponsored conferences on LGBT veteran healthcare, and partnered with gay advocacy groups for guidance on meeting the needs of gay and lesbian veterans.[23]

Despite these efforts, some LGBT veterans have said that mental health and substance abuse treatment programs have not done enough to address all the needs of LGBT veterans. Nongovernment LGBT advocacy groups have tried to fill the void. In 2018, an organization called Strive Health partnered with OutServe-SLDN, an LGBTQ resource group for veterans and active duty military personnel, to offer counseling and substance abuse programs specifically for LGBT veterans and their families. Strive's leaders recognized the unique nature of LGBT vets' experiences and ensured that staff were trained in both military and gay cultures. "People are reluctant to get treatment in general, especially if they don't know if where they're going is going to be a safe place in terms of the culture," said Eric Frieman, co-CEO of Strive Health. "We will hopefully be known as a safe place for the LGBT community and veterans."[24]

VA officials have taken steps to be more educated regarding LGBT veteran issues in response to LGBT needs. Lexi R. Matza, a field coordinator for the VA's LGBT health program, explained that the VA has implemented a program to "help guide staff in creating a welcoming environment for sexual and gender minority veterans."[25] Resources for medical personnel who work with LGBT vets have included online cultural sensitivity training, and VA facilities have attempted to employ at least one LGBT veteran care coordinator. Veterans Administration care has emphasized examining LGBT patients for depression, suicidal thoughts, and substance abuse, noting that LGBT veterans are at a higher risk for developing these conditions than their heterosexual counterparts due to the unique nature of LGBT post-traumatic stress.[26] Gay and lesbian veterans have struggled to move past the years of having to hide their identity and live secret lives, as well as the nagging worry that antigay stigma persists despite the repeal of DADT. The fear and distrust DADT bred in gay and lesbian service personnel has remained entrenched in the minds of many LGBT veterans. A survey of gay and lesbian veterans in 2013 discovered that 30 percent of those surveyed did not feel comfortable revealing their sexual orientation to VA health care employees even though discrimination on the basis of sexual orientation was now illegal.

Reconciling their veteran identity with their LGBT identity involved a long and slow journey for some vets. Ramond Curtis, an army veteran who served in Iraq in 2006, turned to alcohol and drugs after leaving the military in 2009. When he took a friend's advice in 2013 and sought counseling at a VA clinic in New York City, where he lived at the time, Curtis realized that what he needed to talk about but couldn't was his sexuality. He had been so conditioned during his service to keep closeted that he struggled to discuss that aspect of his military service. "A lot of veterans, even of my generation, aren't comfortable being open about their sexuality and their sexual preference at the VA," Curtis said. "A lot of people may still have that fear that was ingrained in you. Like, what if I lose my VA benefits? There's just not that clarity of safety."[27] Christine Black, a veteran who served as an army mechanic from 2005 to 2013, remembered her anxiety about what she considered her dual identity after her military service. When she graduated from law school in 2015, she had earned honors as an LGBT graduate and a veteran graduate, but she did not want the accolades announced. "I had friends in both the veterans center and the queer identity center, and they were maybe forty feet apart, but you would never see me walk from one to the other," Black said. "If I had business in both of them, I went at separate times or I came back another day."[28]

The repeal of "Don't Ask, Don't Tell" did not necessarily make gay veterans feel like part of the military community. The fear and shame they had felt having to keep their identities hidden while serving was not easily overcome by a legal change. Some who had served in silence in the era of DADT and or earlier did not identify as veterans because they integrated into LGBT communities where they could live openly in their true identities. Other LGBT veterans felt mixed emotions at the repeal of DADT. While they welcomed the opening of the military to LGBT service, they did not believe they had earned veteran status either because they had been discharged due to their sexual orientation or because they had chosen to separate rather than continue serving while closeted. Timothy Jones joined the navy in 1998, and he was discharged in 2000 under DADT. He was raped by a fellow sailor, and he spent his final year in the navy enduring harassment and isolation. "I went from being a hard-charging sailor to one that was drinking every weekend to forget what happened," Jones said. "The hazing rose to a level where I had to be removed from my room to another barracks."[29] After his discharge, Jones spent ten years struggling with homelessness, addiction, and jail time. A VA counselor helped him get his life on track, but the repeal of DADT was bittersweet for him. He was happy that gays and lesbians could serve openly, but he mourned for the opportunities that he had lost because of DADT. "Everyone gets supported and decorated when they've done their full service or gone to war, and that wasn't me," Jones reflected. "I didn't feel I had earned the right to be a veteran."[30]

Since the repeal of DADT, a number of gay, lesbian, and bisexual veterans have petitioned the VA to upgrade their veteran status. Doing so has allowed institutionally marginalized vets to gain access to VA and other military benefits previously denied them due to their less-than-honorable discharge status. A study conducted by the UCLA law school think tank the Williams Institute concluded that more than fourteen thousand service members were discharged for their sexual orientation while DADT was in effect. Not long after the VA began implementing its strategic plan to address gay veterans' issues, the organization's efforts earned recognition from the Human Rights Campaign (HRC). In 2013, 121 VA facilities participated in the HRC's Health Equality Index, and the HRC awarded "Equality Leader" status to 76 percent of participants. The award acknowledged patient nondiscrimination policies, equal visitation policies, employment nondiscrimination policies, and training in LGBT patient care. Yet gathering data on gay and lesbian veterans remained challenging for the VA due to lingering fears of discrimination. Veterans who were LGBT did not always self-identify as gay, and VA questionnaires and standard conversations between healthcare providers and patients don't inquire about sexual orientation or gender identity. In that context, LGBT veterans are invisible, and the VA continues to be limited in how it can address gay veterans' health needs.[31]

In the years since 2011, the Defense Department and the VA have implemented programs and strategies to create a military culture accepting of and welcoming to gay and lesbian service personnel and veterans. Transgender Americans comprise the group that continues to fight for inclusions in the armed forces. On June 30, 2016, president Barack Obama and secretary of defense Ash Carter announced that the armed forces would allow transgender people to serve openly. At that time, the US military had approximately 1.3 million active-duty members, and of those, about 2,450, or 0.00188 percent of active-duty personnel, were transgender. A memorandum from Carter announcing the new transgender policy declared, "Service in the United States military should be open to all who can meet the rigorous standards for military service and readiness. Consistent with the policies and procedures set forth in this memorandum, transgender individuals shall be allowed to serve in the military." Carter went on to state that "open service by transgender service members while being subject to the same standards and procedures as other members with regard to their medical fitness for duty, physical fitness, uniform and grooming, deployability, and retention, is consistent with military readiness and with strength through diversity."[32] In a Defense Department press release, Carter said, "This is the right thing to do for our people and for our force. We're talking about talented Americans who are serving with distinction or who want the opportunity to serve. We can't allow barriers unrelated to a person's qualifications prevent us from recruiting and retaining those who can best accomplish the mission."[33] Carter's announcement emphasized that transgender personnel would be held to the same standards as nontransgender service members.

However, in the summer of 2017, president Donald Trump repealed Obama's order and banned open service by transgender personnel. Supporters of Trump's ban asserted that the military affirms innate biological differences between men and women in physical standards, living quarters, uniforms, and bathroom facilities. Supporters of the ban have also argued that transition-related medical care would be an unnecessary financial burden on the military and could result in transgender soldiers not being deployable. Yet a RAND study of transgender military service indicates that only about 0.0015 percent of troops would possibly need transition-related medical services and not be deployable due to transition. By comparison, according RAND, in 2015, approximately fifty thousand active duty army personnel—about 14 percent of the army's active duty strength—were not deployable for various medical, legal, and administrative reasons. In other words, transgender troops make up such a small portion of military personnel that any health care needs specific to transgender people would be negligible in the defense budget.

The issue of transgender medical costs is a front for the real concerns of opponents of open transgender service. They fear that transgender personnel will disrupt unit cohesion, military readiness, and discipline. This is the same argument that opponents of open gay and lesbian service made prior to the repeal of DADT. In both cases, the argument played out in discussions of privacy, barracks, and physical standards. Yet this, too, reveals a deeply rooted ideological opposition some Americans have to envisioning a soldier to be anything but a white, heterosexual, cis-gender male. While that attitude has proven to have staying power, Defense Department studies have debunked the concerns about gay and lesbian military service.[34] Advocates for open transgender service have referred to the integration of gays and lesbians into the military in their efforts to defeat Trump's policy. When the VA composed its five-year strategic plan in 2013 to address the needs of gay and lesbian personnel, it also considered how to be inclusive of transgender veterans by implementing consulting and training programs focused specifically on trans healthcare.[35]

Lessons learned from gay and lesbian veterans will help the VA better assist transgender veterans. In January 2021, president Joe Biden overturned Trump's ban on transgender military service, signing an executive order allowing transgender soldiers to serve openly. Two months after Biden issued his order, the Pentagon announced policies and procedures for military personnel who transition during their service and clinical guidelines for offering medical treatment specific to the needs to transgender personnel. Defense officials also codified Biden's executive order with a policy stating that a serviceman or woman may not be discharged or denied reenlistment due to their gender identity. Opening military service to transgender Americans could embolden transgender veterans who had served closeted to come forward and seek medical care from VA facilities.

Gay, lesbian, and transgender military personnel have all faced legal prohibitions of their right to serve in the US Armed Forces. Legal opposition was grounded in cultural beliefs about who could be a soldier, as well as social attitudes about privacy and sexual danger. Opponents of LGBT service made arguments similar to those articulated by opponents of African Americans and women in the military. They contended that LGBT soldiers would disrupt unit cohesion, military readiness, and lethality, but military necessity outweighed those concerns. In times of war, military authorities were less likely to seek out and punish LGBT troops, because they needed soldiers. As LGBT personnel served with distinction, they provided evidence that their presence did not hurt cohesion or lethality. Although the repeal of DADT and Biden's opening of military service to transgender Americans hasn't completely dismantled the popular image of the US soldier as a white, cis, heterosexual man, legal acknowledgment and protections will help ensure that LGBT personnel have access to the services they need when they separate from the military and become veterans.

NOTES

1. Allan Berube, *Coming Out Under Fire: The History of Gay Men and Women in World War II* (Chapel Hill: University of North Carolina Press, 1990), 230–31.
2. Ibid., 2.
3. Ibid.
4. Margot Canaday, "Building a Straight State: Sexuality and Social Citizenship under the 1944 GI Bill," *Journal of American History* 90, no. 3 (Dec. 2003): 942.
5. Ibid., 943.
6. Ibid., 935–37.
7. Ibid., 950–51.
8. Ibid., 954.
9. Susan Burgess, "Gender and Sexuality Politics in the James Bond Film Series: Cultural Origins of Gay Inclusion in the US Military," *Polity* 47, no. 2, "Entering the System" (Apr. 2015): 227–28.
10. Steve Estes, "The Dream That Dare Not Speak Its Name: Legacies of the Civil Rights Movement and the Fight for Gay Military Service," in *Integrating the US Military: Race, Gender, and Sexual Orientation since World War II*, ed. Douglas Walter Bristol Jr. and Heather Marie Stur (Baltimore, MD: Johns Hopkins University Press, 2017), 202.
11. Randy Shilts, *Conduct Unbecoming: Gays and Lesbians in the US Military* (New York: St. Martin's, 1994), 383–85.

12.   Burgess, "Gender and Sexuality Politics," 227–28.

13.   Elizabeth Kier, "Homosexuals in the US Military: Open Integration and Combat Effectiveness," *International Security* 23, no. 2 (Fall 1998): 10.

14.   Steve Estes, "Ask and Tell: Gay Veterans, Identity, and Oral History on a Civil Rights Frontier," *Oral History Review* 32, no. 2 (Summer–Autumn 2005): 32.

15.   Ibid.

16.   Ibid., 33.

17.   Mary Ann Humphrey, *My Country, My Right to Serve: Experiences of Gay Men and Women in the Military, World War II to the Present* (New York: Perennial, 1991), 262.

18.   Aaron Belkin et al., "A Modest Proposal: Privacy as a Flawed Rationale for the Exclusion of Gays and Lesbians from the US Military," *International Security* 27, no 2 (Fall 2002): 182.

19.   Ibid., 183.

20.   Ibid.

21.   "Developments in the Law: Sexual Orientation and Gender Identity, *Harvard Law Review* 127, no. 6 (Apr. 2014): 1799; Anna Stolley Persky, "Don't Ask, Don't Tell: Don't Work? Courts and Congress Raise New Challenges to Policy on Gays in the Military," *ABA Journal* 94, no. 10 (Oct. 2008): 18–20.

22.   Stephanie Russell-Kraft, "LGBTQ Vets, Uncomfortable with VA, Look to Each Other for Mental Health Care," *Task & Purpose*, June 25, 2018, https://www.taskandpurpose.com/lgbtq-veterans-strive-military-health-care/amp/.

23.   Virginia Ashby Sharpe and Uchenna Uchendu, "Ensuring Appropriate Care for LGBT Veterans in the Veterans Health Administration," *Hastings Center Report* 44, no. 5, "Special Report: LGBT Bioethics: Visibility, Disparties, and Dialogue" (September–October 2014): S53–S54.

24.   Russell-Kraft, "LGBTQ Vets."

25.   Ibid.

26.   Ibid.

27.   Ibid.

28.   Ibid.

29.   Ibid.

30.   Ibid.

31.   Sharpe and Uchendu, "Ensuring Appropriate Care," S54.

32.   Secretary of Defense Ash Carter, Memorandum for Secretaries of the Military Departments, "Military Service of Transgender Service Members," June 30, 2016.

33.   "Secretary of Defense Ash Carter Announces Policy for Transgender Service Members," June 30, 2016.

34.   Aaron Belkin et al., Palm Ctr., *One Year Out: An Assessment of DADT Repeal's Impact on Military Readiness* 4 (2012), http://archive.palmcenter.org/files/One%20Year%20Out_0.pdf; Bernard D. Rostker et al., "Gays in the Military: Eventually, New Facts Conquer Old Taboos," *RAND Review* (Spring 2011), https://www.rand.org/pubs/periodicals/rand-review/issues/2011/spring/gays.html; Bernard Rostker, "A Year after Repeal of 'Don't Ask Don't Tell,' *RAND Blog*, September 20, 2012, https://www.rand.org/blog/2012/09/a-year-after-repeal-of-dont-ask-dont-tell.html.

35.   Sharpe and Uchendu, "Ensuring Appropriate Care," S54.

III.

IN THE SHADOW OF A LOST WAR

Pawns in Their Wars

The Peace Committee of Southeast Asia and the Tumultuous Experiences of Vietnam POWs

JUAN DAVID CORONADO

As the fiftieth anniversary of the end of the Vietnam War nears, the United States is dealing with boiling race relations amid a pandemic that is killing hundreds of thousands of people worldwide. In the summer of 2020, the world witnessed millions of Americans demanding racial equality and an end to white supremacy. Millions more are educating themselves about the plight of Black Americans. In the wake of George Floyd's murder, Black history has been trending on Netflix, and books such as Robin DiAngelo's *White Fragility* and Ibram X. Kendi's *How to Be an Antiracist* are best sellers. Spike Lee joined the conversation with his film *Da 5 Bloods* (2020), which follows the story of a platoon of African American veterans on their journey back to Vietnam. Finally, it seems, American pop culture is ready to grapple with the contradictory experiences of Black veterans. For the most part, however, the nation's racial reckoning with Vietnam remains narrow in its focus, reinforcing a familiar Black-white binary that excludes or misrepresents diverse histories of veterans of color.

This chapter will look beyond the scope of Black and white dichotomy to understand the inherent class-based (and nationalistic) hierarchy of military-veteran's culture. Specifically, it uses the Peace Committee of Southeast Asia (PC) to explore the marginalization of multiracial, class-based soldier's protest from the historical memory of the Vietnam War. All but forgotten today, the Peace Committee of Southeast Asia was a group of enlisted prisoners of war (POW) who protested the war and sympathized with the Vietnamese. The group was composed of eight members of the army and the marines who were held in a prison camp southwest of Hanoi known as Farnsworth.

Of the eight, two were African American, two were Mexican American, and four were white. Unsurprisingly, veterans of the Peace Committee have been marginalized among Vietnam POW narratives that have focused on the upper-stratum POWs shot down over North Vietnam. While names such as Stockdale, McCain, Guy, and Denton remain prevalent in Vietnam POW narratives, names such as Daly, Kavanaugh, Rayford, and Riate have been all but forgotten. Some former POWs have managed to recount their experiences, while others have been forever silenced. Even after their deaths, their memories and stories continue to cause controversy, their service and suffering overshadowed by condemnations both at home and abroad. This chapter dwells on those aberrant voices and perspectives so that they might augment the POW record.

Within a military hierarchy shaped by racial and class division, several factors contributed to the hostility between the PC and their senior rank-ing officers (SROs), many of whom were pilots who had been shot down. Formed at a prison camp in North Vietnam known as Farnsworth around 1967–68, the PC had strong antiwar proclivities, which alienated them from career-oriented officers.[1] Unlike SROs, who would eventually return to the military on release, veterans of the Peace Committee no longer had faith in the military as an institution. The loyalty and trust of the veterans of the Peace Committee were profoundly shaken by their captivity experiences and the harrowing ordeal of their public reception afterward. In addition, members of the Peace Committee and other POWs came from very different backgrounds and had vastly different experiences of the war. The PC was made up of men from the combat infantry, which included more African Americans and Latinos from working-class backgrounds. The multiethnic group contained six sergeants, one army specialist, and one marine private—putting them at the bottom of the chain of command among the officers in camp.[2] When it came to combat, infantry experienced the brutality of war up close, while airmen dropped bombs from thousands of miles away and returned to relatively comfortable quarters. Beyond the normal interservice rivalries, the two groups also had different types of training and different understandings of the Code of Conduct.

While under captivity, the PC began to sympathize with their captors and participated in propaganda campaigns against the American war. They sustained wounds, experienced torture, succumbed to illness, faced prolonged indoctrination, and endured hunger and malnutrition, yet they were ostracized for collaborating with their captors and condemning US war interests. The North Vietnamese and their allies used the PC to produce antiwar propaganda and, once they repatriated, president Richard Nixon used them again to distract from his Watergate scandal, all the while turning POWs into rhetorical fodder to justify the ongoing bombing campaigns.

In summation, the story of the Peace Committee of Southeast Asia demonstrates that the history of Vietnam POWs is more complex and diverse than it has traditionally been presented. No less important, the accounts of Peace Committee POWs remind us that the marginalization of combatant-veterans is an ongoing process, one that usually begins long before they are discharged.

BACKGROUND OF THE POW STRUCTURE: JUNGLE VERSUS HANOI PRISONERS

To understand the Peace Committee of Southeast Asia, one must first have a clear sense of the camps themselves. Over the course of the war, the Vietnamese held nearly 630 American prisoners of wars, of whom only 57 were infantrymen captured in the jungles of South Vietnam. The National Liberation Front (NLF) marched these men to North Vietnam and placed them in several camps. As opposed to the makeshift and small jungle prison camps in the south that often had no more than a dozen Americans, those in the north held up to hundreds of prisoners in a more formal setting. For this reason, "a single camp experience" did not exist in Vietnam. While prisoners in the south often worked in manual labor, prisoners in the north spent their days bored, and were motivated to invent creative ways to keep active. Consequently, prisoners in the north had the energy to develop effective communication methods such as the famous tap code that established a chain of command that enabled them to follow the Code of Conduct. Indeed, jungle POWs—so called because of their capture in South Vietnam—often pointed out that captured flyers enjoyed far greater treatment.

Vietnam has been called a working-class war, yet the demographics of the POW population were widely disparate. According to Joseph Darda, whites comprised 95 percent of the POW population.[3] Eighty-four percent belonged to the air force, while another small percentage came from the navy; in contrast, only 57 of the 629 Americans captured belonged to the infantry and had been captured in South Vietnam.[4] Black and Latino POWs helped form part of this group and were then relocated to prison camps in North Vietnam. The remaining 572 Vietnam POWs were navy and air force aviators, who flew bombing campaigns over North Vietnam.[5] These men were not working-class; they were career officers and mostly all white. These differences came into conflict during and after their captivity.

Among veterans of the Peace Committee, five served in the army and three were marines. The dissimilarities in their backgrounds created conflicts. Having served on the ground and being held in jungle prison camps, the infantry viewed themselves as tougher than the navigators who dropped bombs from thousands of feet away. Excluded from the command structure, enlisted men also took issue with Hanoi POWs disregarding the hard lessons they had learned while being held in the south, where prison conditions tended to be harsher than in the north. "Hanoi, compared to our jungle camp, was like a Holiday Inn," explained Frank Anton, a survivor of the notorious Kushner Camp, where Americans suffered a death rate of about 50 percent. Two members of the PC, Fred Elbert and James Daly, had also been imprisoned at the Kushner Camp. Unlike prison camps in the north, leadership at the Kushner Camp did not depend on rank but rather on who worked the hardest. Corporal Willie Watkins, an African American army enlistee, took over as camp leader because he was the hardest worker and the strongest and healthiest captive.[6]

In this hierarchy that defied military rank, the airmen and enlisted men clashed. With an air of superiority, the officers blamed enlisted men for the high death rates, describing them as "incompetent, undisciplined, and leader-less."[7] Naval and air force officers felt that enlisted men did not resist "as well" and broke the military Code of Conduct.[8] Unlike infantrymen, who received minimal POW instruction (they were taught that the NLF executed captives rather than taking prisoners),[9] fliers received Survival, Evasion, Resistance, and Escape training and followed a stricter Code of Conduct, which established a command structure based on rank. Well-trained airmen set up a command structure, regardless of how tedious or complicated. Even for college-educated officers, the intricacies of command had to be resolved: "What Naval rank was higher than Air Force rank? Should rank at capture plus prison seniority outweigh a new shootdown's higher rank?"[10]

While the command structure was not always clear, it was overwhelmingly white. In situations when SROs could not lead due to being placed in solitary confinement or being tortured excessively, they passed command to the next in line. However, as evidenced by a situation in 1970 between James Bond "Jim" Stockdale, Jeremiah Denton, and Jim Mulligan, the exchange of power "would not be automatic." The command structure was malleable under captivity. Denton's directives to Mulligan passed over a few officers who did not have the experience in leadership "when things were going rough."[11] For men down the chain of command, this caused confusion. The practice contradicted Article IV of the Code of Conduct, which states, "If I am senior, I will take command." The inadequate communication system caused further confusion as prisoners relied on distorted messages being passed along in secrecy.

Experiences of captivity often disrupted the military hierarchy, a power structure that imposes social order by punishment and the threat of exile. The first POW shot down over North Vietnam, lieutenant junior grade Everett Alvarez, wittily called it "the weirdest organization I've ever been in. The longer I stay here, the further down the ladder I go in the chain of command."[12] Where Alvarez, a seasoned officer, could find humor in the frustrating situation, young enlisted men expected to live by the command of SROs from a different branch often rejected the notion. The PCs felt that "stupid, reactionary, racist, or insane officers" used the command structure to demand compliance. Robert Chenoweth, a member of the PC, vocalized his irritation, suggesting that senior POWs "have been subjected to the military mentality for a long time and if there's such a thing as brainwashing, the military does the best job."[13] Enlisted men often held a negative outlook toward their command structure in the south, where a clear division existed between those in the field and those in the rear.

The resentment grunts held for "rear-echelon mother fuckers" shifted to senior command in the north, especially at a prison nicknamed Plantation or Plantation Gardens. The North Vietnamese opened Plantation in the spring of 1967, mainly for the production and circulation of antiwar propaganda.[14] One POW recalled that Plantation Gardens was "sharply divided between officers and enlisted men, with many of the enlisted men opposing the war and many of the officers opposing the enlisted men—but having no access to them to impose their will."[15] Believing that military structure improved morale and empowered the men, the SRO, colonel Theodore "Ted" Guy, enforced rigid command of the Code of Conduct and a hardline stance on not accepting early parole. However, such measures only exacerbated tensions with the jungle POWs, many of whom believed their only hope of surviving captivity was early release. Even nonmembers of the PC disagreed with Colonel Guy. Ike McMillan responded, "Man, you're crazy. If these people call me and tell me I can go home—I'm going home." Others notified Guy through "commo" (communication) that "if offered unconditional release we would take it."[16]

THE PEACE COMMITTEE OF SOUTHEAST ASIA AND THE ANTIWAR MOVEMENT

It was against this backdrop of class-based antagonism that a small multi-ethnic group of POWs turned against the US war effort and the military hierarchies they had been taught to uphold. Their actions can be explained by several factors. First, one of the purposes of the camps was to manipulate the captives and force them to furnish antiwar propaganda. As "master Communist propagandist" Nguyen Khac Vien explained to Jim Stockdale, the most senior navy POW in Hanoi, "We are going to win this war on the streets of New York. And when the American people understand the war and you and your fellow prisoners are going to help them understand it, you will be their teachers. Then the war will go away."[17] The North Vietnamese hoped that American POWs would fuel an antiwar campaign not only in the United States but globally.

Moreover, the North Vietnamese and their allies applied methods of indoctrination similar to the "brainwashing" techniques popularized by the North Koreans and Chinese in the Korean War.[18] In *Broken Soldiers*, Raymond Lech writes about the treatment of American captives who furnished propaganda statements and condemned the US war effort.[19] Eventually twenty-one POWs stayed in North Korea after the war and waived their right to repatriation. Over time, several members of the Peace Committee would ask to remain in North Vietnam or be granted asylum in a different country. Unlike their counterparts in Korea, all of them eventually returned to the United States.

However, because of their racial and class backgrounds, the men of the PC were already primed to look sympathetically on their North Vietnamese "enemies." After being left for dead in a firefight near Khe Sanh, Riate, a Latino marine, was taken captive by the NLF.[20] Like other "jungle prisoners" being transported from South Vietnam, Riate reached Portholes—better known as Bao Cao—a camp along the southern coast of North Vietnam near Vinh. The North Vietnamese methodically placed jungle POWs at Portholes to break them. Nevertheless, several jungle POWs, including Riate, adopted antiwar perspectives. In some cases, the war and captors exacerbated antiwar feelings that had already been brewing. Eventually, Riate and several other men, including John Young, Robert Chenoweth, and Larry Kavanaugh, became sympathetic to the North Vietnamese cause.[21]

Other prisoners grew increasingly critical of the world they had inhabited prior to captivity. Robert Chenoweth, for one, celebrated the day he was captured: "It was a red-letter day for me, the day I began understanding another race."[22] Prior to his time as a POW, he'd been trained to view the Vietnamese as "subhuman. They couldn't help themselves. They lived in dirt floors and grass houses. . . . Plus all the names—gooks and dinks and everything you could imagine."[23] John Young similarly explained, "I was 100% for the war when I went over . . . but after I saw the destruction and the people being killed, I changed my mind."[24] After failed escape attempts, Alfonso Riate embraced socialism and denounced the American war effort. He rose to "room commander" at Bao Cao before tactically being moved to Farnsworth, where the Peace Committee formed, and then to Plantation Gardens.[25] Bao Cao served as a camp that broke down prisoners from the south with the purpose of reorienting them to become sympathetical to the Vietnamese cause. Among prison guards, Riate became known as Tran Van Te, "The Teacher," as he fulfilled the goal mentioned by Nguyen Khac Vien.[26]

At Plantation, James Daly, a Black Jehovah's Witness, became interested in the PC after reading literature they produced, *New Life*.[27] When Daly received his orders for Vietnam, he filed for status as a conscientious objector on moral grounds but was denied.[28] When he was imprisoned at Plantation, his captors fed him magazines and antiwar literature. He joined the Peace Committee after attending their Christmas celebration in 1971. Eventually, Daly joined in the voices of American POWs who made recordings and spoke out against the war. They played a key role in the wider communist propaganda efforts. Of course, many prisoners of war, including senior ranking officers, also produced antiwar statements, gave up information, or made recordings. The PC, however, were maligned for their opposition to the war and to senior command.

In some respects, the trajectory of the Peace Committee POWs parallels the rise of antiwar sentiment at home. By 1967—the year with the highest total number of POWs—attitudes on the war had changed on the home front.[29] Dr. Martin Luther King spoke out against the war publicly, condemning its disproportionate costs on poor people of color at home and in Vietnam. By 1968, senators Robert Kennedy, Eugene McCarthy, Wayne Morse, and Ernest Gruening now openly condemned the war.[30] Lyndon B. Johnson did not seek reelection, and following a summer of assassinations, racial unrest, and antiwar demonstrations, Richard Nixon was elected president, campaigning on "law and order" and "peace with honor." For the first time, the majority of the American public opposed the war. Similarly, by 1970 opposition was widespread in the army. Refusals and a perceived fracturing effort threatened the command structure in Vietnam to the point of collapse.[31] The Nixon administration feared opposition so much that it pressured Westmoreland and the army to transition to an all-volunteer force and end the draft while at war. By the end of the war, Nixon invoked POWs as political rhetoric to justify the ongoing bombing campaigns and as bargaining chips in peace negotiations. Nevertheless, veterans of the Peace Committee would be remembered as traitors and cowards.

RESISTING SENIOR COMMAND

Part of the PC's vilified image can be traced to hierarchical notions of class and race. A double standard existed between officers and enlisted men in POW camps. While officers continued to be held in high esteem after providing information and propaganda, enlisted men received unfair criticism for succumbing to interrogators. Infantrymen were expected to hold the line, to embrace the manly ideals of stoicism and endure the pain. "When POW Steve Leopold heard Robert Risner on Radio Hanoi sounding 'gung ho' on Hanoi's behalf he gave it no credence: officers' statements must have been extorted. However, when he heard two enlisted POWs making similar remarks, Leopold 'was disappointed and depressed': these statements must have resulted from weakness."[32]

Senior ranking officers had other reasons to hold members of the Peace Committee in contempt. As one POW explained of the PC, "None of them [were] officers and some of them [were] Black."[33] Brown, Black, and enlisted white soldiers became scapegoats as SROs focused on the transgressions of the PC in attempts to reestablish order at Plantation. Senior ranking officers grew suspicious of African American and Latino members of the PC, questioning their loyalty and patriotism and seeing them as the "other."

In turn, the PC resisted senior command. John Young grew critical "that there was any attempt to establish a POW command structure that included enlisted men." Young took exception with Colonel Guy and felt "he was trying to earn medals at our expense." Young further criticized Colonel Guy and described him as "a flier who had never seen the war on the ground as we had; a career officer who went by the book whereas we were young enlisted men who still hadn't been influenced that much by the military and were still able to think for ourselves."[34] Senior POWs felt that PCs had sold out for extra liberties. But their real crime lay in rejecting the command hierarchy under prisoner-of-war conditions.[35]

These conflicting hierarchies among the prisoners of war reached a breaking point on August 3, 1971, when captain Edward W. Leonard confronted the Peace Committee: "Kavanaugh, you and your men are to stop all forms of cooperation and collaboration with the enemy. 'We'll do what we want,' Kavanaugh replied. 'Fuck you, Captain Leonard,' shouted . . . Alfonso Riate," who then vowed to protest the war until his death.[36] After the exchange, the group questioned who the real enemy was: the North Vietnamese or the Americans.

Fellow POWs accused the Peace Committee of collaborating with the enemy. Possibly the most incriminating evidence of mutiny came in the form of an alleged letter Alfonso Riate wrote during an American bombing raid of Hanoi. As the B-52s roared through the sky, according to Daly, members of the PC began to cry. In a letter to the camp commander, Riate said he would do "anything possible to help end the war. . . . He was even ready to consider joining the North Vietnamese army, if that was the only way he could help!"[37] Each member of the PC signed the letter that night. Still, SROs received a pass for writing letters condemning the US war effort and for being sympathetic to Hanoi. Members of the PC were accused of cowardice for alleged collaboration.

Further, fellow POWs accused the Peace Committee of betraying the other prisoners. At Plantation in late 1970 and early 1971, the PC informed "the Cheese" (camp commander) that Colonel Guy commanded the camp. Ike McMillan recalls, "[They] beat that man so bad it was a shame. [Guy] was covered with bruises. He lost so much weight he looked like he'd aged fifteen years. And it was all because of the Peace Committee. The PC told the NVA that command came down from the most ranking officer in the camp. Boom!"[38] As hostility grew, the PC came under deep suspicion from their fellow POWs. The camp commander threatened, "Should the POWs be observed in any way to be threatening the survival of other Americans, they were to be eliminated."[39] Guy explained, "There were about a hundred men behind me ready to kill them if I told them to. I'm not being overly dramatic. The PCs were kept alive because I wouldn't let the others kill them, and I'll tell you that."[40] Instead, Guy planned to charge the group once they returned home.

POLITICS, CONFLICT, CAMARADERIE, AND PROPAGANDA

The political ideologies of the PC also caused conflict among the prisoners. The PC were granted access to a private library with extensive Marxist literature. After the confrontation with Captain Leonard, the North Vietnamese segregated the PC at Plantation Gardens. The isolation further alienated them, and from a distance, it appeared that they received special treatment. "But, there were few that were getting special treatments," explained Juan Jacquez. Joe Anzaldúa attested, "We saw a group that was outside all the time [in recreation]. That had more liberties."[41] Fellow jungle POW Hal Kushner, an army doctor, stated similarly, "We all thought they collaborated and we all thought that they got special favors for the collaboration."[42] The North Vietnamese successfully drove a wedge between POWs while extorting propaganda.

Daly believed that his experiences as an oppressed Black American caused the North Vietnamese to be sympathetic to him. Likewise, Daly found commonality with the Vietnamese in their struggles against white supremacy: "And the funny part of it was, as much as our backgrounds, as Negros, might have made it easier to be sympathetic to the Vietnamese at times, I sensed[,] as I often had, an understanding and sympathy for us on their part. Maybe that awareness helped to play a role in my going like I did."[43] Kavanaugh and Riate also became convinced that the NLF and North Vietnamese kept them alive as "Brown-skinned minorities."

In the south, the NLF valued the work ethic of POWs. It seemed that men of color impressed the NLF, as in the cases of Isaac Camacho and Willie Watkins. Though these men did not join the PC, their stories exemplify humane relationships established on a basis of understanding between captors and captives. "Of the four of us, Camacho got along best with the Vietnamese. But he was more familiar with their customs than the rest of us, and he joked with them in sign language and the few words of Vietnamese he knew. He had black hair, and he looked a little bit like them," explained George Smith, who was imprisoned alongside Isaac.[44] Camacho impressed the North Vietnamese with his work ethic, paving a path to better relations and treatment.[45]

The Vietnamese used news reports of the social upheaval in the United States to sow division among the Americans. They made special appeals to African Americans and Latinos, reporting on groups such as the Black Panther Party and highlighting the history of racial violence in the United States. In one of the deadliest prison camps in South Vietnam, Willie Watkins also earned a reputation as a hard worker—no doubt a product of his working-class upbringing.[46] In November 1969, Watkins received early release. In a statement played on Liberation Radio, Watkins talked about racism in the United States and thanked the NLF as Aretha Franklin's "Respect" blasted in the background.[47] Watkins's release played to the antiwar movement and aired on camp radio, where Black soldiers in Vietnam stayed attuned to the struggles of Black Americans in the States, including the assassinations of Dr. Martin Luther King Jr. and Robert Kennedy and the racial unrest that followed.[48] Similarly, the North Vietnamese attempted to use the legacy of Latinos as a conquered people in order to spur anti-imperialist sentiment among Latino POWs.[49]

Such messaging was not limited to POWs. Through Liberation Radio (Clandestine) Broadcasts or Radio Hanoi, the NLF and North Vietnamese disseminated antiwar propaganda to US troops in Vietnam. Hanoi Hannah, a radio personality played by Trinh Thi Ngo, became popular among many GIs. While some men found her informative, others, such as John McCain, found her merely entertaining. "I heard her every day," McCain recalled to the *New York Times* in 2000. "She's a marvelous entertainer."[50] Hanoi Hannah highlighted the racism, inequality, and urban riots prevalent in the United States. After the Detroit riots of 1967, one soldier originally from Detroit stated, "That's when it starts to hit home. We knew what kind of fire power and devastation that kind of weapon can do to people, and now those same weapons were turning on us, you know, our own military is killing our own people. We might as well have been Viet Cong. But Hannah picked up on it and talked about it."[51] This was not a random observation.

The North Vietnamese specifically tailored propaganda to exploit racial divisions among Americans in Vietnam. In a Liberation Radio transcript dated July 5, 1971, a male with an American accent read a letter from a POW group that "hails Negro Opposition to the War" addressed to Black Panther Party leader Bobby Seale. The group, self-identified as being racially and ethnically diverse, stressed the imperialist threat the United States posed on Vietnam: "We have all come here to Vietnam to support a war of aggression against Vietnam and her people. This we now realize, and can no longer remain silent about the destruction and death our government authorities have brought to the Vietnam nation." The group questioned the United States' role in Vietnam given the many problems that existed for Black Americans on the home front. They asked why Black soldiers should serve in Vietnam "instead of contributing to the elimination of our domestic problems such as poverty, racial discrimination, etc. Why must our American black brothers come here to Vietnam to fight a war of aggression and repression against the Vietnamese people, when our American black people have not the total freedom that the Vietnamese people are fighting for!"[52] The radio address clearly spoke to POWs such as King David Rayford Jr., a twenty-one-year-old African American who "suffered bitter racial experiences while growing up in Chicago's ghetto and in the Army."[53] Rayford had been captured by the NLF near Phu Bai in South Vietnam on July 1, 1967, and later joined the PC in North Vietnam.[54]

In a similar radio broadcast from July 16, 1971, Michael Branch, a white PC member, criticized President Nixon for not ending the war, while accusing him of using American POWs as political pawns. "The Vietnamese people care more about the life and the release of the GI's than our American President, Mr. Nixon. Mr. Nixon is using captured GI's as an issue to prolong the war," stated Branch. He continued, "He [Nixon] can no longer use this as an excuse to prolong the war, for the PRG has already guaranteed the release of all captured military men and civilians, including pilots captured in North Vietnam. I, as an American citizen, couldn't ask for anything more than that."[55] Branch, like many Americans on the home front, criticized Nixon for using the POWs to expand the war in Southeast Asia.

Although members of the PC wanted the war to come to an end, the PC faced disputes internally. Daly claimed, "[I] disliked John Young from the first minute I joined the Peace Committee. He seemed to force himself to believe things. He was the type who was ready to give his life for the communist cause totally convinced that it was right yet didn't know what it was all about." Daly compared Young to officers he had conflicts with "who were ready to die for South Viet Nam without understanding anything about the country beyond a few weak clichés."[56] Young went as far as demonstrating his devotion to the North Vietnamese cause on the night of September 4, 1969, at D-1(a POW Camp in Hanoi), by inconsolably grieving the passing of Ho Chi Minh. Young explained to a devastated "Cheese" that he found solace in Uncle Ho's sacrifice, "who gave up everything for his people, [and] had at least lived to see this Independence Day [two days prior, September 2]."[57]

Whether Young was brainwashed, performing, or really mourning the death of Ho Chi Minh is unclear. Early in his captivity, Young wrote an antiwar statement under no duress. It was "just the way I felt," he claimed.[58] Young defended his actions and stated, "It was a strictly patriotic point of view. We felt we were patriots too, but at the same time we felt sorry for the Vietnamese because they had suffered. We felt guilty about what had happened to them."[59]

The brutality faced by jungle POWs may have led to their opposition to the war. Craig Howes, author of *Voices of the Vietnam POWs*, described marine private Fred Elbert as a Kushner POW who "spent his time 'sitting alone, daydreaming, almost in a trance' insisting he was someone else (John Peter Johnson), he was clearly unstable." Howes points out that "naivete, mental illness, and rage account for these PCs" and concludes that Elbert, along with Daly, had been Kushner POWs and thus two of the most brutalized captives in Vietnam.[60] Hanoi POWs took for granted the poor living conditions and cruel lessons learned by jungle POWs early on, and Vietnam POW scholars did the same.

Equally, Larry Kavanaugh sustained severe treatment and torture. At Farnsworth, a guard cut his ear.[61] He often found himself in solitary confinement, and sustained beatings that went on for days. Army chief warrant officer Roy Ziegler recalled Kavanaugh's endurance: "For two years, he was one of the best prisoners. . . . He resisted. He was strong. We admired Larry Kavanaugh."[62] By the spring of 1970, after two years in captivity, Kavanaugh's cellmate, marine sergeant Robert Helle, noticed an "overnight" change in Kavanaugh: "He started telling everybody that he was the 13th Disciple and that he was going to start straightening out all the problems of the world. God sent him . . . that's what he told us."[63]

TENSIONS COMING HOME

In January 1973, after the signing of the Paris Peace Accords, which agreed to the withdrawal of US troops from Vietnam in exchange for American prisoners of war, the nation anxiously awaited the return of its sons under Operation Homecoming. The American public sympathized with American POWs. They had become a focus point in media, as president Richard Nixon used their captivity to defend and expand the unpopular US involvement in Southeast Asia.[64]

"Peace with Honor" became a talking point, and Nixon pointed to POWs to distract from his escalating Watergate scandal. While the public eagerly celebrated POWs as heroes, bestowing on them gifts and honors in appreciation for their service and sacrifice, the White House planned a dinner in May at which Hollywood elites would welcome and entertain returnees and their guests. Headlines quickly covered the extravagant event, and the president's scandal dropped to the back pages of the country's prominent newspapers.[65]

Veterans of the Peace Committee loomed in the shadows of the homecoming celebrations. Unlike other POWs, the PCs did not receive a hero's welcome. Colonel Guy had identified them to military officials upon repatriation. On May 29, 1973, the eight Peace Committee POWs were charged with collaborating with the enemy, disrespecting a superior officer, disobeying a superior officer, conspiracy, and carrying out a conspiracy. They faced court-martial.[66] An undisclosed air force official convinced Colonel Guy to speak to the media, and the PC quickly became guilty in the court of public opinion.[67] While the exhibition of POW parades distracted the media's attention from Watergate, the members of the PC became political pawns once again. Instantly, the PC made headlines distracting from President Nixon's Watergate scandal.

A month later, on June 27, Larry Kavanaugh died from a self-inflicted gunshot wound to the head. Kavanaugh's widow, Sandra, held the government accountable: "I blame Col. Guy and the Pentagon for his death. . . . Without their insistence on pursuing these fictitious charges, my husband would be here today."[68] In a note, Larry wrote that he did not want to be imprisoned again.[69] During a televised press conference, Riate blamed the military for Kavanaugh's death: "I Hope that we have enough intelligence to prevent any more deaths, such as Larry's."[70]

Kavanaugh's suicide exposed the dangers of using prisoners of war as political pawns, and his death rocked the military community. A week later, the Pentagon announced that the secretaries of the army and navy had dropped the charges against the remaining ex-POWs. Sandra Kavanaugh understood this dismissal as admission of the Pentagon's liability in Larry's death. "In bringing these charges, the government murdered my husband and caused indescribable hardship in the lives of the other POWs," claimed Sandra, who was left with a daughter and a baby on the way.[71] In one last Peace Committee–like statement, Sandra expressed gratitude to the North Vietnamese for having kept her late husband alive: "He went to Vietnam and the North Vietnamese kept him alive for five years, then he came back to America and his own people killed him."[72] Six of the seven members of the PCs (except for Michael Branch) served as pallbearers laying Kavanaugh to rest.[73]

Aside from this tragedy, little is known about the veterans of the Peace Committee. Before his untimely death in 1984, Alfonso Riate advocated for the rights of veterans and worked in an outreach program with disabled veterans. He eventually felt vindicated from the maligned treatment he received as a member of the PC.[74] James Daly worked for the US Postal Service for almost twenty years and cowrote two autobiographies, *Black Prisoner of War: A Conscientious Objector's Vietnam Memoir* and *A Hero's Welcome: The Conscience of Sergeant James Daly versus the United States Army.* He passed away in 1998. After the war, Fred Elbert bounced from job to job throughout the country. College seemed tedious for Elbert. He eventually became a deputy sheriff in Orange Country, New York, until he quit, due to the effects of post-traumatic stress disorder.[75] Elbert passed away in 2018 in Canton, Ohio.

Almost fifty years have passed since the Paris Peace Accords, and the remaining members of the PC live in relative obscurity. Not much is known of

John Young, King David Rayford Jr., or Michael Branch. I could not reach them for oral history interviews. In the current digital age, former Vietnam War POWs have an online presence at POWNetwork.org. The POW Network explained that these men were "personae non gratae," and their website provided minimal limited information on the members of the PC.[76] Although the group received honorable discharges from the military, their participation in the Peace Committee would continue to damage their lives and careers. Robert Chenoweth worked at the Smithsonian for nine years as the naval historian. He was allegedly forced to leave his job after an official confronted him, suspiciously: "We know who you are."[77] Chenoweth then became curator at the Nez Perce National Historical Park in Spalding, Idaho. Since the war, he has returned to Vietnam several times, and in 2017, Chenoweth participated in the "Epic Dien Bien Phu in the Air" celebration held at Hoa Lo Prison. His old prison warden, Tran Trong Duyet, greeted Chenoweth, saying he "showed a lot of sympathy for Vietnam, and he believed that the red flag with the yellow star would convey a meaning of justice to Robert."[78]

There are many lessons to learn from the Peace Committee of Southeast Asia. First, we are reminded of the high costs of using military personnel as political pawns. Nixon's eagerness to distract from his own scandals drove Larry Kavanaugh to suicide and forced the remaining Peace Committee members to live in disgrace. To this day, politicians continue to use former military personnel as political capital, a point driven home by former president Donald Trump's pardon of the war criminal Eddie Gallagher in 2019. In addition, the experiences of Vietnam War–era POWs further illustrate the dire effects of solitary confinement and torture. This lesson is especially relevant given the fact that the United States continues to exercise solitary confinement in domestic and military prisons today, especially in the incarceration of a disproportionately high number of African Americans and Latinos. It is also relevant to the thousands of enemy combatants held by the US military facing torture and cruel and unusual punishment. If the United States hopes to remake its image in the world, it must acknowledge the pernicious effects of the torture of military captives and enemy combatants.

However unique the history of the Peace Committee may be, it is also representative of the larger ongoing struggles against inequality in and beyond the military. During the war, men of color were absent from the POW command structure. Today, men and women of color and women in general are still limited in the highest military ranks. Women, Latinos, African Americans, and other underrepresented communities serve the military in great numbers despite their unequal status in the United States. Latinos account for 16 percent of active troops, yet as of 2018, there has been only one Latino three-star general dating back to 1995.[79] Since 1973, the number of women in the military has swelled from 2 percent to nearly 18 percent, a disproportional number of whom are Black and Brown. In the future, veterans studies—including work focused on POWs and other traumatizing experiences—must be intersectional in its analysis to address the changing demography of veterans that comprise the US Armed Forces.

Finally, the histories of these eight Peace Committee members teach us about competing historical narratives that erase Black and Brown veterans and their opposition to the war. In many respects, the Peace Committee POWs were marginalized—by American institutions, by race- and class-based hierarchies, by expectations of military decorum, and by public assumptions about honor under captivity—long before their homecomings. The story of the PC illustrates how historical memory creates a certain type of POW narrative for propaganda and rhetoric. In the end, their histories unravel the myth of the homogenous POW experience.

NOTES

1. Stuart I. Rochester and Frederick Kiley, *Honor Bound: American Prisoners of War in Southeast Asia, 1961–1973* (Annapolis, MD: Naval Institute Press, 1998), 461, 562.

2. Their names were marine sergeant Alfonso Ray Riate, army sergeant King David Rayford Jr., army sergeant James Alexander Daly Jr., army sergeant John Arthur Young, army sergeant Robert Preston Chenoweth, marine sergeant Abel Larry Kavanaugh, army specialist Michael Patrick Branch, and marine private Frederick L. Elbert Jr.; "AP: POW Benefit Claimants Exceed Recorded POWs," *Monitor*, April 12, 2009.

3. Joseph Darda, "Post-Traumatic Whiteness: How Vietnam Veterans Became the Basis for a New White Identity Politics," *Los Angeles Review of Books*, November 21, 2017, https://lareviewofbooks.org/article/post-traumatic-whiteness-how-vietnam-veterans -became-the-basis-for-a-new-white-identity-politics#; Christian Appy, *Working-Class War: American Combat Soldiers and Vietnam* (Chapel Hill: University of North Carolina Press, 1993).

4. Craig Howes, *Voices of the Vietnam POWs: Witnesses to Their Fight* (Oxford: Oxford University Press, 1993) 211, 4; Darda, "Post-Traumatic Whiteness."

5. Darda, "Post-Traumatic Whiteness."

6. Howes, *Voices of the Vietnam POWs*, 200, 109, 215.

7.   Ibid., 200–201.

8.   Ibid., 34.

9.   Rochester and Kiley, *Honor Bound*, 442–43.

10.   Howes, *Voices of the Vietnam POWs*, 211.

11.   Ibid., 26.

12.   Everett Álvarez and Anthony S. Pitch, *Chained Eagle: The Heroic Story of the First American Shot Down over North Vietnam* (Dulles, VA: Potomac Books, 2005), 250.

13.   Howes, *Voices of the Vietnam POWs*, 26.

14.   Rochester and Kiley, *Honor Bound*, 340; Juan David Coronado, *"I'm Not Gonna Die in This Damn Place": Manliness, Identity, and Survival of the Mexican American Vietnam Prisoners of War* (East Lansing: Michigan State University Press, 2018), 81–82.

15.   Howes, *Voices of the Vietnam POWs*, 218.

16.   Ibid., 218–19.

17.   James Bond Stockdale in *Return with Honor*, dir. Freida Lee Mock and Terry Sanders, video (Washington, DC: PBS, 2001). Stockdale was the highest-ranking navy POW during the Vietnam War. He received the Congressional Medal of Honor after being released from captivity. Howes, *Voices of the Vietnam POWs*, 247–48; Coronado, *"I'm Not Gonna Die,"* 82.

18.   Raymond B. Lech, *Broken Soldiers* (Chicago: University of Illinois Press, 2000), 81.

19.   Lech, *Broken Soldiers*, 5.

20.   Defense Prisoner of War/Missing in Action (DPMO) file on Alfonzo Riate, Department of Defense, Pentagon, Washington, DC, "Investigation Report" June 10, 1967 (previously classified secret).

21.   Rochester and Kiley, *Honor Bound*, 461.

22.   Peter Arnett, "POWs Who Opposed the War Find Battle Goes on at Home," *Washington Post*, August 29, 1978, 1.

23.   Michael E. Ruane, "Traitors or Patriots? Eight Vietnam POWs Were Charged with Collaborating with the Enemy," *Washington Post*, September 22, 2017.

24.   "POWs Accused of Treason," *Highway 13* (Chicago), July/August 1973, 3.

25.   Rochester and Kiley, *Honor Bound*, 461.

26.   "US Pilots in Vietnam: Preparing for the Day to Return to the U.S," *Nguoi cao tuio* (Vietnam), June 17, 2010. See Coronado, *"I'm Not Gonna Die"* for details on Alfonso Riate and Larry Kavanaugh.

27.   James A. Daly and Lee Bergman, *Black Prisoner of War: A Conscientious Objector's Vietnam Memoir* (Lawrence: University Press of Kansas, 2000), 183.

28.   Ibid., 43.

29.   Howes, *Voices of the Vietnam POWs*, 5.

30.   Lewis L. Gould, preface to *1968: The Election That Changed America* (Chicago, IL: Ivan R. Dee, 2010); and Howes, *Voices of the Vietnam POWs*, 107.

31.   Appy, *Working-Class War*, 246–47.

32.   Howes, *Voices of the Vietnam POWs*, 108; John G. Hubbell, *P.O.W.: A Definitive History of the American Prisoner of War Experience in Vietnam* (New York: Reader's Digest, 1976), 529; Coronado, *"I'm Not Gonna Die,"* 98.

33.   Howes, *Voices of the Vietnam POWs*, 217–18.

34.   Ibid., 34 and 218.

35.   Ibid., 218.

36. Ibid., 109; Zalin Grant, *Survivors: American POWs in Vietnam* (New York: Berkley, 1975), 265.

37. Daly and Bergman, *Black Prisoner of War,* 208.

38. Howes, *Voices of the Vietnam POWs,* 219.

39. Ibid., 109.

40. Grant, *Survivors,* 326.

41. Coronado, *"I'm Not Gonna Die,"* 96.

42. Ruane, "Traitors or Patriots?"

43. Daly and Bergman, *Black Prisoner of War,* 137; quote from 180–81.

44. Billy Waugh, *Isaac Camacho: An American Hero* (Tampa: Digital Publishing of Florida, 2010), 90; George Smith, *P.O.W.: Two Years with the Vietcong* (Berkeley, CA: Ramparts, 1971), 202.

45. Ibid., 118.

46. Howes, *Voices of the Vietnam POWs,* 215.

47. Ibid., 131; Grant, *Survivors,* 196.

48. Appy, *Working-Class War,* 18–21; Kimberly L. Phillips, *War! What Is It Good For? Black Freedom Struggle and the US Military from World War II to Iraq* (Chapel Hill: University of North Carolina Press, 2012), 205–6.

49. Waugh, *Isaac Camacho,* 272.

50. Mike Ives, "Trinh Thi Ngo, Broadcaster Called 'Hanoi Hannah' in Vietnam War, Dies," *New York Times,* October 4, 2016, available at https://www.nytimes.com/2016/10/05/world/asia/trinh-thi-ngo-hanoi-hannah-vietnam-war.html.

51. Matt Miller, "Spike Lee's Da 5 Bloods Brings Hanoi Hannah's Haunting, Real Vietnam War Radio Broadcasts to Life," *Esquire,* June 12, 2020.

52. *POW Message Hails Negro Opposition to War,* from Liberation Radio (1971), manuscript/mixed materials, https://www.loc.gov/item/powmia/pw147576/.

53. Howes, *Voices of the Vietnam POWs,* 109.

54. *RAYFORD, KING D./Prisoner of War Debriefing,* 1973, manuscript/mixed materials, https://www. loc.gov/item/powmia/pwo80282/.

55. *RVN: POW Michael P. Branch Questions Nixon's Concern for POW's, from Liberation Radio,* 1971, manuscript/mixed materials, https://www.loc.gov/item/powmia/pw147576/.

56. Daly and Bergman, *Black Prisoner of War,* 291; Howes, *Voices of the Vietnam POWs,* 219.

57. Hubbell, *P.O.W.,* 512.

58. Ibid., 412.

59. Howes, *Voices of the Vietnam POWs,* 218.

60. Ibid., 109.

61. "Fellow Prisoner Tells How Kavanaugh Changed as POW," *Rocky Mountain News,* June 29, 1973, 5–6.

62. "Kavanaugh Victim of War, Laments Ex-POW Comrade," *Rocky Mountain News,* June 28, 1973, 12.

63. Ibid., 12.

64. Michael J. Allen, *Until the Last Man Comes Home: POWs, MIAs, and the Unending Vietnam War* (Chapel Hill: University of North Carolina Press, 2009), 5, 14.

65. Coronado, *"I'm Not Gonna Die,"* 118.

66.   Suzanne Weiss, "Pentagon Drops POW Charges; Kavanaugh Vindication Claimed," *Rocky Mountain News,* July 4, 1973, 1; Hubbell, *P.O.W.,* 602.

67.   Grant, *Survivors,* 315–16.

68.   Suzanne Weiss, "Sergeant's Widow Blames Pentagon for His Death," *Rocky Mountain News,* June 29, 1973, 5.

69.   Arnett, "POWs Who Opposed the War."

70.   "*US PRISONER OF WAR HOLDS PRESS CONFERENCE,*" AP Archive, June 30, 1973, https://www.aparchive.com/metadata/youtube/3f7f2f8326bf6a9994e9652 217d5d *d63.*

71.   Ibid.

72.   "Here Is a Text of Statement by Widow of Kavanaugh," *Rocky Mountain News,* June 29, 1973, 87.

73.   "7 Enlisted Men Cleared: POW Charges Dropped," *Evening Star and Washington Daily News,* July 3, 1973, A1, A6.

74.   Arnett, "POWs Who Opposed the War."

75.   "Former POW Honors Those Who Did Not Make It Home," *Morning Journal,* September 28, 2014, https://www.morningjournalnews.com/news/local-news/2014/09 /former-pow-honors-those-who-did-not-make-it-home/.

76.   P.O.W. Network: Mary and Charles Schantag, email in discussion with author, February 5, 2010.

77.   Ruane, "Traitors or Patriots?"

78.   "Tears of American Former POW as He Returns to Hoa Lo Prison," *Nhan Dan,* December 24, 2017, https://en *.nhandan.org.vn/culture/item/5733202-tears-of-american -former-pow-as-he-returns-to-hoa-lo-prison.html.*

79.   Rafael Bernal, "Latinos Aren't Reaching Top Military Positions, Study Shows," *Hill,* July 22, 2018, https://thehill.com/latino/398139-latinos-arent-reaching-top -military-positions-study-shows.

Our First Sister

Lynda Van Devanter and the Vietnam Veterans of America's Women's Project

KARA DIXON VUIC

Lynda Van Devanter was an average, all-American girl who played softball, cheered at high school football games, and from a young age felt destined to be a nurse. She was fifteen when president John F. Kennedy challenged her generation of Americans to "ask what you can do for your country," and immediately after graduating from nursing school, she did just that. Motivated by national pride and idealism, she joined the US Army Nurse Corps and volunteered for an assignment in Vietnam. She landed in country in June 1969 and served at the 71st Evacuation Hospital in Pleiku, then the 67th Evacuation Hospital in Qui Nhon. As an operating room nurse, Van Devanter worked long hours trying to save men often younger than herself who endured harrowing injuries. Soon, she began to question why her patients were suffering and dying, and whether the war was worth their sacrifices. The idealism that had led her to the war steadily faded with each casualty. By the end of her year's tour in Vietnam, Van Devanter opposed the war and questioned the policy makers who had sent her and 2.7 million other Americans to wage it. When she returned home, she tried to reintegrate into her old life, but struggled with debilitating depression, substance abuse, and flashbacks that curtailed her ability to hold lasting employment. For many years, she felt isolated and alone, feelings that many veterans would have recognized but that were intensified simply because she was a woman.

In 1979, however, a chance meeting shifted the trajectory of Van Devanter's life and the lives of many other women like her. Van Devanter's husband, a radio writer, was recording a project on a new veterans advocacy group called the Vietnam Veterans of America (VVA) and asked her to tag along.

She sat silently while her husband interviewed its founder, Bobby Muller, and Joe Zengerle, a member of the executive committee, about the organization and their own experiences as veterans. When Zengerle described his struggles readjusting to life after coming home from the war, Van Devanter began crying. Surprised, the men asked why she was upset, and Van Devanter explained that they made her remember her own homecoming and ongoing struggles. Instantly, Muller and Zengerle realized that in all of their planning and organizing, in all of their thinking about the particular needs of Vietnam veterans, they had forgotten the women with whom they had served. Soon after that meeting, Muller asked Van Devanter to create a Women Veterans Project within the VVA to lobby for government research on the particular needs of women veterans, advocate for reform in the Veterans Administration (VA) to guarantee women the care and benefits to which they were legally entitled, and to train counselors on how to work with women veterans.[1]

This chapter examines the Women's Project, and particularly the work of Van Devanter and other Vietnam veterans who advocated for a fundamental reconsideration of women in the veterans, psychological, and medical communities. Through their advocacy and collaboration with a growing women veterans community, the Women's Project and the VVA challenged the conventional image of veterans as male. They accomplished much. As Van Devanter crisscrossed the country, she brought other women veterans out of the shadows and into the public eye, where they began to speak about women veterans' particular health care needs. They insisted on making veterans' health care facilities more accommodating and welcoming for women. And they successfully agitated for the creation of the VA's Women's Advisory Committee, which continues to advise the government on women veterans' issues today.

Even as they enjoyed many successes, those involved in the Women's Project discovered that expanding the public's and the government's image of veterans to include women would be a long and difficult journey. As the face and voice of that effort, Van Devanter personally bore much of the criticism that emerged. Her autobiography about her experiences in Vietnam and afterward brought much-needed public attention to the plight of women veterans, but it also spawned a vitriolic public backlash from critics who judged Van Devanter and the women she described as being too unconventional, too unfeminine. The Women's Project thus walked a fine line between pushing for change and not pushing too hard. Theirs was a fight framed by the particular historical era of the early 1980s, but it was also a fight about issues that women veterans of all eras would recognize: How to be both veterans and women? What does equality mean for veterans who have physical and mental needs particular to their sex and their gender?[2]

The 1970s and early 1980s were an opportune time for women veterans, who benefitted from the accomplishments of second-wave feminism, even if they did not claim the mantle. The Civil Rights Act of 1964 had led to several rulings and laws that required equal educational, death, and loan benefits for women veterans and their dependents. Revisions to Title 38 of US Code in 1972 required the VA to adopt gender-neutral pronouns in its literature to avoid confusion about the benefits to which women were entitled.[3] In 1977, Congress finally granted military status and veteran benefits to the Women Airforce Service Pilots of World War II.[4] And, by January of that same year, thirty-five of the required thirty-eight states had ratified the Equal Rights Amendment. Women were also becoming a larger and more integral part of the military. Since the ending of the draft in 1973, the military had dramatically increased the number of women in uniform, integrated women into regular branches and promotion lists, and opened previously closed military occupational specialties.

But even as women made strides within the military and as veterans, they encountered a public that was still ambivalent about women's military service. For example, although the ERA appeared well on its way to being ratified, conservative activist Phyllis Schlafly rallied opposition to the amendment in large measure by suggesting that its passage would require women to be conscripted for combat service. Schlafly's point might have remained theoretical, but when president Jimmy Carter proposed the reinstatement of Selective Service registration in 1980, he initially proposed that women register alongside men. Even with his qualification that women could be conscripted only for noncombatant service, the proposition of requiring women's service at all sparked consternation, especially among conservative military leaders, about their expanding place in the armed forces. The following year, after the election of president Ronald Reagan, the military halted its recruitment of women, and many leaders tried to reverse the gains women had made.[5]

In these tumultuous years, Vietnam veterans as a whole were finding some success in focusing public awareness on service-connected health concerns, mental health, and the appalling conditions of VA hospitals. Outraged by the bureaucratic red tape they encountered and feeling unwelcomed by staff accustomed to working with older veterans of earlier wars, they lobbied for the creation of community-based outpatient mental health clinics known as Vet Centers that promised "help without hassles," fought for increased educational benefits, and advocated in the psychological community to better understand what was then popularly known as "Vietnam stress syndrome."[6] Especially after the dedication of the Vietnam Veterans Memorial in 1982, the nation as whole seemed much more open to public conversations about the meanings of the war and the experiences of those who served.

For the most part, though, those conversations focused on men. More specifically, the popular image of Vietnam veterans centered around stories of close combat, battlefield heroics, and hypermasculine men, to the exclusion of all other experiences and stories.[7] Few Americans thought of women when they thought of veterans at all. Despite a long history of women's military service, mainstream veterans' organizations excluded women, which left them isolated from each other, unaware of common struggles, and without a support network. The Veterans of Foreign Wars excluded women outright until 1978, and the American Legion largely relegated even women who had served in uniform to ladies' auxiliaries.[8] Groups such as the Vietnam Veterans Against the War (VVAW) had no formal exclusionary practices, but many women felt unwanted nonetheless. Van Devanter had been vocal about her opposition to the war even when stationed in Vietnam, but when she showed up at a VVAW parade, another veteran told her that she shouldn't march because she didn't "look like a vet."[9]

Women veterans who sought solidarity in feminist organizations seldom found it. Many radical feminist organizations opposed the Vietnam War and saw women in uniform as being complicit in a patriarchal institution that had waged an unjust war.[10] Some liberal feminist organizations, including the National Organization for Women, argued that women should have equal opportunities in the military but hesitated to actively support women veterans. One of the great ironies, perhaps, of the history of the VVA's Women's Project is that feminist organizations repeatedly denied Van Devanter's appeals for funding, yet the Playboy Foundation donated ten thousand dollars for the first study of female Vietnam veterans' mental health.[11]

Many female veterans even felt disconnected from women their age. "Maybe if I didn't go to Vietnam," nurse Jill Mishkel considered, "I'd be married and have a house in the suburbs and a two-car garage. That's what I planned on doing before I went to Vietnam."[12] Army nurse Joan Garvert found that when she returned home from Vietnam, her "friends were all into their own little world. . . . They wanted to talk about their babies, their lives now, who they were dating, whether so-and-so would call them," Garvert explained, and she "just couldn't deal with it because there were people dying on the other side of the world. I thought, don't you all understand what's going on in the world?"[13] Essentially, women veterans belonged to no obvious cohort: they did not "look like vets" to most veterans, but their experiences did not neatly conform to the typical lives of women, either.

In part because of this lack of a group identity, many women had come home from Vietnam, separated from the military, and not mentioned the fact that they were veterans. Army nurse Kate O'Hare Palmer even married without ever telling her husband that she had been an operating room nurse in Vietnam.[14] The first task of the Women's Project, then, was simply to find the women. That should have been a fairly straightforward task, but as Van Devanter quickly discovered, neither the US Department of Defense nor the Veterans Administration had any idea how many women had served in Vietnam. The secretary of Defense for Health Affairs reported that a total of 269 women served in Vietnam throughout the war, including six in Pleiku at the time that Van Devanter had been there. These numbers were so low as to be laughable; as Van Devanter pointed out, there were seven women in her hootch alone.[15]

To find the women—however many of them there were—Van Devanter launched a publicity campaign in the fall of 1980 and began traveling the country. She reached out to the VVA's journalist contacts who wrote news articles and feature stories that described women veterans' particular struggles. Army veteran Sara McVicker was working at the Dayton, Ohio, VA Medical Center when she read one of those articles in *Parade* magazine. She had not told any of her colleagues that she had served in Vietnam, but when she read about Van Devanter and heard that she was going to be attending a local conference on PTSD, McVicker reached out.[16] Countless other women did the same. Many women veterans credited Van Devanter with giving them the courage to speak openly about their experiences and their struggles, often for the first time.[17] As air force nurse Linda Spooner Schwartz put it, Van Devanter was "our first sister."[18] She made other women veterans feel comfortable sharing their stories, a necessary first step for women veterans who slowly began to find each other and advocate for their common needs.

As she gathered a group of "sister" veterans around her, Van Devanter focused the Women's Project's attention on improving women's access to and reception in Vet Centers and VA hospitals. For women who found it difficult to publicly identify as veterans, seeking help for mental or physical health needs proved even more problematic. Many male veterans welcomed the camaraderie and counseling they received at Vet Centers, but women veterans seldom found the same. When army nurse Peggy Mikelonis went to her local Vet Center seeking counseling, the staff greeted her with the question that was posed countless times to countless women who sought health care, home loans, and counseling: "Who's your husband?"[19] Even if women veterans were accepted into Vet Center groups, they seldom felt included in conversations that focused on firefights, patrols, and the terrors of combat. Many counselors, in fact, subscribed to the notion that women could not suffer from war stress because they had not been in combat. Many women veterans supposed the same. For years, Van Devanter had failed to see how the traumas that haunted her dreams were shaping her daytime struggles. Even after she sought therapy in the late 1970s, she did not tell her therapist that she had served in the war.[20]

Her reluctance made some sense, given contemporary associations between war stress and combat. But these were also the years when Vietnam veteran counselors were actively pressing for a revision of what was then formally called "gross stress disorder" to recognize that war stress did not always nor necessarily result from direct engagement of the enemy. When the third edition of *The Diagnostic and Statistical Manual of Mental Disorders* was published in 1980, it attributed the newly renamed "Post Traumatic Stress Disorder" to having endured a "recognizable stressor that would evoke significant symptoms of distress in almost everyone." In disassociating PTSD from combat, the *DSM* made it possible for women (and indeed, most of the men who had served in Vietnam who had also not served in combat positions) to connect their postwar struggles to the war.[21]

With a new understanding of PTSD to support her, Van Devanter traveled the country, seeking to make Vet Centers more welcoming to women veterans. Among her biggest supporters was Shad Meshad, an army veteran who had served as a counselor in Vietnam, lobbied for the creation of the Vet Center program, and worked in the 1970s for the inclusion of a broadened definition of PTSD to the *DSM*.[22] Meshad immediately recognized Van Devanter's struggles when the pair met in 1979 and then led her through a counseling program that she credited with helping her confront her struggles with the war.[23] Together, Van Devanter and Meshad worked to increase the number of female counselors at Vet Centers and to make the centers more responsive to women veterans. Van Devanter served as faculty at staff training that emphasized the particular needs of women veterans, some Vet Centers issued public service ads targeting women, and female Vietnam veterans joined Vet Center staffs as counselors and directors.[24]

As Van Devanter worked on improving women's access to Vet Centers, she expanded her sights and gained allies. Although the early 1980s witnessed a growing cultural resistance to the changes brought on by second-wave feminism, legally, women had made significant strides in a short span of time. One did not have to be an ardent feminist to support the removal of legal and practical discriminations against women. In that environment, Van Devanter's publicity campaign caught the eye of senator Daniel Inouye (D-HI), who, after reading an article about her work and asking how he could help, requested a US Government Accountability Office (GAO) report on the VA's care of women veterans.[25] The Women's Project also found an ally in representative Tom Daschle (D-SD and chair of the Vietnam Veterans in Congress, an early ally of the VVA). Daschle called a subcommittee hearing of the House Committee on Veterans' Affairs in July 1981 and invited Van Devanter to testify.

In the first of several testimonies before Congress, Van Devanter pointed out that although women veterans were legally entitled to the same care as male veterans, VA hospitals regularly failed to provide basic women's health care and did not include women in studies of veterans' health. She explained that while traveling to raise awareness for the Women's Project, she had called local VA hospitals, identified as a veteran, and asked if she could receive a gynecological exam. Of the fifteen hospitals she called, fourteen had no gynecologist on staff. Only once did hospital staff inform her that she could be reimbursed for getting the exam in a civilian facility, but only after she had pushed the matter all the way to the hospital's chief of staff.[26] When the GAO report came out a little over a year later, it confirmed what Van Devanter had been saying. Only seven gynecologists worked on staff at VA hospitals across the country.[27]

Van Devanter's efforts to reform Vet Centers and VA hospitals pointed to a central question that framed women veterans' fight for mental and physical health care: what did it mean to offer women and men equal care? Although women had endured many of the same wartime experiences and postwar struggles as male veterans, they also confronted issues particular to their sex and to their gender. As Van Devanter and Meshad explained in news articles about the Women's Project, whatever women's specific job in-country, men often looked to them as maternal and romantic symbols and even as sexual partners. They endured harassment and assault. Women who had been nurses cared for others while ignoring their own needs. And women typically buried their frustrations both during the war and afterward because that was what women of their generation were supposed to do.[28] Moreover, in all of the studies about Vietnam veterans, not one had included women, and the VA had no plans to include them in an upcoming study of Agent Orange.[29]

Ronald Reagan's first and short-lived VA director, Robert P. Nimmo (1981–82), insisted that that the administration treated all veterans "without regard to sex," but the matter was not quite that simple. When pressed, officials insisted that the VA did not need to provide women's health care in hospitals because the number of women veterans was small, and it did not need to offer women fee-basis care (by which they could receive care at a civilian facility and be reimbursed by the VA) because any health care concern particular to women was unlikely to be service-connected. Any sex-specific care such as a gynecological exam or mammogram constituted a "special" service, according to VA officials, and therefore discriminated against men.[30]

Veterans Administration officials must have been caught off-guard, then, by women veterans who argued that sex-specific care was necessary for equality.

These were women of the sixties generation who had grown up in the era of second-wave feminism, and they were not going to sit idly by and accept that their needs were irrelevant. When army nurse Sara McVicker came home from Vietnam, she explained, "We had a new culture that said it was okay to do unheard-of things like question authority or debate the legitimacy of the war." Nurses such as herself had witnessed the worst of war, and "none of these women, me included," she noted, "thought we should just tolerate things as they had always been."[31] After all, men could expect prostate exams at VA hospitals, despite the fact that prostate health was seldom service-connected.[32] Despite the resistance they faced, the women were getting noticed. In August 1981, a *Boston Globe* reporter inquired about whether the VA had conducted studies on women Vietnam veterans. "I wish I could tell you there are some," one unnamed "VA bureaucrat" responded. "Then we could shut up that little group of 50 women veterans who are always appearing on television and complaining about that."[33]

Van Devanter was making slow but steady progress, and in the spring of 1983 published her autobiography *Home Before Morning: The Story of an Army Nurse in Vietnam* to great acclaim. A *Washington Post* advertisement described the book as "Deeply moving . . . awesome . . . an eloquent guide by one 'who knows dearly the cost of war.'"[34] But the book also sparked an intense backlash that revealed just how deeply some were committed to the image of military women that Van Devanter challenged. *Home Before Morning* upturned the conventional, popular image of wartime nurses as modern-day Florence Nightingales, angels in white wiping fevered brows.[35] Van Devanter described her affairs with physicians, chronicled drug and alcohol use among medical staff, laced the text with plenty of four-letter words, and critiqued military policies and the war itself. In many ways, her book paralleled the accounts of many male veterans who had written about similar issues and expressed similar disillusionment.

But while many were willing to grant male veterans the artistic license to tell their stories, they were unwilling to extend the same to Van Devanter.[36] Many of her harshest critics were other women veterans, particularly older women whose formative experiences in the military had occurred in an era when women in uniform were even less accepted than they had been during the Vietnam War or in the 1980s, women who had had to very carefully craft an acceptable public image of servicewomen as professional, sexually respectable, proper ladies.

In particular, critics charged that Van Devanter was too feminist, too radical in her opposition to the war, too sexually liberated. One especially vocal critic alleged that Van Devanter was "trying to turn the war into a battleground for women's rights," of pursuing antiwar and feminist goals at the expense of wounded soldiers.[37] The combination of sexual liberation and antiwar protest was just too much for one "high-ranking official" at the VA who alleged that the book cast the Army Nurse Corps "in a disparaging light."[38] Nora Kinzer, special assistant to VA administrator Harry Walters, who led the VA between 1983 and 1986, went on television to criticize the book and Van Devanter. To Kinzer, Van Devanter's frank discussions of sexuality only reinforced common tropes of army nurses as being either lesbians or whores.[39] Edith Knox, chief nurse at the 67th Evacuation Hospital, Van Devanter's second assignment, complained, "This book makes us look like a bunch of bed-hopping, foul-mouthed tramps."[40]

According to those who knew her, Van Devanter felt the criticism personally and deeply.[41] And it impeded her work for women veterans. For several years, the Women's Project had worked with the American Veterans Committee, a politically liberal veterans organization founded in World War II, to lobby for the creation of a Women's Advisory Committee at the VA that would provide advice on all matters related to women veterans. Although several VA directors had nodded their endorsement of the committee, none had actually created one, and advocates had turned to Congress for support. In July 1983, Congress mandated the creation of the committee and required that the VA report biennially about the needs of women veterans as well as the programs and activities it had enacted to meet those needs.[42] Five VA staffers, headed by Nora Kinzer, appointed the committee's inaugural eighteen members. Lynda Van Devanter—who had led the charge to force the VA to pay attention to women veterans—was not among them. No member of the VVA was appointed until 1987.[43] Very likely, the snub was intentional, a deliberate decision to prevent a vocal VA critic from serving on the committee. Even without her, however, the committee struggled with the very issue that Van Devanter had raised: what did equality mean for women veterans who had sex- and gender-specific needs?[44]

Still, Van Devanter and the VVA continued to press on in their fight for women veterans, and perhaps this is where Van Devanter's legacy is most visible. From its founding in 1979 until 1983, the VVA operated as a loosely organized advocacy group directed and controlled primarily by its founder, Bobby Muller. In November 1983, the organization held its founding convention, adopted a constitution, voted to approve a series of resolutions, and elected officers and a board of directors. Two of the nineteen inaugural members of the board of directors were women—army nurse veterans Saralee McGoran and Lily Adams, whom Van Devanter had met during her travels and encouraged to become involved in women veterans' issues.[45]

Among the resolutions unanimously adopted by delegates were three that indicated the VVA's stance on women's position within the organization and as veterans at large. One resolution, noting the "traditional inequities in the draft laws and their administration during the Vietnam War," declared that "any future draft be equitable . . . irrespective of . . . sex, sexual preference, social and economic position."[46] The organization also referenced the historical exclusion of women from most veterans' organizations and popular conceptions of veterans as being men. To correct these injustices, the VVA directed that "all literature or outreach materials coming from or pertaining to the Vietnam Veterans of America be written in non-gender-specific language and be indicative of the membership of women veterans in the Vietnam Veterans of America." It also called for a monthly column in its national newsletter on women veteran issues and committed the VVA to working to "correct the inequities in the health care system."[47]

Most controversial, however, was the resolution supporting the Equal Rights Amendment. Noting the VVA's commitment to "equal responsibility for all citizens of the United States under any future draft" and its "support of complete and equitable recognition of women veterans," the resolution committed the VVA to "support the passage of the Equal Rights Amendment by the Congress, and its ratification by the states, affording equal responsibilities, rights and protections to female citizens under the United States' Constitution"[48] Jack Devine, a delegate from Michigan who was elected to the board at the meeting, had proposed the resolution to the Government Affairs Committee, where it was initially defeated. He took it to another committee, where it passed and was ultimately approved by the convention.[49]

Then the VVA's membership director, Mary Stout, attributed the VVA's support of such progressive gender policies to Van Devanter's influence. Many of the resolutions had been written by the VVA national staff—including Van Devanter—and they appealed to the political leanings of many in attendance. Delegates came from all sides of the political spectrum, but the national staff and many in positions of power at the convention fell more toward its left side.[50] Still, the male veterans in the primarily male VVA respected Van Devanter and the women they had served with in Vietnam.[51]

The next spring, in May 1984, Van Devanter resigned from the VVA. Publicly, she attributed her resignation to the "pressure of mounting commitments since the publication of her book . . . and the rapid growth of the VVA this past year." She had also committed herself as an adviser to Columbia Pictures, which was then considering making *Home Before Morning* into a film, and thus, she had little time for political work.[52] Behind the scenes, she had been forced out by VVA president Bobby Muller and vice president John Terzano, who believed that she lacked a clear agenda and mission.[53] Perhaps if Van Devanter had been appointed to the Women's Advisory Committee, she might have had more concrete plans for the Women's Project. Perhaps personality conflicts played a role in her dismissal. Nonetheless, the VVA remained committed to advocating for women veterans. In 1987, the membership elected the organization's second president. By a three-to-one margin, they elected army nurse Mary Stout. She was the first woman to head a national veterans' organization.[54] "Veteran," Stout declared, "is no longer a male word."[55]

Together, Lynda Van Devanter, the Women's Project, and the VVA expanded government, medical, and psychological communities' understandings of the definition of "veteran," of PTSD, and of the gendered nature of military service in ways that have had lasting effects. After Van Devanter left the Women's Project, it ceased to exist as a special project. Under Stout's leadership, the membership assumed more of the work of the organization than it had done under Muller, and a new standing Women Veterans Committee took up the charge. Kate O'Hare Palmer, who had married without telling her husband that she was a veteran, now chairs the committee and works to raise awareness about women's issues and advocate for women veterans at all levels of government.[56] She and the countless other women who have advocated for women veterans are Van Devanter's legacy.

NOTES

Thanks to Jorden Pitt, Mokie Porter, and John Baky for research assistance, and to Rick Weidman, Joan Furey, Mary Stout, Linda Spooner Schwartz, Lily Adams, and W. D. Ehrhardt for the privilege of talking with them about Lynda Van Devanter, the VVA, and women veterans.

1. Lynda Van Devanter with Christopher Morgan, *Home Before Morning: The Story of an Army Nurse in Vietnam* (New York: Beaufort Books, 1983), 287–89; Lynda Van Devanter, "VVA's Women Veterans Project Carries Issues to Congress and to Public," *Minerva* 1, no. 1 (Mar. 1983): 14, accessed August 7, 2019, http://library.tcu .edu/PURL/EZproxy_link.asp?http://search.proquest.com/docview/222789704 ?accountid=7090. For more on organizations that had advocated for women veterans before and alongside the Women's Project, see Susan Sweetnam, "Women Veterans: A Different Road Home from Vietnam," *Christian Science Monitor*, November 17, 1981; Amy Rebecca Jacobs, "Redefining 'Veteran': The Vietnam War and the Making of Women Veterans 1979–1997" (PhD diss., University of Virginia, 2013); June A. Willenz, *Women Veterans: America's Forgotten Heroines* (New York: Continuum, 1983); Jean Dunlavy, "A Band of Sisters: Vietnam Women Veterans' Organization for Rights and Recognition, 1965–1995" (PhD diss., Boston University, 2009).

2. For an excellent study of how women veterans and the VA understood "equality," see Jacobs, "Redefining 'Veteran.'"

3. Willenz, *Women Veterans*, 193–95; "Words and Statements Denoting Gender," 72 Stat. 1114, 38 USC 210.

4. *GI Bill Improvement Act of 1977*, Public Law 95–202, November 23, 1977.

5. Kara Dixon Vuic, "Conscription and Combat in a Volunteer Force," in *The All-Volunteer Force: Fifty Years of History, Impacts, Challenges, and Implications*, ed. William A. Taylor (under contract with University Press of Kansas); Beth Bailey, *America's Army: Making the All-Volunteer Force* (Cambridge, MA: Harvard University Press, 2009); Jeanne Holm, *Women in the Military: An Unfinished Revolution* (Novato, CA: Presidio Press, 1992).

6. *Veterans Health Care Amendments of 1979*, Public Law 96–22, July 13, 1979; Wilbur J. Scott, *Vietnam Veterans since the War: The Politics of PTSD, Agent Orange, and the National Memorial* (Norman: University of Oklahoma Press, 2004); Mark Boulton, *Failing Our Veterans: The G.I. Bill and the Vietnam Generation* (New York: New York University Press, 2014).

7. See Gregory A. Daddis, "Mansplaining Vietnam: Male Veterans and America's Popular Image of the Vietnam War," *Journal of Military History* 82, no. 1 (Jan. 2018): 181–207, for a review of literature on this topic.

8. Dunlavy, "Band of Sisters," 110–11.

9. Van Devanter, *Home Before Morning*, 231.

10. Some radical feminists later connected women's military service to women's equality and power. Kathie Sarachild wrote in 1989 wrote that "military duty was and is a power" both to defend the nation and to refuse to participate in unjust wars. See Kathie Sarachild, "Taking in the Images: A Record in Graphics of the Vietnam Era Soil for Feminism," *Vietnam Generation* 1, no. 3–4 (1989): article 19.

11. Betty Cuniberti, "'Forgotten' Vietnam Veterans: Women," *Los Angeles Times*, October 10, 1982; Diane Kiesel, "Women Also Carry Pain of Vietnam," *Frederick (MD)*

News-Post, September 2, 1981. The donation funded the first scholarly study of female Vietnam veterans' mental health: Jenny Ann Schnaier, "Women Vietnam Veterans and Mental Health Adjustment: A Study of Their Experiences and Post-Traumatic Stress" (master's thesis, University of Maryland, 1982).

12. Jill Mishkel, in Keith Walker, *A Piece of My Heart: The Stories of Twenty-Six American Women Who Served in Vietnam* (New York: Ballantine Books, 1987), 132–33.

13. Joan Garvert, in Ron Steinman, *Women in Vietnam* (New York: TV Books, 2000), 111.

14. Kara Dixon Vuic, *Officer, Nurse, Woman: The Army Nurse Corps in the Vietnam War* (Baltimore, MD: Johns Hopkins University Press, 2010), 8.

15. *House Committee on Veterans' Affairs, Issues Concerning Vietnam Veterans: Hearing Before the Select Subcommittee of the Committee on Veterans' Affairs,* 97th Cong., 1st Sess., July 16, 1981, 46–50. Neither the military nor the VA knows, even now, an exact number of servicewomen who served in Vietnam. Estimates range from 7,500 to 11,000.

16. Richard Currey, "Sara McVicker," *VVA Veteran*, January/February 2019, http://vvaveteran.org/39-1/39-1_saramcvicker.html.

17. Winnie Smith, *American Daughter Gone to War: On the Front Lines with an Army Nurse in Vietnam* (New York: Pocket Books, 1992), 7; Kathryn Marshall, *In the Combat Zone: An Oral History of American Women in Vietnam, 1966–1975* (Boston, MA: Little, Brown, 1987), 3–4; Leslie McClusky (pseudonym), in Marshall, *In the Combat Zone*, 60; Lily Adams, in Marshall, *In the Combat Zone*, 227; Dan Freedman and Jacqueline Rhoads, *Nurses in Vietnam: The Forgotten Veterans* (Austin: Texas Monthly Press, 1987), x; Walker, *Piece of My Heart*, xii; Anne Simon Auger, in Walker, *Piece of My Heart*, 104–5; Lily Jean Lee Adams, in Walker, *Piece of My Heart*, 403–4; Georgia Duella, "Like Men Who Fought, They Tell of Anxiety and Painful Recall," *New York Times*, March 23, 1981, B12.

18. Linda Spooner Schwartz, interview by author, August 12, 2019, phone interview, recording.

19. Peggy Mikelonis, interview by author, December 22, 2003, Tampa, FL, tape recording and transcript, The Vietnam Archive, Texas Tech University, Lubbock TX, 21.

20. Van Devanter, *Home Before Morning*, 262. See also Jacobs, "Redefining 'Veteran,'" 121–22.

21. PTSD diagnostic criteria in Allan V. Horwitz, *PTSD: A Short History* (Baltimore, MD: Johns Hopkins University Press, 2018), 99, see also 85–106 for a brief history of the revision of the *DSM* in response to the Vietnam War. For an excellent study of how a broadened understanding of PTSD enabled women veterans to make claims as veterans, see Jacobs, "Redefining 'Veteran,'" 55–69.

22. See Scott, *Vietnam Veterans since the War*, chapters 2 and 3.

23. Van Devanter, *Home Before Morning*, 295–97.

24. Joan Furey, interview by author, August 2, 2019, telephone interview, recording; Kathleen Hendrix, "After the War: Women Vietnam Vets Seeking Peace of Mind," *Los Angeles Times*, January 11, 1981; "Veterans News," *Clovis News-Journal*, September 23, 1981, 19; Kiesel, "Women Also Carry Pain"; Dunlavy, "Band of Sisters," 135–39; Willenz, *Women Veterans*, 228–29.

25. Dunlavy, "Band of Sisters," 125.

26. Lynda Van Devanter testimony, *House Committee on Veterans' Affairs, Issues Concerning Vietnam Veterans*, 46–50.

27. Government Accountability Office, *Actions Needed to Ensure that Female Veterans Have Equal Access to VA Benefits* (Washington, DC: Government Printing Office, 1983).

28. See Hendrix, "After the War"; David Grunwald, "Crying Need," *Boston Globe*, August 23, 1981.

29. Van Devanter testimony, 49.

30. Pete Earley, "Forgotten Women: Effects of War on Female Vietnam Veterans Are Only Now Emerging," *Washington Post*, March 25, 1981.

31. Currey, "Sara McVicker"; also see Sara J. McVicker, "Invisible Veterans: The Women Who Served in Vietnam," *Journal of Psychosocial Nursing & Mental Health Services* 23, no. 10 (Oct. 1985): 12–19.

32. For a much longer discussion of the VA's understanding of equality for men and women in medical care, see Jacobs, "Redefining 'Veteran.'"

33. Grunwald, "Crying Need."

34. Display ad 116, *Washington Post*, May 8, 1983, BW8; quotes from Carol Van Strum, "Healing and Hurting in Vietnam," review of *Home Before Morning*, *Washington Post*, April 11, 1983, B6.

35. VVA sold copies of *Home Before Morning* and advertised it in the *VVA Veteran* from December 1983 through December 1987. See VVA Product Sales Division ad, *VVA Veteran*, December 1983, 19; Warner Books full-page ad, *VVA Veteran*, March 1984, 18.

36. For a lengthy critique of Van Devanter's accounts of her wartime experiences, see Gary Kulik, *"War Stories" False Atrocity Tales, Swift Boaters, and Winter Soldiers—What Really Happened in Vietnam* (Washington, DC: Potomac Books, 2009). I examine the criticism Van Devanter faced in *Officer, Nurse, Woman*, chapter 7.

37. "Nurses Against Misrepresentation," three-page statement, 3, 314.7 History, Vietnam, Comments on Studies, Books—"Home Before Morning" and "Forever Sad the Hearts," Army Nurse Corps Archive, Fort Sam Houston, San Antonio, TX (ANCA).

38. Boodman, "War Story"; also Michael McLeod, "Vietnam's Horrors Endured by Women, Too," *Cincinnati Enquirer*, June 8, 1983.

39. Boodman, "War Story"; Pete Earley, "Inside: The Veterans Administration," *Washington Post*, August 24, 1983.

40. Sandra G. Boodman, "War Story: Ex-Army Nurse's Book on Horrors of Vietnam Renews Old Controversy," *Washington Post*, May 23, 1983; also see Virginia Knox, interview by Connie Slewitzke, October 1992, ANC Oral Histories, ANCA, 5.

41. Rick Weidman, interview by author, September 18, 2019, Silver Spring, MD, recording; Furey interview, August 2, 2019; Schwartz interview.

42. *Veterans' Health Care Amendments of 1983*, Public Law 98–160, November 21, 1983; Willenz, *Women Veterans*, 213–23, 226, 240; Furey interview.

43. "VA Establishes Advisory Committee on Women Veterans," *VVA Veteran*, 3, no. 3 (June 1983): 3; Earley, "Inside"; Dunlavy, "Band of Sisters," 161. Several individuals I spoke with who knew Van Devanter and were aware of the situation all believed that VA officials' opposition to *Home Before Morning* and to Van Devanter's confrontational style led to her not being appointed to the Women's Advisory Committee. Weidman interview; Mary Stout, interview by author, August 22, 2019, telephone interview, recording; Furey interview.

44. Jeanne M. Holm, "Report of the Veterans Administration Advisory Committee on Women Veterans July 1988," *Minerva* 6, no. 4 (Dec. 1988): 1; Stout interview.

45. Saralee McGoran, "Vietnam Veterans of America Show Respect for Women at Founding Convention," *Minerva* 2, no. 1 (Mar. 1984): 8, accessed August 7, 2019, http://library .tcu.edu/PURL/EZproxy_link.asp?http://search.proquest.com/docview/222788917 ?accountid=7090.

46. Draft, G-4, adopted at Founding Convention, November 6–10, 1983, quoted in *VVA Veteran*, December 1983, 10.

47. Women Veterans and Public Policy Positions, adopted at Founding Convention, November 6–10, 193, quoted in *VVA Veteran*, December 1983, 14.

48. Equal Rights Amendment, adopted at Founding Convention, November 6–10, 193, quoted in *VVA Veteran*, December 1983, 14.

49. Michael Keaton, "Glory Days: VVA's Founding Convention," *VVA Veteran*, May/June 2018, http://vvaveteran.org/38-3/38-3_foundingconvention1.html.

50. Weidman interview; Stout interview; Keaton, "Glory Days."

51. Weidman interview; Stout interview; Schwartz interview.

52. "Van Devanter Resigns from VVA Top Slot," *VVA Veteran*, August 1984, 3.

53. Weidman interview.

54. "Woman Takes Command," *New York Times*, August 3, 1987; "Ex-Nurse Leading Veterans' Body Recalls Her War," *New York Times*, August 12, 1987; Lee Hockstader, "Woman to Lead Charge for Viet Veterans Group," *Washington Post*, August 3, 1987; Elizabeth Mehren, "New President of Vietnam Veterans—She's Been There," *Los Angeles Times*, July 31, 1987.

55. "Woman Takes Command."

56. "Women Veterans Involvement in VVA," M-WV-11–93, *VVA Veteran*, September 1993, 22.

"The Wrong Man in Uniform"

Antidraft Republicans and the Ideological Origins of the All-Volunteer Force, 1966–73

JOHN WORSENCROFT

The years from about fifteen to twenty-five are the crucial formative years of a man's life. . . . And it is these years that an allegedly humanitarian society forces him to spend in terror—that any road he takes can be blocked at any moment by an unpredictable power, that, barring his vision of the future, there stands the gray shape of the barracks, and, perhaps, beyond it, death for some unknown reason in some alien jungle.

—Ayn Rand, *Capitalism: The Unknown Ideal*

In the messy popular memory of the fight to end the draft during the Vietnam War, there is a recurring cast of characters: unwashed hippies, who famously attempted to "levitate" the Pentagon in 1967; privileged college students, who protested a war that they would probably never see because their deferments kept them safe; and the radicals, who burned their draft cards, broke into draft board offices, and, in the words of Mario Savio, put their "bodies upon the gears and upon the wheels" of the state to stop the war machine. But the history of how the draft ended in 1973 also contains characters who might have felt more comfortable in Merle Haggard's vision of Muskogee, Oklahoma. Largely forgotten today, Republicans, as early as 1965, began making the case that the draft was un-American, that it forced men to make hasty life choices to avoid getting drafted. These unusual antidraft activists used midcentury representations of American masculinity to send a clear message: the draft infringed on every man's liberty to chart his own course in life, and compulsory military service was a waste of time and a formidable roadblock to the American Dream. As one critic argued, "Draftees are the lowest caste of a caste-conscious estate and wield no influence whatever, and heaven help us if American liberty . . . rests on their helpless shoulders."[1] Getting drafted meant being stuck in uniform while the rest of society continued to move forward—or worse, getting left behind at war's end.

On top of that, right-wing critics of the draft argued that the Selective Service System cast a shadow over American men, damaging their psyche. A nation that valued individualism and freedom could not countenance the "involuntary servitude"—the slavery—of conscription, they argued. Like a dam on a river—a recurring metaphor in conscription debates—the draft blocked the natural flow of young men's lives, forcing some men to go to college when they might not have, forcing others to get married and have children sooner than they might have, and forcing those men who did get drafted to put off marriage, family, and a career, forever diminishing their chance to chart their own destiny.[2] It was all terribly unfair—an injustice that needed to be remedied.

Over time, these clean-cut antidraft Republicans would join libertarian economists such as Milton Friedman and Martin Anderson to convince the Nixon administration to abandon the draft and move to a volunteer military in 1973.[3] These younger members of the Republican Party developed a robust critique of the draft, not in 1968 or 1969, when the war was becoming politically untenable for politicians on both the right and left—but as early as 1965 and 1966, when Americanization of the war effort was just beginning. They honed arguments that would ultimately appeal to Richard Nixon. First, they argued that compulsory military service, and the Selective Service System that "channeled" young men through its complicated manpower system, was psychologically damaging to young men. Second, they charged that conscription was antithetical to liberty, that the draft constituted a "hidden tax" on thousands of young men, crippling their chances of success in the civilian economy. Some went so far as to equate conscription with "involuntary servitude"—or slavery. Finally, they argued that the draft made noble military service cheap, reducing what might be a worthy voluntary pursuit to a waste of time. As Bruce K. Chapman, a conservative editorialist for the *New York Herald Tribune,* lamented, the only feeling that the draft inculcated into draftees was "the desire to get out as soon as possible."[4]

This chapter tells the story of a group of Americans who did not want to become veterans. Even as the civil rights struggle raged, when questions of freedom were at the forefront of national consciousness, when activists and policy makers grappled with solutions to the problems of racism and poverty in America, a small yet influential group of white male conservatives demanded the right to avoid veteran status. To be sure, we can understand their hesitancy. By the late 1960s, the war had become increasingly unpopular. Over the following years, racial conflict, fragging, AWOL, and desertion rates increased and threatened the ability of the army to achieve objectives in Vietnam. Within this context, people across the ideological spectrum grasped the potency of the idea of marginalization as a political weapon.[5] As African Americans struggled to eliminate the Jim Crow injustice of the poll tax, these Republicans argued that the draft constituted a "hidden tax" on young American men. As liberals expanded the power of the federal government in the 1960s, younger Republicans began to view conscription as another iteration of government overreach. Nurturing these ideas were broader anxieties, felt by many Americans, about the family, the status of the breadwinner, and the meaning of manhood.[6] The draft placed an enormous burden on young men who might not be ready to make consequential life choices—to go to school, to marry and have kids, to enlist rather than be drafted according to the needs of the military, or to go into a draft-exempted career. Conversely, for those who were drafted, it meant putting off school, or vocational training, or on-the-job experience, for two years—meaning a loss of potential wages and time gaining experience and seniority in a job. The free market, critics argued, not the Selective Service System, was the proper arena for making men better providers, husbands, and productive members of society.

The story of conservative antidraft activism is significant for a number of reasons. For starters, it upsets our understanding of American politics as neatly divided between left and right, Democrat and Republican. It was the Republicans, the party of national defense, that radically upset how the military functioned in the United States—while the nation was still at war in Southeast Asia, no less. This history reminds us that today's era of "thanking the troops" is a somewhat new development. As recently as the 1960s, within the context of the Cold War and the Vietnam conflict, there was a remarkable amount of debate across the political spectrum. And many of its most consequential voices were not obscure people on the fringes—the men (and they were overwhelmingly men) who participated in this debate would become foot soldiers in the Reagan revolution. Most of the names in this story became entrenched figures in Washington for the rest of the twentieth century, writing American policies in areas ranging from economics and finance to war and peace. They became the intellectual backbone of the Republican establishment from Reagan, through the Bush years, all the way to Donald J. Trump.

For our purposes, though, this chapter shines further light on Americans' anxieties about Vietnam-era veterans. As numerous historians have observed, the Vietnam War in so many ways fundamentally changed the status of veterans in US culture and national identity. Even as the war was being fought, Vietnam veterans were assigned (and, in some cases, embraced) a narrative of victimization that cast them as the war's primary casualties, betrayed by the government, spat on (figuratively) by the public, and isolated from the rest of society—marginalized in the country for which they fought, often with little choice. In this chapter, I explore efforts to mobilize this narrative in the service of a small, elite, white male cohort—the sort who never experienced the sting of inequality themselves. Horrified at the thought of becoming veterans—of putting their bodies on the line in service of their nation—they argued that the answer to society's problems, from racism to war fighting, could be found in the market. Inequality, they believed, was a function of government getting in the way of citizens making rational economic choices. The draft picked winners and losers, rather than the "impartial" marketplace. And, if African Americans joined the new volunteer military in droves, then that was a rational market choice, a logical solution to social inequities.

To be certain, some readers will no doubt wonder about the relative scarcity of *actual* veterans in the narrative that follows. Indeed, in their paeans to free-market economics, conservative draft critics rarely evoked the experiences of flesh-and-blood vets—the hungry Bonus Marchers of the 1930s or the Korean War vets stigmatized as inadequately victorious. Moreover, conservative draft critics avoided the theatricality of the pre–World War II youth group the Veterans of Future Wars, which frequently larded their discourse with gruesome references to looming hardships. Nevertheless, the ghosts of veterans—both past and future—haunted this entire episode, shadowy figures representing the lives draft critics hoped to avoid. In the end, these men created a bogeyman out of veterans, and weaponized it for their ideological purposes, contributing to the very real marginalization of veterans of the Vietnam era. Occasionally cloaked in metaphors of "statism" and the "free market," what these men believed was that military service was beneath them, that it was a waste of time. Marginal men joined the army, not successful men. Their ideas would have lasting consequences—not least a civil-military divide that widens to this day.

THE RIPON SOCIETY AND THE IDEOLOGICAL ORIGINS OF THE ALL-VOLUNTEER FORCE

It has become axiomatic that Richard Nixon saw ending the draft as a political opportunity in the 1968 presidential election, and being a master at political opportunism, he seized on it in the waning days of the campaign. But what made 1968 different? Other presidential candidates on both sides of the political spectrum—Adlai Stevenson in 1956 and Barry Goldwater in 1964—had tried to make an opportunity out of ending the draft, but the idea failed to gain traction. Vietnam is clearly a major factor, but even though Americans were turning on the war, support for the draft was still strong at the time of the election: a Gallup poll conducted in the first week of 1969 found that 62 percent of Americans favored continuing the draft, and only 31 percent supported a volunteer military.[7]

Still, an unusually tight election forced Nixon to try anything he could. But unlike when Stevenson tried in 1956, or Goldwater in 1964, Nixon could tap into a robust antidraft movement—not one that started on the political left but one that began among a small group of young, moderate Republicans called the Ripon Society. The Ripon Society would gain influence with a cadre of Republican congressmen, the "Wednesday Group," so-called because they met for lunch on Wednesdays. When Richard Nixon appointed the Commission on an All-Volunteer Armed Force, often referred to as the Gates Commission after its chairman, Thomas Gates, members of the Wednesday Group and the Ripon Society joined libertarian economists who were popular among

Ripon's members, namely Milton Friedman and Alan Greenspan, to write the commission report that would allow Nixon to end conscription in America.

Although the Ripon Society was formed in 1962, the assassination of John F. Kennedy in 1963 and the nomination of Barry Goldwater as the Republican candidate for president a year later gave the group greater purpose and direction. Like many Americans, Ripon members were deeply moved by Kennedy's aspirational politics of voluntary service to country, and they were profoundly shaken by his tragic death. Their signal statement that they sent out to all Republican members of Congress on January 6, 1964, at the beginning of that year's election season, echoed the moderate politics that Kennedy's long-time adviser, Arthur M. Schlesinger Jr., championed in his midcentury treatise *The Vital Center:* "We believe that the future of our party lies not in extremism, but in moderation. The moderate course offers the Republican Party the best chance to build a durable majority position in American politics."[8]

Headquartered in Cambridge, right on Harvard Square, the Ripon Society set out to make conservatism, and the Republican Party, the intellectual center of American politics, and they soon started hammering out those ideas in the *Ripon Forum,* their semimonthly newsletter. Over the course of the next decade, the Ripon Society would become an intellectual home for center-right, libertarian-leaning politicos. The *Forum* would publish critical and engaging articles about issues that mattered to young people—student activism, higher education, civil rights, and, most importantly, Vietnam and the draft. The draft in particular became a signature issue, and the *Forum* would become the site for Republicans interested in honing a serious Republican critique of conscription in America.

In the December 1966 issue, the *Forum* published a new vision for military service. Calling the draft an injustice of "first prominence"—alongside racism and urban poverty—the editors of the *Forum* urged "the Federal Government to eliminate the draft . . . and to establish a 2.7 million man volunteer army." Instead of a burden to be foisted on young men, they argued that military service should be more like a career—one that would provide a sufficient salary and benefits for men to comfortably support a family. "Good wages," they argued, "unquestionably are an important inducement," but draftees brought home amounts comparable to "Rumanian peasants on a collective farm." This was no way to convince a man to make a career out of the military, they argued. "If a man does make a career out of the service he and his wife frequently find themselves living in unattractive military communities. . . . Psychologically, such an environment cannot help but have an influence on a potential careerist's attitude toward the services."[9]

The *Forum*'s call for a volunteer military was released two months before the publication of the Burke Marshall Commission's report "In Pursuit of Equity: Who Serves When Not All Serve?," which president Lyndon B. Johnson ordered to quell growing criticism of his draft policies. In 1966, when over 382,000 Americans were drafted—the most inductions of the entire war—the *Forum* argued that the commission was a political farce, meant to shore up Johnson and the Democrats' flank before the midterm elections, not to seriously consider reforming the draft. Tongue-in-cheek, the editors commented, "Undoubtedly the distinguished members of the commission are sincere in their desire to find ways to improve the draft system," but then pondered why the "distinguished" members had met only twice since they were empaneled. They mused, "Perhaps the very skilled staff men have gleaned information and opinions from knowledgeable people on all sides of the draft question" in such a short time.[10]

To the editors of the *Ripon Forum*, the commissions' assumptions were the problem. "Few people truly favor the present practice of conscription," they argued. The editors appealed to youth: "Particularly in the undergraduate community—where the draft is subject to fraternity bull-sessions, student government polls, and 'New Left' petitions—resentment is high." While most draft reformers focused on two alternatives, a national lottery or expanding the notion of obligatory "national service" to include other options, such as VISTA or the Peace Corps, the *Forum* editors likened the former to a perverse game of "Russian roulette," and believed the latter was unfeasible due to the enormity of the manpower pool. There simply could never be enough VISTA, Peace Corps, or other service jobs for the number of eligible citizens of draft age.[11]

The editors also objected to expanding compulsory national service because it would necessitate a massive growth of the federal government. Drawing on well-rehearsed Cold War arguments, they wrote that time—two years of compulsory service instead of a lifetime—was the only difference between government-mandated national service and communism. Finally, they asked whether women would be compelled to serve in some capacity. The draft aside, they asked, if the government was going to compel its citizens to perform what would essentially be social service functions, shouldn't women participate? And, if so, would that be fair to men, a percentage of whom would still be required to fight in the time of war?[12]

Now, even as late as 1967, the Ripon Society was a tiny movement within the larger Republican Party. In an article published in June, the *Boston Globe* estimated that their membership was "not much more than 1,000."[13] Ripon's unorthodox positions also put it at odds with the broader Republican coalition: its members advocated for a guaranteed income through a negative income tax plan, supported the Civil Rights Act of 1964, and were warning their fellow Republicans of "creeping Reaganism"—by which they meant a raft of complaints including anti-intellectualism, the rise of celebrity politicians, and a more conservative turn for the Republican Party—as early as 1965.[14]

But in the *Ripon Forum,* these liberal-leaning Republicans were able to slowly hone their opposition to the draft, using themes that were drawn from broader conservative critiques of the welfare state, of taxation, and of government intrusion into the "free market." First, they argued that the draft was an infringement on liberty and antithetical to a free society. Rehearsing old arguments about continental versus British ideas about conscription, they argued that the postwar peacetime draft smacked of "Napoleonic" ideals and "Prussian virtues." Conversely, "in Britain and the United States impressment has always been seen as unjustifiable except when the security of the state required it."[15] Second, citing the work of economists associated with the University of Chicago, namely Walter Oi, the editors argued that the draft was, in effect, a tax on the young men who had the misfortune of getting conscripted. The draft-as-tax argument would gain particular traction among Republicans and disaffected Democrats within the context of the rising cost of the war in Vietnam and expanded social welfare programs associated with the Great Society in the late 1960s. And, third, they argued that the draft produced an inferior product: a costly military, with high turnover, and poorly motivated troops.[16]

One particularly well-connected Ripon man was Bruce K. Chapman. Chapman had made a name for himself in conservative circles through his regular editorials in the *New York Herald Tribune*. A founding member of the Ripon Society, Chapman would spend the latter third of the twentieth century within earshot of the halls of power in Washington. He eventually founded the Discovery Institute (famous for its "intellectual" pursuit of the "science" of creationism over evolutionary biology) in 1990 with his Harvard roommate (and fellow Ripon member) George Gilder, the economist who wrote the "supply-side" economic policies of the Reagan administration.

In 1967, Chapman published a book on the inequities of the draft titled *The Wrong Man in Uniform: Our Unfair and Obsolete Draft—and How We Can Replace It*. Chapman's book was the culmination of months of research he conducted for his recurring editorials on the draft for the *Herald Tribune*. Although Chapman echoed many of the Ripon Society's arguments against the draft, in *The Wrong Man in Uniform* he wasted no time cutting down what he thought were baseless shibboleths about military service. Chapman, who never served in uniform, scoffed at the idea that "the Army builds men." The "many old veterans" who "cherish the memory of what benefits military discipline brought them" were suffering from amnesia, Chapman mused. He argued that the type of training that most draftees got would be "useless to a man in his civilian career, for draftees are not the men on whom the military lavishes its famed training programs." Instead, the drafted soldier learns "to suffer boredom endlessly, to take orders, to feel responsibility only for a tight and small area of assignment, to take their pleasures on the run and where they can."[17] Chapman reserved most of his disdain for the question of "duty" or responsibility to country. To the liberal proponents of compulsory national service, he sneered, more convincingly than any disillusioned vet, "There is something about such an argument that has a fashionable, democratic tone in the speech of a politician or between the covers of a weekly magazine. But from the perspective of any Army post it is most palpably foolery, for if there is a military establishment, it is made of up career officers, not draftees. Draftees are the lowest caste of a caste-conscious estate and wield no influence whatever, and heaven help us if American liberty from undue military influence rests on their helpless shoulders."[18] To Chapman, military service was at best a nuisance, and at worst an immoral appropriation of a young man's time by an overreaching government. "Men who have been through basic training in most areas of the modern American military know," Chapman concluded, "boot camp is designed to make soldiers out of civilians; except by accident, and that rarely, it does not and cannot make better civilians of civilians. Any argument that it does is freighted with ignorance, quarter-truths or fraud."[19] The question, for Chapman, was not how to make the lives of ex-soldiers better; the question was how to make sure that society's best avoided the inevitable marginalization that being a veteran entailed.

Chapman was not alone in this intellectual universe. Ayn Rand, perhaps the most widely read libertarian thinker of the twentieth century, and an intellectual inspiration to many within the Ripon Society, wrote that conscription was tantamount to slavery. In her 1967 essay collection *Capitalism: The Unknown Ideal*, she argued, "Of all the statist violations of individual rights in a mixed economy, the military draft is the worst. It is an abrogation of rights. It negates man's fundamental right—the right to life—and establishes the fundamental principle of statism: that a man's life belongs to the state, and the state may claim it by compelling him to sacrifice it in battle. Once that principle is accepted, the rest is only a matter of time."[20] Beyond an abrogation of fundamental rights, compulsory military service wreaked untold damage on men's psyches. Men of draft age were at a critical phase in their psychological development, a "time when he confirms his impressions of the world, of other men, of the society in which he is to live, when he acquires conscious convictions, defines his moral values, chooses his goals, and plans his future." And right at this formative moment, "an allegedly humanitarian society" forced men to live "in terror." Unable to plan for his future in the shadow of the draft, knowing "that any road he takes can be blocked at any moment by an unpredictable power," and blocking the American man's vision, "there stands the gray shape of the barracks, and, perhaps, beyond it, death for some unknown reason in some alien jungle."[21]

To Rand, the conclusion to this psychological damage was a hopeless nihilism, in which men would develop "searing contempt for the hypocrisy of his elders, and a profound hatred for all mankind," and his only recourse to "escape from that inhuman psychological pressure" would be to turn to "the beatnik cult of the immediate moment, by screaming: 'Now, Now, Now!' (he has nothing else but that 'now'), or by dulling his terror and killing the last of his mind with LSD." Once a man went down this path, Rand warned, "don't blame him. Brothers, you asked for it!"[22]

THE WEDNESDAY GROUP

Who was most terrified about joining the ranks of ex-soldiers? As it turns out, draft opposition made bedfellows out of ideological strangers, and although the Ripon Society represented a central node in a growing network of Republican organizations opposed to the draft, the young members of Ripon were willing to make alliances with all political stripes to end conscription. Bruce Chapman, for example, helped form the Council for a Voluntary Military, which brought together groups from the entire political spectrum, from the Young Americans for Freedom to the Americans for Democratic Action. By declaring all other political issues off-limits (including the merits of the Vietnam War), the Council for a Voluntary Military provided a forum for a lively debate among thinkers and activists interested in ending conscription, including Sanford Gottlieb of the National Committee for a Sane Nuclear Policy, James Farmer of CORE, and Milton Friedman, the University of Chicago economist who, at that time, was perhaps the most influential voice on the right in the debate over ending the draft.[23]

Ripon men also gravitated toward the halls of power, where policy was made. Take Ripon member Stephen Herbits. Like other young men in the 1960s, Herbits had to make calculated life choices in the shadow of the draft. He graduated from Tufts University in 1964 and worked as a congressional staffer in Washington, DC, before entering Georgetown Law in 1967. Although Herbits opposed the draft, like many Americans at the time, he disdained protestors in particular and radical politics in general. He considered himself a lifelong Republican when he went to work for Congress, and he found a home with a group of Republican representatives who began meeting for lunch on Wednesdays to discuss political strategy and the direction of the party.

In May 1966, this group of twenty-five congressmen began pressuring the Democratic chairman of the House Armed Services Committee, L. Mendel Rivers, to open an investigation into inequities in the draft and the broader Selective Service System. Although Rivers consented to creating a panel to study the issue, most observers agreed that he never really intended to rock the boat. The year 1966 was shaping up to be a tough midterm election year for Democrats, and no Democratic leader wanted to open the floodgates on the Vietnam question, or the draft, in this political climate.[24]

After the unsatisfactory results of the Armed Services Committee's hearings, the Wednesday Group went to work on their own study of the draft and alternatives to conscription, hiring Stephen Herbits as a researcher. Toward the end of 1967, after the Burke Marshall Commission released its report, the Wednesday Group published its own findings in a short monograph titled *How to End the Draft*. Written by Vermont congressman Robert T. Stafford and four other Republican congressmen, *How to End the Draft* was endorsed by seventeen other members of Congress, including Robert Taft Jr., and a young congressman from Illinois named Donald Rumsfeld. In the book, the Wednesday Group put forth a plan to reduce draft calls dramatically, ultimately transitioning to an all-volunteer military within five years.

How to End the Draft echoed Ripon arguments about liberty, choice, and the free market: conscription was antithetical to a free society; it was "evil" and "unnecessary and repulsive." It concluded, dramatically, "If our society ever reaches the stage that its needs cannot be met through the free commitment of its people, then our society is doomed."[25] But the Wednesday Group also argued there were benefits of military service—if it was a choice, not compulsory. If the military was to be a job, these Republicans envisioned it as entry-level work. For instance, the Wednesday Group recommended "a significant expansion in the in-service training opportunities for technical skills" and that "a broad program similar to available civilian apprenticeship programs could be established." They argued that the military's unique ability to train people should be expanded "to include such civilian career categories as construction, brick laying, heating engineering, electrical engineering, public utility maintenance, etc."[26] Using census survey data, the Wednesday Group pointed out that young men (between ages sixteen and thirty-four) viewed military service as both an opportunity and a burden. Although respondents believed that the military promised a steady job, the chance to be a leader, and good retirement benefits, most also believed it meant lower pay, less chance for advancement, and less autonomy. Young men were also generally concerned about what the Wednesday Group awkwardly described as "the interesting nature of the work," by which they might have meant combat.[27]

Critics of an all-volunteer military pointed to the already higher propor-
tion of African Americans serving in the Vietnam-era military, as compared
to their overall share of the population. And, while this disparity evened
out as the war dragged on (because manpower officials, reacting to political
pressure from civil rights groups, worked assiduously to correct it), in 1967,
when *How to End the Draft* came out, the overrepresentation of Black men in
uniform was front-page news, and this fact was a major point of contention
between civil rights leaders and policy makers in the Johnson administration.

But in the view of the members of the Wednesday Group, the high number of African Americans serving in uniform was a simple function of the
market. They correctly pointed out that one major reason that there were
more Black men in uniform was that African Americans reenlisted more
often than white soldiers. Moreover, Black men volunteered for hazardous
jobs in higher proportions than their overall share of the population, thus
contributing to their outsized share of combat casualties in Vietnam. Black
men gravitated toward the military, the Wednesday Group argued, simply
because the military provided a job opportunity that was unavailable to Black
men in the civilian world. Unfortunately, even this proved too optimistic.
The recession of the 1970s devastated Black veterans, especially those with
other-than-honorable discharges, sentencing thousands of Black families to
lives of poverty.[28]

While the Wednesday Group was adamant that "military services should
not be operated for the purpose of offering a better life to those in society
who are deprived of the opportunity to share meaningfully in the nation's
prosperity," they could admit that the realities of racism in America distorted
the functions of the market. Directly contradicting their stated belief that the
military should not be involved in social engineering, the authors countered
those who argued that a volunteer military would increase the number of
African Americans in uniform by saying, "There is nothing wrong with the
fact that military service in an all-volunteer army might offer some Negroes
better living conditions, better education, more secure employment, a better
chance of assuming responsibility, and a more dignified life than the civilian
economy can offer." They concluded, "It is not our military system which
should be condemned for offering a chance to the Negro, it is the civilian

sector of our society which should be condemned for failing to allow the Negro to share fully in the fruits of America's prosperity."[29]

RICHARD NIXON AND THE INSTITUTION OF THE ALL-VOLUNTEER FORCE

By 1968, a small circle of younger members of the Republican Party, all self-described intellectuals of the right, had developed a robust critique of the draft—one that depended on an often unspoken, yet unremitting, belief in veteran marginalization. One can see the seeds of arguments that would later be convincing to those in power, especially Richard Nixon: the idea that conscription was antithetical to liberty, the notion that the draft constituted a "hidden tax" on thousands of young men, and that the military could be better and more efficiently served through free-market solutions. During his 1968 acceptance speech for the Republican Party's nomination for president, Richard Nixon did not mention the draft once, and his "secret plan" to end the war was still very much a mystery. The Ripon Society always viewed Nixon coolly, and its members overwhelmingly supported Nelson Rockefeller in the primaries. The *Ripon Forum* took the members' temperature after the convention—and opinion on Nixon had only gotten colder. On the topic of Vietnam, 45 percent of Ripon's membership believed Nixon did not have a "clear-cut" vision for American victory; only 26 percent believed he was even knowledgeable on the subject.[30] In their tepid endorsement of Nixon a month after the convention, the *Forum*'s editorial board chided Nixon for his lack of candor on the war: "Any man who wants to lead the country during the next four years should have a position on it."[31]

Representatives from the Ripon Society attended the Republican National Convention that year, but it is unclear if any members had any official role. Ripon published a bound convention biography, titled *Ripon's Republican Who's Who at Convention '68*, which it distributed to delegates and convention-goers. In the introduction, written in the days before the convention, the authors remained hopeful that the party would adopt some of their positions, especially concerning the draft.[32]

Ripon members certainly celebrated when the Republican Party added a plank to its platform officially adopting the position that the United States should move to a volunteer military "when military manpower needs can be appreciably reduced." Still, the Ripon people knew what party platforms represented, calling them at best "a statement of principles," and at worst, "a propaganda piece designed to help win an election" in the convention biography. And like Richard Nixon's own opportunistic and vague musings on the draft in the months between the convention and the election in November, the plank was light on details.[33]

The draft plank reflected the Ripon Society's contention that people were quietly opting out of the traditions of their parents. The Republicans added the plank in 1968 not because Nixon wanted it—candidate Nixon would not come out against the draft until October, a month before the election—but because many Republicans in power, some associated with the Ripon Society, others who were members of the Wednesday Group, had been advocating for it for years. The political Left animated much of the broader Vietnam antiwar movement, including spectacular protests that were directed at the Selective Service System and the draft. But the antidraft movement spanned the political spectrum. Religious groups, libertarians, and "vital center" politicians in both the Republican and Democratic parties formed a loose coalition around the draft issue, often disagreeing on tactics, and usually operating from differing, even contradictory, political philosophies. As scholars of this era have rightly pointed out, Nixon's support for ending the draft was pure political opportunism, born out of an unpopular war.[34] But by 1968, it was not a vague or nebulous afterthought—or worse, to Nixon at least, an idea cooked up by the radical left. The idea to end conscription was ripe for Nixon to pluck because reformist Republicans had spent years cultivating and circulating it within the halls of power.

For its part, the Ripon Society still remained committed to helping the new Republican administration enact an agenda that, in its words, forwarded "progressive policy recommendations based on identifiable Republican themes."[35] And, when the time came for the new president to turn his attention to the draft, the society was ready with more than just advice from afar. Ripon member Stephen Herbits landed a spot as the youngest member (by a generation) on the Gates Commission, which would advise Nixon to end conscription and move the country to a volunteer military. After this, he returned to Congress as a staffer to help the administration shepherd the All-Volunteer Force through the legislative process, and eventually he became the Pentagon's "special assistant" in charge of the force.[36]

Although some called Herbits the "token" student, ostensibly put on the commission because he had "skin in the game" as a man of draft age, he was no accidental choice. Herbits was a player in the growing conservative intellectual movement to end the draft, and his role as a congressional researcher for *How to End the Draft* provided him with the necessary credentials: five congressmen, all members of the Wednesday Group, wrote to President Nixon recommending Herbits to the commission.[37]

As one scholar of the All-Volunteer Force put it, when Nixon commissioned a study on ending the draft, he may not have wanted to "stack the deck" with supporters of ending conscription, but he certainly stacked it with intellectuals "cut from the same cloth."[38] The Gates Commission was chock-full of economists of a certain flavor. Commission members Milton Friedman and Alan Greenspan, and their respective advisers, made for a Venn diagram of University of Chicagoans and Ayn Rand followers with a remarkable amount of overlap. The cochairman of the commission, congressman Thomas Curtis, was a member of the Wednesday Group, and a signatory to *How to End the Draft*. (Curtis also wrote the introduction to Bruce Chapman's *The Wrong Man in Uniform*, rounding out his antidraft bona fides.) Antidraft reformers from the Ripon Society's orbit were overrepresented, and it would soon become apparent. Undersecretary of defense Alfred Fitt, a holdover from the Johnson administration, called the commissioners, and Friedman in particular, "fanatic opponents of the draft." In a memo to the new secretary of defense, Melvin Laird, he warned, "My concern is that the economists (whom I respect greatly as a general rule) with the President's ear do not stack the deck against a thoughtful, careful objective study of the problem."[39]

Although there were several notable differences, the commission's report looked an awful lot like *How to End the Draft* and the Ripon Society's proposal before that. But it veered off course from previous antidraft arguments on pay, as well as military benefits such as housing, commissary privileges, and other fringe benefits. Whereas earlier antidraft reformers advocated "civilizing" military pay and benefits packages, which included increasing base pay (or salary) and dialing back the myriad enlistment bonuses, clothing allowances, and varying pay increases for types of duty (hazardous duty or combat pay, for example), they nonetheless understood that there were certain aspects of military life that fundamentally differed from civilian life. For example, the

Wednesday Group pitched increasing the budget for on-base construction and off-base housing allowances so that servicemen could "live with their families in comfort and convenience."[40] They also called for increasing educational benefits for service members, and even extending those benefits to military family members. The Gates Commission, in stark contrast, advocated gutting these programs in favor of lump cash payments to service members. They recommended against "general increases in such benefits or in income-in-kind items of pay" because they "would be an inefficient means of compensating military personnel." They went on, "Providing compensation in cash has an inherent advantage . . . it allows each individual to decide how he or she will use whatever he earns."[41]

Antidraft Republicans convinced Nixon to end the draft and move to the All-Volunteer Force in 1973. For the first decade of its existence, the new volunteer military looked an awful lot like the worst of Bruce Chapman's characterizations. The military of the 1970s, especially the army, suffered from widespread disciplinary problems, failed to recruit quality volunteers, and garnered a reputation as an employer-of-last-resort—a proverbial choice given to defendants facing jail time. Antidraft reformers succeeded in portraying military service as an undesirable waste of time, and this, coupled with the disastrous Vietnam War, tarnished the image of the military and marginalized those who served in it. The military struggled mightily, but as it rebuilt its image in the 1980s, much of its rebranding revolved around changing the narrative that the military was only for failures—for marginal people who could not cut it in the modern economy. To overcome this image of marginalization that Ripon men had weaponized to end the draft, the military paid millions of dollars to Madison Avenue advertising agencies. Successful ad campaigns, such as the army's "Be All You Can Be," sold job skills, technical training, and the promise of a college education, all tailored to combat the belief that military service was a waste of time and that only flunkies joined the army.[42] Today, Americans worship the military and its service members through extravagant public rituals. Absent a draft to compel service, fewer Americans spend time in uniform, and the military institution has drifted from the everyday of American life. In its place we created a civic religion of hero worship, in which the military and soldiers are above reproach, immune to even the most pedestrian of criticisms.

Historians describe this as a process of remilitarization and place this conservative project within the context of the backlash against social changes associated with the Left, principally the women's movement and the broader sexual revolution. We forget that much of the post-Vietnam struggle over the place of the military in American society was an intraparty fight among Republicans, and that, of all the changes during this era, perhaps the most radical was the right-wing project to end the draft, which severed the notion of obligation from the meaning of American citizenship.[43] No less important, this moment left a profound legacy for the post-Vietnam military and those who, in later wars, would enter and exit service. Without the draft to compel Americans into enlisting, the military learned to recruit from populations that in many ways were *already* marginalized—less likely to have the social, economic, and political resources needed to push back against state intervention in their lives. As a result, today's military is more diverse—which, undoubtedly, is a social good. The end of the draft marked a watershed moment in veterans' history if only because it fundamentally reshaped the demography of the military and veteran populations. But the success of antidraft conservatives has done little to help the lives of today's vets, those who, seeking opportunity or lacking few other options, are "taxed" with the burdens of national service. If anything, the end of the draft has made it easier to create new populations of marginalized veterans—just not the kind that read Ayn Rand.

NOTES

The author would like to thank Drew McKevitt and David Anderson for their comments and feedback on this essay, and the editors for their willingness to let me tell this story.

1. Bruce K. Chapman, *The Wrong Man in Uniform: Our Unfair and Obsolete Draft—and How We Can Replace It* (New York: Trident, 1967), 78.

2. Amy J. Rutenberg, *Rough Draft: Cold War Military Manpower Policy and the Origins of Vietnam-Era Draft Resistance* (Ithaca, NY: Cornell University Press, 2019).

3. The history of the move to the All-Volunteer Force has been well documented. See Beth Bailey, *America's Army: Making the All-Volunteer Force* (Cambridge, MA: Harvard University Press, 2009); Robert K. Griffith, Jr., *The U.S. Army's Transition to the All-Volunteer Force, 1968–1974* (Washington, DC: Center of Military History, 1996); Jennifer Mittelstadt, *The Rise of the Military Welfare State* (Cambridge, MA: Harvard University Press, 2015); Bernard Rostker, *I WANT YOU! The Evolution of the All-Volunteer Force* (Santa Barbara, CA: RAND, 2006).

4. Chapman, *Wrong Man in Uniform,* 77.

5. On civil rights and debates over marginalization, see Steve Estes, *I AM A MAN! Race, Manhood, and the Civil Rights Movement* (Chapel Hill: University of North Carolina Press, 2005); Daniel Geary, *Beyond Civil Rights: The Moynihan Report and Its Legacy* (Philadelphia: University of Pennsylvania Press, 2017). On the conservative right's deployment of the idea of marginalization, see Grace Elizabeth Hale, *A Nation of Outsiders: How the White Middle Class Fell in Love with Rebellion in Postwar America* (New York: Oxford University Press, 2011).

6. See Robert Self, *All in the Family: The Realignment of American Democracy since the 1960s* (New York: Hill & Wang, 2012); Natasha Zaretsky, *No Direction Home: The American Family and the Fear of National Decline, 1968–1980* (Chapel Hill: University of North Carolina Press, 2007).

7. George Q. Flynn, *The Draft, 1940–1973* (Lawrence: University of Kansas Press, 1993), 237.

8. "A Call to Excellence in Leadership," in *The Ripon Papers, 1963–1968,* ed. Lee W. Huebner and Thomas E. Petri (Washington, DC: The National Press, 1968), 5.

9. "Politics and Conscription: A Ripon Proposal to Replace the Draft," *Ripon Forum* 2, no. 9 (Dec. 1966).

10. Ibid.

11. Ibid.

12. Ibid.

13. Fred Pillsbury, "Full-Time Chief for Ripon Society: Big Doings in Only 2 Small Rooms," *Boston Globe,* June 25, 1967, 6A.

14. The phrase "creeping Reaganism" would accompany nearly every story about the former president of the Screen Actors Guild after 1965, when Reagan began to gear up for the California governorship.

15. "Politics and Conscription," *Ripon Forum.*

16. As Robert Self argues, "The conservative definition of 'family values' represented an antiwelfare-state ideology. It was consistent with attacks on social democracy, the emphasis on market-based policies, and a general advance of neoliberalism—meaning a 'new' version of classical liberalism's idea of free markets"; Self, *All in the Family,* 10.

17. Chapman, *Wrong Man in Uniform,* 77.

18. Ibid., 78.

19. Ibid., 98.

20. Ayn Rand, "The Wreckage of the Consensus," reprinted in *The Military Draft: Selected Readings on Conscription,* ed. Martin Anderson (Stanford, CA: Hoover Institution, 1982), 172.

21. Ibid., 174.

22. Ibid., 175.

23. Russell Freeburg, "All-Volunteer Army Urged by New Group," *Chicago Tribune,* May 19, 1967, A11; Neil Sheehan, "Draft Is Uniting Right with Left," *New York Times,* May 22, 1967, 17.

24. Rostker, *I WANT YOU!,* 30–31; Rutenberg, *Rough Draft,* 169–70.

25. Stafford et al., *How to End the Draft: The Case for an All-Volunteer Army* (Washington, DC: The National Press, 1967), 10–11.

26. Ibid., 71.

27. Ibid., 64.

28. *Veterans' Unemployment Problems: Hearing Before the Subcommittee on Readjustment, Education, and Employment of the Committee on Veterans' Affairs, United States Senate,* 94th Cong., 1st Sess., Sess. on S. 760 and Related Bills, October 22, 1975, 879. Also see James Westheider, *Fighting on Two Fronts: African Americans and the Vietnam War* (New York: New York University Press, 1997), 63.

29. Stafford et al., *How to End the Draft,* 14–15.

30. *Ripon Forum* 4, no. 10 (Oct. 1968): 17.

31. *Ripon Forum* 4, no. 9 (Sept. 1968): 22.

32. The Ripon Society, *Ripon's Republican Who's Who at the Convention '68: A Biographical Directory of Delegates to the 1968 Republican National Convention at Miami, Florida, August 5–8* (Cambridge, MA: The Ripon Society, 1968).

33. The Ripon Society, *Biographical Directory,* 15–17; Republican Party Platforms, "Republican Party Platform of 1968," *American Presidency Project,* August 5, 1968, https://www.presidency.ucsb.edu/ws/?pid=25841.

34. Bailey, *America's Army,* 2; Mittelstadt, *Rise of the Military Welfare State,* 22.

35. *Ripon Forum* 4, no. 10 (Oct. 1968): 14.

36. Rostker, *I WANT YOU!,* 66–67.

37. Robert T. Stafford et al. to Richard Nixon, March 11, 1969, Rostker Archive (L0040, L0039).

38. Rostker, *I WANT YOU!,* 66.

39. Alfred Fitt memo to Melvin Laird, January 29, 1969, Rostker Archive (G0260).

40. Stafford et al., *How to End the Draft,* 67.

41. *Report of the President's Commission on an All-Volunteer Armed Force* (Washington, DC: Government Printing Office, 1970), 63.

42. Bailey, *America's Army.*

43. Andrew J. Bacevich, *The New American Militarism: How Americans Are Seduced by War* (New York: Oxford University Press, 2005); Mittelstadt, *Rise of the Military Welfare State*; Rutenberg, *Rough Draft*; Michael Sherry, *In the Shadow of War: The United States since the 1930s* (New Haven, CT: Yale University Press, 1995).

IV.

CENTERING MARGINALIZED VETERANS IN A TIME OF FOREVER WAR

"The Patriot Penalty"

National Guard and Reserve Troops,
Neoliberalism, and Manufactured Precarity
in the Era of Perpetual Conflict

DAVID KIERAN

By 2005, Nevada national guardsman Joseph Perez had been on active duty for four years. First, he was called up for Operation Noble Eagle, which provided infrastructure and airport security after the September 11 attacks.[1] That deployment lasted eighteen months; "two stop-loss orders" extended his service.[2] Afterward, Perez took a civilian firefighting job but was recalled and sent to Iraq, where at one point his unit received incoming mortar fire every day for three weeks.[3] His real struggles began, however, after "an uprising from insurgent detainees led to a prison riot" left him with a knee injury and a concussion; later, he witnessed an IED explosion and developed symptoms of post-traumatic stress.[4] Bounced from Nevada to Iraq to Washington and caught up in army, national guard, and air force bureaucracy, Perez languished in deplorable conditions at Fort Lewis.[5] His wife and children "went 3 months without military IDs, Tri-Care health [and] pay" and couldn't take advantage of the post exchange's bargains.[6] "Not being able to work, I had to borrow money from family members to make ends meet," Perez told Congress.[7] Increasingly feeling "that maybe I did something wrong and I was being punished," he contemplated suicide.[8] His story, however, wasn't unique. In the same hearing, master sergeant Daniel Forney, a Pennsylvania reservist, explained that many hospitalized guardsmen and reservists faced uncertainty about their benefits when active-duty orders ended. "The Reserves and Guard are fighting next to the active duty," he complained, "and still we treat them like second class citizens."[9]

This chapter tracks the economic marginalization of part-time soldiers during the Iraq and Afghanistan Wars. Military service in the era of the All-Volunteer Force has often been understood as an engine of economic security, if not mobility.[10] This has remained true throughout the twenty-first-century wars, particularly as the military offered ever-larger bonuses to attract and retain personnel.[11] Yet the twenty-first-century wars have also constituted "the largest ongoing mobilization of Reserve components since World War II."[12] These deployments in fact made US military operations in Iraq feasible; as the national guard noted, "At one point in 2005, Army National Guard units contributed half of the combat brigades on the ground in Iraq."[13] For those troops, deployments often had financial consequences alongside the more obvious physical and psychological dangers. As the national guard touted its role in Iraq, newspapers highlighted the financial precarity that guard and reserve troops faced as debts mounted because their military salaries were substantially lower than their civilian pay or businesses collapsed in their absence. In short, the financial challenges that many guard and reserve troops faced after being called to active duty during the twenty-first-century wars highlight that even as the military functions, in Jennifer Mittelstadt's terminology, as "a vast, comprehensive, and effective safety net unique in American life," the benefits that it provides do not always extend equally to all service members.[14] Some part-time soldiers whose service may have been motivated in part by a promise of greater economic security instead found that military service in the twenty-first century threatened, rather than reinforced, their financial stability.

Guard and reserve precarity resulted from the choices of military leaders and legislators who failed to construct and endorse policies that would protect part-time service members' economic well-being. The United States sent guard and reserve troops to war under antiquated policies that were never intended to ensure troops' financial security over long deployments or during lengthy hospital stays. Simultaneously, conservative legislators repeatedly refused efforts to provide soldiers bonuses or to shield them from predatory financial practices. Instead, they lauded corporate volunteerism as a form of patriotic citizenship best suited to addressing troops' fiscal challenges.

The economic immiseration of part-time troops was thus the product of two intersecting forces that define contemporary US culture: the ascendency of neoliberal economic policies and a commitment to perpetual war.[15] According to Judith Butler, "Precarity designates that politically induced condition in which certain populations suffer from failing social and political networks of support and become differentially exposed to injury, violence and death," including "poverty."[16] Such precarity is an inherent feature of contemporary neoliberal capitalism. As Lisa Duggan explains, over the past four decades "the overall direction of redistribution of many kinds of resources, in the US and around the world, has been upward."[17] That redistribution was hardly "universally inevitable"; it was midwifed into existence by politicians who are "pro-corporate capitalist guarantors of private property relations."[18] Neoliberalism's impact has been most evident in the racial disparities inherent in mass incarceration and the withdrawal of social services from majority nonwhite urban areas.[19] Yet the dismantling of the social safety net, the rise of austerity politics, and upward wealth redistribution have also had pernicious effects on middle-aged white Americans without college degrees, particularly those living in rural areas, who are increasingly dying "deaths of despair."[20]

The rise of neoliberal austerity has coincided with a moment in which, Andrew Bacevich explains, "Americans have come to define the nation's strength and well-being in terms of military preparedness [and] military action."[21] The most notable twenty-first-century consequences of this infatuation have been two poorly managed, prolonged wars in which very few Americans have actually served.[22] Although service members have been customarily celebrated during these conflicts, such celebrations overlook, and in fact mask, the reality that for many part-time service members, military experience has been an engine not of opportunity but of precarity.

The intersection of these two phenomena has enhanced the economic precarity of guard and reserve troops. By 2005, it was becoming clear that the Iraq War would last longer than policy makers had promised. As part-time troops shouldered an increased burden—lengthy deployments and, often, long hospitalizations—they also confronted lost wages and jobs, closed business, and mounting debt. Yet legislators, particularly Republicans, consistently refused to protect these troops or ameliorate their suffering. The economic immiseration of national guard and reserve troops was thus not an inevitable byproduct of contemporary warfare. It was, rather, the product of the nation's simultaneous commitment to perpetual warfare and neoliberal austerity, an intersection that places people at risk while offering few safeguards to their well-being.

"THE WEEKEND IS GONE FROM WEEKEND WARRIORS"

When Joseph Perez testified to Congress, there were more guard and reserve soldiers than active component troops serving overseas.[23] This figure represents a striking departure from the guard and reserve's historical use. Lyndon Johnson's refusal to send guard and reserve troops to Vietnam, for example, rendered those units what Gregory A. Daddis terms "havens for those hoping to avoid service."[24] After Vietnam, the military reimagined the role of these units, and they became, as former army officer and historian John Sloan Brown puts it, "increasingly critical to plans for rapid deployment and operations other than war," with "the Army reserve committed to focus even more heavily on combat service support, whereas the National Guard committed to orient more on combat units."[25] By 2001, a considerable portion of the army's war-making capacity rested with part-time soldiers; as Brown notes, "Half of the maneuver brigades in the Army were in the National Guard."[26] As a result, guard and reserve soldiers quite quickly came to play significant roles in both Iraq and Afghanistan.[27] Perez's Nevada national guard was among the smallest in the nation, but in 2006, it reported that "nine of the Nevada Army Guard's 14 deployable units, or 64 percent, have deployed since 2001."[28] In Kansas, the fraction deployed was three-quarters.[29] As the *New York Times* put it, "The weekend is gone from Weekend Warriors."[30]

For the many men and women who had enlisted expecting to deal with "floods and hurricanes and missions clearing snow from the highway," these lengthy deployments were both a surprise and a frustration.[31] Certainly, guard and reserve troops had deployed overseas throughout the 1990s—for example, on peacekeeping missions in the Balkans—but, as Brown notes, these missions were "in effect voluntary."[32] In the twenty-first century, by contrast, "the very act of joining the reserve component implied deployment," often for longer periods, more frequently, and in more dangerous roles.[33] These deployments thus also differed substantially from many service members' expectations. An article about the New York National Guard's 42nd Infantry Division, for example, acknowledged "an undercurrent of regret and dread evident in many

National Guard troops who acknowledge that they have found themselves in a situation they neither imagined nor wished for: real live combat against a mercurial enemy in a war with an uncertain course."[34] Americans increasingly criticized these deployments, particularly as casualties mounted.[35] One critic of the war explained his opposition by pointing out that "there are people from Vermont who have been sent to Iraq who have been called upon to do things which they wouldn't choose to do."[36]

"THE PATRIOT PENALTY"

Alongside worries about the duration and risk of guard and reserve deployments came concerns about the economic precarity that those deployments generated. As Brown notes, most part-time soldiers "had civilian careers," which meant that they "wanted to know [they] could pick up job and career upon returning."[37] In most cases, their ability to do so was guaranteed by the United Services Employment and Reemployment Rights Act of 1994, which specifies that a deployed service member "shall not be denied initial employment, reemployment, retention in employment, promotion, or any benefit of employment by an employer."[38] That was about as far as the legislation went in protecting service members, though, and as the wars continued, financial realities created a range of hardships.

The Employment and Reemployment Rights Act, for example, applied only to service members who worked for others and whose employers stayed in business while they were gone. In fact, the law made an exception for employers if their "circumstances have so changed as to make such reemployment impossible or unreasonable," so some guard and reserve members returned to find that their employers no longer in business and themselves in distress.[39] Guardsman Mike Dickenson's employer went bankrupt during his deployment, leaving him "facing mortgage payments, hospital bills, car payments and no job" on his return.[40] The possibility of job loss was even more acute, Brown notes, "for small businesses and the self-employed," adding that "dentists and physicians running small businesses, for example, were likely to lose those practices if they deployed for a year."[41] As the *New York Times* put it in February 2005, federal law did little for "for the self-employed who are compelled to entrust their businesses to relatives, partners or friends, maintain them from afar or, at times, helplessly watch them collapse."[42] Newspapers profiled a Vermont convenience store forced to close because a deployed guardsman's mother was "unable to handle the business alone"; a Michigan taxi company transformed from a business that "was bringing in about $175,000 a year" to one that was "$110,000 in debt"; and a Washington State entrepreneur was "unable to obtain the government loan that would have allowed him to train someone else to run his bookstore."[43]

Having a job to return to was one thing; maintaining financial stability during a deployment was another. As Stephen Lendman and J. J. Asongu point out, "About half of all reservists and Guard members report a loss of income when they go on active duty" and that "most of the soldiers lose at least $4,000 a year, but others loss over the $50,000 [sic]."[44] This is because when part-time soldiers are activated, they become federal employees paid according to their "rank and length of service" and "are paid just like their Active Duty counterparts," though they may earn additional money because they have particular skills (for example, fluency in a language) or because of the nature of their assignment.[45] When the Iraq War began, a soldier deployed to Operation Enduring Freedom or Operation Iraqi Freedom likely received $225 per month for being "assigned to duty in a designated imminent danger location," up to $150 in "Hardship duty location pay," and, if they had dependents, an additional "Family Separation Allowance" of $250.[46] For active-duty troops, this money constituted additional income, over and above their standard military salaries, and, presumably, additional monies into their monthly budgets. In 2006, for example, soldiers from the 3rd Infantry Division "estimated they earned an extra $700 to $800 per month while in Iraq, totaling up to an extra $9,600 for some from their year overseas," and the Associated Press reported that "business has been booming" near Fort Stewart, Georgia, "because of thousands of 3rd Infantry Division troops . . . returning from a yearlong tour in Iraq and finding their bank accounts flush with combat pay, tax breaks and bonuses."[47]

Even with those additional stipends, such windfalls were less common for part-time troops. Rather, most activated guard and reserve troops took a significant pay cut, and there was no mandate that employers backfill the lost wages. To understand the magnitude of this difference, consider that in 2005 the average police officer in the United States earned $50,180, while the average secondary school teacher earned $49,400, salaries that amount to slightly more than $4,100 per month.[48] The average tractor-trailer driver for a grocery store earned $37,670 per year, or about $3,100 per month.[49] If those individuals held the rank of staff sergeant in the reserves or guard with ten years of service and were called to active duty, they would earn $2,687.10 per month, plus, perhaps, an additional $625 of imminent danger, hardship duty location, and family separation allowance pay. While the trucker would come out about even, or perhaps a bit ahead, the others would be almost $1,000 short each month.[50] For the teacher or police officer to make the equivalent to their civilian salary while on active duty, they would have had to have held an enlisted rank of E-8 (first sergeant in the army, a master sergeant in the marine corps, a senior master sergeant in the air force, or a navy senior chief petty officer) and have twenty-two years of experience or, if they were an officer, hold a 0–3 rank (in the army, air force, and the marines, a captain; in the navy, a lieutenant, all with four years of service).[51] Unsurprisingly, many part-time soldiers did not have the combination of rank and tenure.

Brown's assertion that "many found themselves making more money while serving on active duty than they had as civilians, and some much more" notwithstanding, news stories presented dire accounts.[52] Six months into the Iraq War, the *New York Times* profiled the California national guard's 870th Military Police Company, a group of men and women who were cast as unexpectedly thrust into a lengthy combat deployment, noting that "for those with children, mounting bills and a reduced income, the hardships have become almost unbearable."[53] One unit member reported that "His employer is not paying his salary and with what he is earning for his military service, he estimated the couple was losing $2,000 a month."[54] Over the coming year, a common theme emerged. In February 2005, the paper reported on Arkansas guardsman David Qualls, explaining that "in his civilian life" the truck driver was "earning far more than what he has earned as a radio operator in Iraq for more than a year."[55]

Media coverage cast these deployments as a bait and switch. Members of the national guard, the *London Times* argued, had been "attracted by the old sales pitch: give us two weeks a year and a weekend a month, and we will give you cash, job training and the chance to fight fires or help local towns hit by natural disasters," but then they were sent to Iraq, where "it is the massive impact that these long deployments have on their lives back home that is breeding the greatest resentment." One reservist blamed these economic losses on the war's operational tempo: "You're told you'll be going for six months. You tell your employer that and then, boom, you're extended: you don't come back. Then you come back and six months later you're deployed again. We're frequently coming across people who have lost their businesses."[56] One national guardsman's wife, who had to "to scrape by with half as much money," worried, "If he doesn't come back soon, we're going to lose it all."[57] The *Christian Science Monitor* told readers that "financial problems back home . . . [are] so common that some critics call it the 'patriot penalty.'"[58]

"THE SYSTEM WAS UNDER STRAIN AND BREAKING"

Stories of service members returning financially worse off than before they had left ran counter to both public celebrations of their service—particularly by conservative policy makers and Iraq War supporters—and long-standing assumptions that military service was a path to economic independence. That troops returned to face these challenges was not, however, inevitable. Rather, they were the product of the combination of two intersecting realities. First, the Iraq War was a catastrophe. Even the US Army admits that the conflict, which policy makers promised would be brief but which lasted nearly a decade—costing the lives of nearly 4,500 US troops (and perhaps two and a half million Iraqis) while injuring countless others—was poorly planned and executed, resulting in "thinly stretched units and over-taxed headquarters often . . . undertaking unexpected missions for which they were doctrinally, materially, and perhaps intellectually ill-prepared."[59] Many of those stretched, unprepared units came from the guard and reserve, who deployed more, for longer periods, and in more dangerous conditions than ever before. Second, the conditions under which the units mobilized significantly heightened the likelihood of economic precarity. In particular, their deployments were governed by Department of Defense policies that had been constructed without imagining the nature of the missions that guard and reserve troops were being asked to undertake, and conservative lawmakers repeatedly refused to accede to any legislation that would offer financial relief to these soldiers and instead insistently celebrated corporate volunteerism as the best avenue for alleviating service members' suffering.

One issue was whether service members were appropriately paid in the first place. Six months into the Iraq War, the General Accounting Office (GAO) decried "the complex, cumbersome processes used to pay soldiers from their initial mobilization through active-duty deployment to demobilization."[60] Ideally, ensuring soldier pay is straightforward: an automated system and manual data entry ensures that a soldier's active duty pay kicks in on mobilization.[61] The GAO found, however, that a staggering 93 percent of soldiers whose cases they studied "had at least one pay problem associated with their mobilization"; in one unit, only one deployed soldier *didn't* have a problem.[62]

The nature of these problems varied. Some soldiers "did not receive the correct amount of Hardship Duty Pay," while others "did not receive payments for up to 6 months after mobilization."[63] The reasons for the errors were likewise diverse, with some seeming paradigms of bureaucratic inefficiency, as when "forty-eight of 51 soldiers in a California National Guard military police unit received late payments because the unit armory did not have a copy machine."[64] Most significantly, the system had not been built for this level of deployment; it "was originally designed to process payroll payments to Army Reserve and Army Guard personnel on weekend drills, [or] on short periods of annual active duty (periods of less than 30 days in duration)." Guard troops' longer deployments, the GAO concluded, meant that "the system is now stretched to the limits."[65]

For some units, this created significant suffering. The improper calculation of one Colorado guardsman's pay "reduced the soldier's net pay to less than 50 percent of the amount he had been receiving," to the point that "the soldier's wife had to obtain a grant of $500 from the Colorado National Guard's Family Support Group to pay bills."[66] Another complained that "not having this resolved means that my family has had to make greater sacrifices and it leaves them in an unstable environment. This has caused great stress on my family that may lead to divorce."[67] Guard and reserve precarity was thus not the inevitable result of deployments; it was another casualty of the poor planning endemic to the wars.

Soldiers who had been hospitalized also suffered financially. Officially, injured soldiers remain on active duty, with the accompanying benefits, while receiving medical care.[68] In practice, however, this was not always the case. The GAO noted that four Virginia guardsmen injured in Afghanistan "experienced pay disruptions because existing guidance was not clear" and thus "experienced gaps in receiving active duty pay and associated medical benefits."[69] Injured guard and reserve troops who had been placed on "medical hold status" or an active-duty medical extension but "removed from active duty status in the automated systems" because of a convoluted, mismanaged system—what representative Tom Davis (R-VA) termed "financial and medical friendly fire"—were the topic of the hearing at which Perez spoke in February 2005.[70]

The GAO had found that a third of reservists who requested otherwise had been removed from active-duty status, often with dire consequences: "Soldiers and their families denied medical and dental care, loss of access to the post exchange and commissary, negative impact on credit due to the late payment of bills, soldiers borrowing money from friends and family to pay bills, added stress for soldiers that already had serious medical conditions, and injured soldiers spending incredible amounts of time to obtain entitled pay and benefits."[71] Rodger Shuttleworth, a Maryland guardsmen, was pointed in his critique: while "the number of injured soldiers in these programs prior to 2001 was manageable," the demands of the post-2001 combined with a system "not specifically designed for GWOT," meaning that "soldiers were being denied eligibility, fell off pay systems, and lost benefits for their families."[72]

John Allen, a New Jersey police officer who had been wounded in Afghanistan, made this point vividly, decrying "a broken and dysfunctional system" that created "a multitude of problems for me and my family—no pay, no access to the base, no medical coverage for my family, and the cancellation of all my scheduled medical appointments."[73] Pointing out that "the hospital administrators are also doctors," he reflected, "What surprises me is their own motto: cause no further harm. How can you allow Reserve Component soldiers to go months without pay, nowhere to live, their medical appointments canceled, and not even being paid?"[74] "In the Special Forces," he bitingly added, "we have our own motto: free the oppressed. In this case, the oppressed are the Reserve Component disabled veterans."[75]

Asked to explain how this had happened, Defense Department official Daniel B. Denning admitted that the GAO's findings, and Allen's complaint, were accurate. Having gone to war with a system "designed to take care of soldiers injured during their 2 weeks of active duty a year," he acknowledged, "it took us, frankly, some time to realize the system was under strain and breaking."[76] That guard and reserve troops suffered such strains underscores the multiple ways in which those who are neither fully soldier nor fully civilian were immiserated during the twenty-first-century wars. While some faced hardship because their military salaries couldn't keep pace with their civilian budgets, others suffered because they did not receive the benefits to which they were entitled as full-time soldiers.

"COMPANIES ARE REAL HEROES TO ME"

Listening to Allen's and Denning's testimony, representative Chris Shays (R-CT) expressed frustration. "This has been a longstanding problem," he acknowledged. "We have too many of our Guardsmen and Reservists risking their lives, and they get treated like dirt. That is the bottom line."[77] But rhetoric was not matched by action. Throughout 2005, guard and reserve precarity was exacerbated by repeated instances in which conservative politicians who purported to support the troops instead enacted neoliberal economic policies that benefitted corporations while blocking initiatives that might have eased service members' financial burdens.

In 2003, for example, congressman Bart Stupak (D-MI) asked his House colleagues to consider an amendment that would "grant a $1,500 bonus" to those deployed.[78] A single payment was a nice gesture but a thin reed, given the economic hardships that many military personnel and their families were facing; for the teacher or cop imagined earlier, the payment would make up a single month of lost wages, potentially still leaving them twenty-three months behind. Yet even this modest effort failed to gain traction in Congress. Six months into the Iraq War, it failed again; seven Democrats in the chamber voted against it, while only fourteen Republicans favored it.[79] The amendment likewise went nowhere in 2005. In 2007, Stupak introduced it as a stand-alone bill, but it found only two Republican cosponsors among the forty-four legislators who supported it and never came to a vote.[80]

Repeated Democratic attempts to attach amendments that would extend special bankruptcy protections to national guard and reserve service members also failed on party-line votes. In March 2005, the Senate debated the Bankruptcy Abuse Prevention and Consumer Protection Act of 2005, which Democrats condemned as "the dream of the credit card industry."[81] The bill made it more difficult for individuals to declare Chapter 7 bankruptcy, and offered greater protection to creditors.[82] When president George W. Bush signed the bill into law in April 2005, he complained that "too many people have abused the bankruptcy laws" and "walked away from debts even when they had the ability to repay them," while declaring that "America is a nation of personal responsibility where people are expected to meet their obligations."[83] Unsurprisingly, the bill was roundly supported by the financial services industry.[84]

On March 7, senator Dick Durbin (D-IL) introduced an amendment that would have protected some military personnel from means testing in bankruptcy proceedings and that, in part, offered protections if "the debtor or the debtor's spouse is a reserve of the armed forces, and the indebtedness occurred primarily during a period of not less than 180 days, during which he or she was . . . on active duty."[85] The amendment offered protections to small business owners or families who lost their homes because active-duty military pay was too low to meet expenses, but it was quickly defeated, and Durbin raged on the Senate floor at his conservative colleagues' hypocrisy: "I offered an amendment that said if one served in the Guard or Reserve, if they are in the military and they are serving their country overseas and as a result of their service their family or their business goes into bankruptcy, we are not going to be so harsh on them. . . . I thought that was a reasonable amendment. I hear all my fellow Senators praising our men and women in uniform. . . . [But] I lost that amendment 58 to 38. Every Republican Senator voted against it."[86] Durbin returned to the amendment moments later, asking his "friends on the Republican side of the aisle, for one last time, to be sensitive to some of the real hardships that have been created for families of Guardsmen and Reserves who have been activated."[87] His conservative colleagues were unmoved. Senator Jeff Sessions (R-AL) summarily dismissed his plea, blithely noting that "these amendments, for the most part, have been up before. I do not believe that most are going to be accepted. But there is every right of my colleague's side to offer them."[88] That Republican senators were content to rest on patriotic platitudes was evident moments later, when Charles Grassley (R-IA) "[rose] in tribute to a noble Iowan who has given his life for his country." Praising guardsman Brian Gienau, Grassley gravely intoned, "We are forever in his debt."[89]

Democrats were not ready to let the matter go. The next morning, Ted Kennedy (D-MA) argued that the legislation "favors the worst of the credit industry" but "hurts real people who . . . suffer major loss of income because they were called up for duty in Iraq or Afghanistan" and "leav[e] their families and their jobs and their small businesses behind to suffer the economic consequences, but this Senate said no to the Durbin amendment."[90] Other Democratic lawmakers made explicit what was implicit in Kennedy's comment, couching their support for the amendment in military exceptionalism, arguing that service members were particularly worthy of financial protections. The amendment's purpose, Durbin explained, was to "take a category of Americans to whom we all owe such a great debt of gratitude and say if their debts overwhelm them because they are serving our country, we are going to give them a break."[91] This was a theme that he had already touched on. After Kennedy spoke, he had risen to rhetorically ask, "Should not the harshest aspects of this bill not apply to men and women in uniform serving our country?" before providing his own answer: "The Republican side of the aisle said no; apply the law as harshly as possible to these soldiers as you would to everyone else."[92] Moments later, senator Chuck Schumer (D-NY) rhetorically asked, "Do we want to come down like a hammer on these people the same as we would come down on somebody who squandered whatever money they had in Las Vegas gambling?"[93] Durbin had also voiced this notion, calling guard and reserve members "people who really should be treated differently."[94] "For goodness' sakes," he inveighed, "these people aren't morally deficient; they're our best."[95]

The notion that service members are more virtuous than other citizens is, of course, problematic, but Democrats linked this notion to critiques of guard and reserve deployments and Republican claims to support the troops. "They joined thinking: once a year I may have to serve my State, my country for a month or so. Now we are calling them into battle for a year, a year and a half, and no end in sight," Durbin argued the next day, adding, "you are called into combat and leave behind your family and your business. And what if the business fails while you are gone?"[96] Durbin thus cast active-duty service for part-time troops as a bait and switch; having joined on the premise of short, regional deployments, they were first misused by their government and then not shielded from the financial ruin that those deployments produced. More icily, he condemned the hypocrisy inherent in the tension between conservative admonitions to "support the troops" and what Wendy Brown terms the "corporate domination of political decisions and economic policy."[97] "Many of the Senators who go back home and cheer the troops," he had noted a day earlier, "couldn't wait to vote with Visa and MasterCard and against the Army, Navy, Marine Corps, Air Force, and Coast Guard."[98] In the end, and despite assertions that "the Act contains special accommodations for active duty military personnel," there were only two mentions of the military in nearly two hundred pages of the law's text.[99] One provision asserted that service members deployed to combat zones could not be considered debtors if they missed credit counseling sessions; the other established that a person on active duty could petition for an additional lowering of their debt burden by demonstrating that they faced "special circumstances."[100]

Conservative policy makers' willingness to defer to corporate interests rather than endorse policies that might have had a widespread impact on alleviating guard and reserve precarity was perhaps best illustrated in a hearing in October 2005 in which Republican senators noted guardsmen and reservists' continued struggles but lauded companies' voluntary efforts to assist deployed employees rather than endorsing structural relief for those troops. Senator Johnny Isakson's (D-GA) opening statement, in which he intoned that "the companies that are here today and those that are here in support of our men and women are real heroes to me," was a paean to neoliberalism. Isakson cast private enterprise as enabling the nation's military strength, arguing that "because of the employers that we have" the nation had "the best trained, best equipped, best staffed Reserve and Guard anywhere in the world"—an assertion, it bears noting, with which innumerable drill instructors might take issue. Next, he argued that benefits that might otherwise be described as rights—such as a living wage and healthcare—were appropriately the product of corporate benevolence. He noted that while federal law required that employers hold a deployed service member's job for them, "thousands upon thousands of employers like the three represented here today go well above and beyond the call of duty" through "voluntary" programs that "take the extra step" by providing differential pay, maintaining health care for families, and sending care packages. Finally, he cast deployed troops as not only patriotic citizens but also content workers who "talked specifically about their employer and about how much their support had meant to their families while they were deployed to Iraq."[101]

Unsurprisingly, senator Patty Murray (D-WA), wasn't having it. In her opening statement, she embraced conclusions that had emerged in earlier hearings and in the debate over the Durbin amendment. "The Cold War is over," she complained, "yet we are holding on to programs that were built for veterans of that era."[102] Hers was a lonely voice. Only Ted Kennedy joined her, complaining that "servicemembers' rights are at risk of being mired in a bureaucracy that can't communicate with itself" and proposing congressional action to ensure that those rights weren't violated.[103] Most Republicans on the panel called for allowing employers to count differential pay as wages, which would have been more tax-friendly.[104] Such sentiments are again unsurprising in an era when government officials' primary goal has become "cut[ting] back public, noncommercial powers and resources that might impede or drain potential profit-making."[105]

One witnesses happily joined Isakson in extolling corporate virtue. One told of a Walmart manager who called a deployed soldier's wife each week and sent her flowers on Valentine's Day and a community college where the "automotive department made repairs to his family's vehicle, reducing the stress on his wife" before concluding, "If National Guardsmen and Reservists are indeed 'twice the citizen,' then their civilian employers are 'twice the patriot.'"[106] Home Depot's executive vice president, Dennis Donovan, described voluntarily providing differential pay and healthcare "as our responsibility to our country" and "a valuable investment to our company's future."[107] Ronald Fry, a Wachovia Bank employee and national guardsman, extolled his employer's willingness to pay his salary and benefits for a year as well send him so many care packages that "the regular Army soldiers were amazed when I told them I had received all the items from work, and I was proud to tell them about the company."[108] His employer, he concluded, "was a partner to me in the deployment."[109]

Flowers, auto repairs, and care packages are nice gestures, but they don't close a pay gap. Voluntarily providing a pay differential does, but few guard and reserve troops are fortunate to have an employer willing or able to do so. Murray did her best to highlight this reality, getting Fry to acknowledge that only a few people in a unit of more than one hundred received differential pay.[110]

Another witness, Lisa Nisenfeld of the Southwest Washington Workforce Development Council, who had likely been invited at Murray's behest, argued, "Employers certainly are anxious to tell, say that they support our troops. When it comes down to individual businesses, particularly small businesses, they are hesitant."[111]

The other comments were more insidious. In particular, the notion that paying a soldier's differential pay was a "valuable investment" and that a bank—an entity, it bears pointing out, that the Durbin amendment was designed to protect struggling guardsmen and reservists from "partnered with [soldiers] during [their] deployment[s]" comports with what Brown identifies as another neoliberal imperative. "'Caring,'" Brown explains, has "[become] a market niche" because it "attracts consumers and investors."[112] It also, apparently, attracts senators. Closing the meeting, Isakson thanked Wachovia and Home Depot "for what you do for your country."[113]

Economic precarity was a built-in feature for guard and reserve troops mobilized to fight the United States' twenty-first-century wars. More heavily deployed than at any point in the preceding half century and facing call-ups that often stretched to a year and a half between training, deployment, and redeployment, they lost wages and businesses, their families suffered, and they were unsure if they would have jobs to which they could return. The emergence of this population of marginalized veterans resulted from two intersecting policy shifts. First, the force structure of the national guard and army reserve, shaped in the aftermath of the Cold War, was not designed to withstand the deployments that the Iraq and Afghanistan Wars necessitated. Differentials between civilian and military pay, as well as the strain that absences placed on businesses, created substantial economic problems, from mounting consumer debt to foreclosure, that could not easily be overcome. Relief, however, was not quick in coming. Although Democratic members of Congress proposed initiatives that ranged from one-time relief checks to financial protections and employer incentives, a legislative branch enthralled by neoliberalism—embracing deregulation and privatization while celebrating corporate citizenship—refused almost all reform efforts.

It took until 2008 for legislation—the National Guard and Reservists Debt Relief Act of 2008, which protected guard and reserve troops who had incurred debt while deployed and filed for bankruptcy from means testing—to become law.[114] The passage of this law was a relatively thin reed, and applied "only with respect to cases commenced during the three-year period beginning on December 19, 2008," meaning that earlier bankruptcies were not covered.[115] Still, guard and reserve troops won a victory that could assuage some financial suffering.[116] The economic suffering of guard and reserve troops, however, has not been quick to abate. Ten years after the Iraq invasion, the *New York Times* reported that deployed guardsmen had been the victims of improper home foreclosures, and Congress was holding hearings on national guard unemployment.[117]

During the COVID-19 pandemic, however, the struggles of part-time soldiers continued. Two months into the mobilization of nearly forty thousand national guardsmen to assist in fighting the COVID-19 pandemic, *Politico* reported that the Trump administration had ordered "a 'hard stop' on their deployments on June 24—just one day shy of many members becoming eligible for key federal benefits."[118] And in June 2021, the *Washington Post* reported that, largely as a result of the call-ups that the COVID pandemic necessitated, guard and reserve members were "report[ing] more food insecurity than nearly any other group, regardless of household income, education, age or race" and that "nearly one in five Guard members report sometimes or often not having enough to eat."[119] The reasons for this were the same as those that had shaped the economic struggles of part-time soldiers during the Iraq and Afghanistan Wars: "The spike in days worked takes Guard members and reservists away from their jobs, with many soldiers not drawing that income if they're away on military duty."[120] The history and continuing reality of guard and reserve precarity, and the policy failures that create and exacerbate it, thus reveal that veterans are not marginalized only in the aftermath of their service. Rather, the policies that shape their service and the political will of those who send them to fight play a significant role in determining their economic stability and, with it, their postservice life chances. Considering this history thus demands a reckoning with the consequences of the nation's simultaneous embrace of neoliberal economics and permanent war.

NOTES

1. House Committee on Government Reform, *Wounded Army Guard and Reserve Forces: Increasing the Capacity to Care*, 109th Cong., 1st Sess. (2005), 98.
2. House Committee on Government Reform, *Wounded Army Guard*, 98

3. House Committee on Government Reform, *Wounded Army Guard*, 98.

4. House Committee on Government Reform, *Wounded Army Guard*, 98–99.

5. House Committee on Government Reform, *Wounded Army Guard*, 99.

6. House Committee on Government Reform, *Wounded Army Guard*, 100.

7. House Committee on Government Reform, *Wounded Army Guard*, 100.

8. House Committee on Government Reform, *Wounded Army Guard*, 100. On the Nevada Guard in this era, see *Nevada National Guard Biennial Report 2005–2006* (Carson City: Nevada Office of the National Guard Public Affairs Office), 19, http://epubs.nsla.nv.gov/statepubs/epubs/470325-2005-2006.pdf.

9. House Committee on Government Reform, *Wounded Army Guard*, 123–24.

10. Jennifer Mittelstadt, *The Rise of the Military Welfare State* (Cambridge, MA: Harvard University Press, 2015); Beth Bailey, *America's Army: Making the All-Volunteer Force* (Cambridge, MA: Harvard University Press, 2009).

11. Bailey, *America's Army*, 251.

12. House Committee on Government Reform, *Wounded Army Guard*, 144.

13. National Guard Bureau, *Annual Review, Fiscal Year 2005*, 7, accessed November 19, 2021, https://www.nationalguard.mil/About-the-Guard/Historical-Publications/Annual-Reports/FileId/134575/.

14. Mittelstadt, *Rise of the Military Welfare State*, 11.

15. On the latter, see Mary L. Dudziak, *War Time: An Idea, Its History, Its Consequences* (Oxford: Oxford University Press, 2012).

16. Judith Butler, *Frames of War: When Is Life Grievable?* (London: Verso, 2009), 25.

17. Lisa Duggan, *The Twilight of Equality? Neoliberalism, Cultural Politics, and the Attack on Democracy* (Boston, MA: Beacon Press, 2003), x.

18. Duggan, *Twilight of Equality?*, xiii, xii.

19. Ibid., 18, 39.

20. Anne Case and Angus Deaton, *Deaths of Despair and the Future of Capitalism* (Princeton, NJ: Princeton University Press, 2020), 28.

21. Andrew J. Bacevich, *The New American Militarism: How Americans Are Seduced by War* (Oxford: Oxford University Press, 2005), 2.

22. Andrew J. Bacevich, *Breach of Trust: How Americans Failed Their Soldiers and Their Country* (New York: Metropolitan Books, 2013), 13.

23. House Committee on Government Reform, *Wounded Army Guard*, 169.

24. Christian G. Appy, *Working-Class War: American Combat Soldiers in Vietnam* (Chapel Hill: University of North Carolina Press, 1993), 36.; Gregory A. Daddis, *Withdrawal: Reassessing America's Final Years in Vietnam* (Oxford: Oxford University Press, 2017), 145.

25. John Sloan Brown, *Kevlar Legions: The Transformation of the United States Army, 1989–2005* (Washington, DC: US Army Center for Military History, 2011), 127.

26. Ibid., 259.

27. Ibid.

28. *Nevada National Guard Biennial Report, 2005–2006*, 8.

29. Adjutant General's Department, *Annual Report, 2005*, 3, 7, http://kansastag.gov/AdvHTML_doc_upload/Annual%20Report%202005.pdf; Robert G. F. Lee, *Department of Defense Annual Report: Fiscal Year 2005* (Honolulu: Hawaii Army National Guard, 2005), 5, n.p.

30. Alan Feur, "Regular Citizens with Regular Army," *New York Times*, February 6, 2005.

31. Ibid., ; Bailey, *America's Army*, 246–47.

32. J. S. Brown, *Kevlar Legions*, 259.

33. J. S. Brown, *Kevlar Legions*, 259; Eric Schmitt and Thom Shanker, "Rumsfeld Seeks Broad Review of Iraq Policy," *New York Times*, January 7, 2005.

34. Kirk Semple, "Part Time Warriors, Fully Committed," *New York Times*, February 14, 2005.

35. J. S. Brown, *Kevlar Legions*, 265.

36. Pam Belluck, "Vermonters Vote on Study of National Guard's Role," *New York Times*, March 2, 2005.

37. J. S. Brown, *Kevlar Legions*, 377.

38. United Services Employment and Reemployment Rights Act of 1994, Public Law 103–353, 5, https://www.congress.gov/103/bills/hr995/BILLS-103hr995enr.pdf.

39. Ibid., 6.

40. Tim Reid, "US Weekend Troops Pay Price of Time as Virgin Soldiers in Iraq," *Times* (UK), February 26, 2005.

41. J. S. Brown, *Kevlar Legions*, 378.

42. Kirk Sample, "Deployed: Lives Left Behind; Interrupted by War, the Struggle to Care for Family and Business," *New York Times*, February 22, 2005.

43. Pam Belluck et. al., "Vermonters Vote on Study of National Guard's Role," *New York Times*, March 2, 2005; Elizabeth Olson, "War Service Is Taking Toll on the Self-Employed," *New York Times*, August 25, 200; Brad Knickerbocker, "Money Woes on the Homefront: Call-Ups Mean Lower Pay and Hardship for National Guard and Reserve Troops," *Christian Science Monitor*, August 11, 2005. See also Stephen Lenham and J. J. Asongu, *The Iraq Quagmire: The Price of Imperial Arrogance* (Lawrenceville, GA: Greenview, 2005): 26.

44. Lenham and Asongu, *The Iraq Quagmire*, 26.

45. "Guard and Reserve Benefits," Military.com, June 1, 20202, acccessed November 19, 2020, https://www.military.com/deployment/deployment-pay.html; "Basic Pay," MyArmy Benefits, accessed November 19, 2001, https://myarmybenefits.us.army.mil/Benefit-Library/Federal-Benefits/Basic-Pay?serv=120.

46. For a soldier without dependents, the amount was less. See General Accounting Office, *GAO-04-89: Army National Guard Personnel Mobilized to Active Duty Experienced Significant Pay Problems* (Washington, DC: General Accounting Office, 2004), 10, https://www.gao.gov/assets/250/240624.pdf.

47. Russ Bynum,Troops Return from Iraq with Money to Burn," *Associated Press*, January 22, 2006, https://acikradyo.com.tr/arsiv-icerigi/troops-return-iraq-money-burn.

48. US Department of Labor, "Bulletin 2585: Occupational Employment and Wages, May 2005," May 2007, 76, 133, https://www.bls.gov/oes/bulletin_2005.pdf.

49. Ibid., 102.

50. "2005 Military Pay Scale," Military Factory, 2020, https://www.militaryfactory.com/pay-scales/2005_military_pay_scale.asp; "2005 Military Pay Scale," Military Factory, n.d., accessed November 19, 2021, https://www.militaryfactory.com/pay-scales/2005_military_pay_scale.php.

51. "2005 Military Pay Scale," Military Factory.

52. J. S. Brown, *Kevlar Legions*, 379.

53. Sarah Kershaw, "The Struggle for Iraq: Citizen Soldiers," *New York Times*, September 15, 2003.

54. Ibid.

55. Monica Davey, "Soldier Protesting Extended Deployment Drops Suit and Re-enlists," *New York Times*, February 6, 2005.

56. Reid, "US Weekend Troops Pay Price of Time as Virgin Soldiers in Iraq."

57. Andrew Jacobs, "With Breadwinners Overseas, Guard Families Face Struggle," *New York Times*, April 25, 2004.

58. Brad Knickerbocker, "Money Woes on Home Front," *Christian Science Monitor*, August 11, 2005.

59. John D. Rayburn et. al. *The US Army in Iraq*, vol. 1 (Carlisle, PA: The US Army War College, 2019), xxxii, https://publications.armywarcollege.edu/pubs/3667.pdf; Brian Glyn Williams, *Counter Jihad: America's Military Experience in Afghanistan, Iraq, and Syria* (Philadelphia: University of Pennsylvania Press, 2016); Medea Benjamin and Nicolas J. S. Davies, "The Staggering Death Toll In Iraq," *Salon*, March 19, 2018, https://www.salon.com/2018/03/19/the-staggering-death-toll-in-iraq_partner.

60. General Accounting Office, *GAO-04–89*, 3.

61. Ibid., 12–14.

62. Ibid., 17–18. Notably, not all of the errors were failures to pay guardsmen; there had been nearly seven hundred thousand dollars in overpayments.

63. Ibid., 19.

64. Ibid., 20.

65. Ibid., 5.

66. Ibid., 29.

67. Ibid., 35.

68. Ibid., 34.

69. Ibid.

70. House Committee on Government Reform, *Wounded Army Guard*, 1–3.

71. Ibid., 35–36.

72. Ibid., 112.

73. Ibid., 73.

74. Ibid., 75.

75. Ibid., 75.

76. Ibid., 202.

77. Ibid., 141.

78. Representative Stupak of Michigan, speaking on "Support Our Troops: $1,500 Bonus Bill," *Congressional Record*, October 1, 2003, H9080.

79. "On Agreeing to the Amendment: Amendment 19 to HR3289," GovTrack, October 17, 2003, https://www.govtrack.us/congress/votes/108-2003/h554.

80. The bill was H.R. 3051 (108th Cong.). See "H.R.3051: To Pay a One-Time Bonus to Members of the Armed Forces Who Served or Serve in a Combat Zone Designated for Operation Iraqi Freedom or Operation Enduring Freedom, and for Other Purposes," ProPublica, 2017, https://projects.propublica.org/represent/bills/108/hr3051.

81. Senator Durbin of Illinois, speaking on S.256, *Congressional Record*, March 9, 2005, S2326.

82. Meghann Cotter, "New Bankruptcy Laws Expected to Limit Abuse of the Program," *Free Lance-Star* (Fredericksburg, VA), April 29, 2005.

83. "Remarks by President Bush in Signing the Bankruptcy Abuse Prevention, Consumer Protection Act," White House, April 20, 2005, https://georgewbush-whitehouse.archives.gov/news/releases/2005/04/20050420-5.html.

84. Wendy Kaufman, "New Law Would Increase Consumer Liability in Bankruptcy," National Public Radio, April 12, 2005.

85. Senator Durbin of Illinois, S.A. 111, *Congressional Record*, March 7, 2005, S2139.

86. Senator Durbin of Illinois, speaking on S. 256, *Congressional Record*, March 7, 2005, S2141.

87. Senator Durbin of Illinois, speaking on S. 256, *Congressional Record*, March 7, 2005, S2142.

88. Senator Sessions of Alabama, speaking on S. 256, *Congressional Record*, March 7, 2005, S2143–44.

89. Senator Grassley of Iowa, speaking on "Honoring Our Armed Forces," *Congressional Record*, March 7, 2005, S2143–44.

90. Senator Kennedy of Massachusetts, speaking on S. 256, *Congressional Record*, March 8, 2005, S2200–2201.

91. Senator Durbin of Illinois, speaking on "Amendment No. 40 Withdrawn," *Congressional Record*, March 8, 2005, S2218.

92. Senator Durbin of Illinois, speaking on S. 256, *Congressional Record*, March 8, 2005, S2203.

93. Senator Schumer of New York, speaking on S.256, *Congressional Record*, March 8, 2005, S2205. This quote was taken from the March 8 issue—highlighted in yellow in text.

94. Senator Durbin of Illinois, speaking on S.256, *Congressional Record*, March 8, 2005, S2216.

95. Senator Durbin of Illinois, speaking on S.256, *Congressional Record*, March 8, 2005, S2216–17.

96. Senator Durbin of Illinois, speaking on S.256, *Congressional Record*, March 9, 2005, S2326.

97. Wendy Brown, *Undoing the Demos: Neoliberalism's Stealth Revolution* (Brooklyn, NY: Zone Books, 2017), 29.

98. Senator Durbin of Illinois, speaking on S.256, *Congressional Record*, March 8, 2005, S2217.

99. Leslie Bonacum and Neil Allen, "Major Bankruptcy Reform Means Changes for Many Professionals, CCH Says," Wolters Kluwer CCH, April 14, 2005, https://www.cch.com/Press/news/2005/20050414b.asp.

100. Public Law 109–8, "Bankruptcy Abuse Prevention and Consumer Protection Act of 2005," 119 STAT. 29 and 119 STAT. 37, https://www.congress.gov/109/plaws/publ8/PLAW-109publ8.pdf.

101. Subcommittee on Employment and Workplace Safety of the Senate Committee on Health, Education, Labor, and Pensions, "Enhancing Cooperation between Employers and Guardsmen/Reservists," 109th Cong., 1st Sess. (2005), 2.

102. Ibid., 5.

103. Ibid., 11.

104. Ibid., 6. The bill, "The Uniformed Services Differential Pay Protection Act," did not become law.

105. Duggan, *Twilight of Equality*, xiii.

106. Subcommittee on Employment and Workplace Safety, "Enhancing Cooperation," 16.

107. Ibid., 17.

108. Ibid., 30.

109. Ibid.

110. Ibid., 32.

111. Ibid., 33.

112. W. Brown, *Undoing the Demos*, 27.

113. Ibid., 40.

114. *National Guard and Reservists Debt Relief Act of 2008*, Public Law 110–438, https://www.congress.gov/110/plaws/publ438/PLAW-110publ438.pdf; see also "Hall Helps National Guardsmen and Reservists Achieve Debt Relief," States News Service, June 24, 2008 and "Cohen Introduces Bipartisan National Guard & Reservist Debt Relief Extension Act," Congressman Steve Cohen, June 15, 2011, https://cohen.house.gov/press-release/cohen-introduces-bipartisan-national-guard-reservist-debt-relief-extension-act.

115. *National Guard and Reservists Debt Relief Act of 2008*, 122 Stat. 500. The law has since expanded the window of time in which cases can be filed with this protection; US Bankruptcy Court of Southern Mississippi, "National Guard and Reservists Debt Relief," https://www.mssb.uscourts.gov/robohelp/ecf_docketing_guide/Miscellenaous/National_Guard_and_Reservists_Debt_Relief.htm.

116. It warrants noting that this law constituted a benefit that civilians did not enjoy, thus reaffirming discourses of military exceptionalism.

117. Jessica Silver-Greenberg and Ben Protess, "Banks Find More Wrongful Foreclosures among Military Members," *New York Times*, March 4, 2013.

118. Alice Miranda Ollstein, "'Hard Stop:' States Could Lose National Guard Virus Workers," *Politico*, May 19, 2020, https://www.politico.com/news/2020/05/19/national-guard-coronavirus-267514.

119. Laura Reiley, "The Rising Cost of Being In the National Guard: Reservists and Guardsmen are Twice as Likely to be Hungry as Other American Groups," *Washington Post*, June 22, 2021.

120. Reiley, "Rising Cost."

Prisoners after War

Veterans in the Age of Mass Incarceration

JASON A. HIGGINS

INTRODUCTION

Oral history has unique potential to document unrecorded experiences and amplify the voices of those forgotten in the margins of society. Since the days of interviewing combat soldiers in World War II, this methodology has come a long way toward creating more socially diverse military histories.[1] Today, the Library of Congress, for example, contains over 110,000 interviews in the Veterans History Project. Yet, most veterans' oral histories rarely become veterans history. Too often, they recollect military experiences from the perspectives of former soldiers, centered primarily on wartime. These constraints limit scholarly imagination to the possible ways oral history can be used to analyze collective memory and intergenerational trauma.

The Incarcerated Veterans Oral History Project has recorded the memories of nearly sixty US military veterans involved in the criminal justice system, providing an analytical lens through which to historicize the consequences of military-related trauma, racial inequality, and systemic injustice.[2] A preview of this project, this chapter traces the wake of intergenerational trauma through the oral histories of three African American veterans caught up in US wars and the prison system.[3]

Against the backdrop of centuries of inequality, the histories of incarcerated veterans have been expunged from American national memory.[4] For much of the nineteenth and twentieth centuries, African American soldiers were more likely to be punished, imprisoned, dishonorably discharged, or executed by the military justice system.[5] Black military masculinity challenged the ideological foundation of white supremacy, which categorically excluded African Americans from constructions of manhood. Generations of Black soldiers and veterans clashed with white authorities. After war, veterans organized politically, defended their communities, and often became successful business leaders.[6] Consequentially, many also became the victims of police brutality, imprisonment, and lynching.[7]

The historic roots of mass incarceration can be traced back to slavery, the Civil War, and Jim Crow.[8] After Reconstruction, white Southerners overturned or circumnavigated the political and legal rights of freed people. Southern Democrats passed a series of "Black Codes" that criminalized unemployment, vagrancy, and petty property theft, entrapping formerly enslaved people in a system of control that functioned like slavery by another name. The convict leasing system created a new form of legal bondage, designed to force freed people to return and work on plantations.[9] By the 1890 US Census, statistical evidence indicated that African Americans comprised 12 percent of the population of the United States but made up 30 percent of the prison population.[10] These statistics were interpreted as proof of Black people's supposed "natural predisposition" for crime. Taken out of context of the Jim Crow legal system, statistics on Black criminality provided the ideological justifications that fueled the rise of mass incarceration during the twentieth century.[11] Discourse on Black crime and unemployment would have profound consequences during the Vietnam War, when Daniel Patrick Moynihan described the root cause of urban crime as "pathological."[12]

Historically, African Americans were excluded from veteran's status. The GI Bill essentially created the suburban middle class, but the denial of Veterans Administration (VA) entitlements and home loans to Black families constrained many to urban areas, with little access to economic opportunity.[13] Labor and housing markets failed to absorb the second wave of migrants from the South.[14] "The resulting concentration of poverty and unemployment in predominantly black inner-city neighborhoods . . . led to the explosion of urban crime rates a generation later."[15] The children of the Second Great Migration experienced harsh economic inequality, police brutality, and disproportionate incarceration rates.[16] Socially engineered segregation perpetuated generational urban poverty and violent crime, laying the foundation for the pipeline to prison. In the 1960s, it also funneled poor and disproportionately Black men into combat in Vietnam. From 1966 to 1971, more than four hundred thousand mostly poor, semiliterate African Americans served in combat units in Vietnam under Project 100,000. From 1965 to 1967, Black troops were twice as likely as whites to die on the battlefields of Vietnam.[17] By 1970, Black soldiers were disproportionately imprisoned in military jails and discharged without benefits.[18]

PART I

Discriminatory practices in the military, the VA, and the US criminal justice system led to the incarceration of hundreds of thousands of veterans since the Vietnam War era. In the 1970s, veterans were more likely than nonveterans to be incarcerated in US prisons.[19] Data from 1973 indicated that over half of the veteran prison population had received "less-than-honorable" discharges; half of these were Black Vietnam veterans.[20] The Department of Justice series on "Veterans in Prison and Jail," first published in 1981, indicated that Vietnam veterans were more likely to have "less-than-honorable" discharges, more likely to be convicted of a violent crime, and more likely to serve a longer prison sentence.[21] Punitive discharges could bar veterans from receiving disability benefits, counseling services, and GI Bill entitlements. At the height of the global economic recession in 1974, the unemployment rate of African American veterans was also three times higher than average.[22] By 1979, one in four prisoners in the United States were military veterans.[23] This occurred at a moment when domestic policy was simultaneously turning to the prison-industrial complex to address social problems. The Incarcerated Veterans Oral History Project shows this historic relationship between military-related trauma, inequality, and imprisonment.

Born the son of a coal miner in West Virginia, Henry Burton joined the US Marine Corps for the promises of opportunity and experience. In late 1967, he deployed to Vietnam. "I stayed there," Burton said. "I stayed a total of nineteen months, and in Vietnam, I became a different person."[24] In 1970, he reintegrated from the war with all the problems that veterans face today—with none of the resources. He did not know about the VA or disability benefits. When he returned to the United States, Burton got a job in a Detroit factory but lasted only a few months. His wife and baby were waiting on him back in the world, but undiagnosed combat trauma permanently damaged his ability to provide for them financially or emotionally.

In desperation, he robbed a grocery store; then he hit a bank. No one was hurt, but he was sentenced to fifteen years in a federal prison in Atlanta. In the criminal justice system, Burton has always been a Black male first and foremost. If his veteran status mattered, it did not help his case. If anything, it made him look more dangerous.

Burton, however, had never been in trouble with the law before joining the military. Like hundreds of thousands of teenage boys before and since him, Burton underwent the marine corps' rite of passage into manhood. "They break you down to nothing. I mean, you're not even an individual." The military severs contact with the outside world, restricting calls and letters from family. The marine corps becomes the new family. It provides and protects. "They broke me down," recalled Burton. "When they gave me a pair of socks and pants, I thought I had a tuxedo. They looked good! I remember coming out of the camp, thinking I could take on the whole wide world. I went to [Fort Polk] Louisiana, and my chest stuck out so bad." He said, "I couldn't wait to get to Vietnam to kill . . . that's how my mind frame was" at that time.

In late 1967, Burton arrived in Da Nang. It had a "peculiar smell that I'll never forget," he recalled. "I can still smell the atmosphere. It was different. I know what it was now—it was death that I was smelling." "And the people were smaller," he thought. "They looked strange to me, but death was in the air," he said. "It still lingers today of death." Burton arrived by himself, the only one from his platoon to be shipped to Vietnam. He had orders to join the 2nd Battalion, 7th Marines.

Weeks later, Burton's father died of black lung disease. Burton flew home to attend the funeral. While back stateside, he met Marquette, the woman who became his wife and the mother of his child. He filed for "a hardship discharge from the Marine Corps because [he] was the oldest one of the family," but the appeal was denied. He rejoined the 1st Battalion, 5th Marines in 1968 on the eve of the Tet Offensive. Burton recounted his first major combat experience: "They hit us on the bridge on the way to Hue City," he said. "After the combat, they asked me to go up to a place where all the dead bodies was to identify the men from our platoon. I get there, and it's like a football field of bodies, from one end to the other. There wasn't a path in between, so you have to step on the bodies to get to the people to identify them." He remembers "stepping on the bodies. I kept saying 'excuse me, excuse me.' But yet, I had no feelings for them at that time. All kinds—races and different countries—had been killed. That still haunts me today."

Over the next year and a half, Burton's body and behavior adapted to the conditions of war—long periods of boredom and intense moments of violence, death, and moral injury. At war, Burton learned to survive by isolating. He created emotional distance between himself and other men. "When I got to Vietnam, I was the only one in my platoon, so I had to make friends from the men that I met." Over time, he came to expect sudden death by ambush. "When we got new men in the platoon, we really didn't care about them because they wouldn't survive long enough. . . . I lost that compassion for human beings." Afterward, Burton found it difficult to reconcile his losses in a senseless war: "I can remember the face of death." But memorializing is a conflicting process. "If my friends died," he said, "I couldn't think about them. All I could think about was the living. The dead had no meaning." The strategies that helped Burton survive in combat became detrimental to his life in civilian society.

After receiving a third Purple Heart, Burton was administratively discharged by the marine corps. "They give them three chances to kill you. If they can patch you up, they send you back into combat. But if you lose an arm, leg, or something critical, then they send you home. But if they can patch you back up, they give them three chances to kill you. After a third time, they may take you out the field," he believes. "So that's how I got out of the field the third time." Burton was suddenly booted out of the marines with no time for adjustment, no job training, and no support. "I didn't know anything about disability. I didn't know anything about the VA." On April 15, 1970, Burton returned to the United States, but "was stuck with a wife, a child, no job, nothing—stuck."

After the war, Burton and his wife moved to Detroit. He got a job at a motor company in Wayne County, Michigan, installing upholstery in Ford station wagons. "I was putting the floorboard in there with twelve screws and an air gun. And I had just come from Vietnam. I didn't last six months," he said. "I just could not adjust to having an air gun in my hand because it reminded me too much of combat." In 1972, Burton left. "I abandoned my home in Detroit, and that's how I ended up in Roanoke, Virginia. I told Marquette I didn't want to be married." Afterward, he bounced around from employment services and various jobs but hit a dead end. "I had only two marketable skills, combat or supermarkets," he thought. "This is how I ended up turning to crime."

No one was hurt during the robberies of the grocery store or the bank—and it was his first offense—but based on the nature of Burton's crimes and his military service record, the court sentenced him to fifteen years in a federal penitentiary. He recounted the trial: "The judge gave me life, and my lawyer said, 'Your Honor, he never killed nobody.'" The judge responded, "'He's dangerous. Get him out of my court room.' It looked like my military service became my enemy. All I did was take the money, but that still didn't matter. 'His military record makes him dangerous.'" It was not that Henry Burton was simply a combat veteran from an unpopular war; he was a Black man who had been an agent of state violence. "I joined the military because I believed in our country . . . and almost died three times." He asked, "What happened to me? But that's not a question." Burton admitted, "I broke the law . . . but why do I get life?" "Give me another life," he said, repeating, "Give me *another life*."

Over the last few decades, Burton became institutionalized. "In the early part of prison, I became a prisoner of war. In my mind, that's how I coped." He learned to survive in prison by isolating himself. "My post-traumatic stress went dormant. It went to sleep on me," he thought. After serving fourteen years, Burton was released from prison. Once more, the veteran came home to the world. But the post-traumatic stress disorder resurfaced; he recidivated. Since then, Burton and his family have fought for recognition of his status as a veteran; he receives partial disability benefits for combat-related PTSD and a lifetime of trauma.[25] He said, "I've been buried in prison the last forty years."[26]

PART II

The end of the Vietnam War marked the start of the war on drugs. Civil rights and the Great Society programs were the priority of the national agenda in the first half of Lyndon Johnson's presidency, but by 1965, attention turned to Vietnam. Paradoxically, Johnson ushered in the Voting Rights Act and then launched a new war on crime.[27] Following the 1965 Watts riots, the Johnson administration began redirecting resources away from the war on poverty to fund war efforts in Vietnam.[28] He also commissioned a study on the causes of racial unrest; the resulting Kerner Report and the federal legislation that followed in 1968 transformed policing and laid "foundations of the carceral state: aggressive policing, mass incarceration, and engulfing the state's welfare capacities."[29]

Richard M. Nixon defunded Great Society programs and turned to punishment, militarizing police forces and targeting predominately poor Black urban areas.[30] States redirected federal funding from community resources to expand police forces and prison systems. The war on drugs extended prison sentences and introduced mandatory minimum sentences. In 1973, the Nixon administration created the Drug Enforcement Agency to conduct drug investigations within and beyond US borders. Launching the war on drugs in 1971, Nixon's "Public Enemy Number One" speech blamed heroin-addicted soldiers for US losses in Vietnam,[31] while simultaneously stigmatizing and stoking public fear of Vietnam veterans.

Since the Vietnam War, the US prison population has multiplied from three hundred thousand to over two million.[32] Incarcerated veterans populations doubled.[33] Heather Ann Thompson noted, "Between 1970–2010 more people were incarcerated in the United States than were imprisoned in any other country, and at no other point in its past had the nation's economic, social, and political institutions become so bound up with the practice of punishment."[34] In the 1980s, president Ronald Reagan further escalated the global drug war, while intensifying domestic enforcement.[35] To combat the "crack epidemic," the US Department of Justice launched, in the words of Doris Marie Provine, a "new—blacker—war on drugs."[36] Crack cocaine was criminalized more severely than powder cocaine.[37] Mandatory minimum laws removed the discretion of judges on sentencing. For a generation of veterans self-medicating with unrecognized and undiagnosed trauma, these laws entrapped them in the criminal justice system.

Born and raised in Harlem, Haywood Fennell Sr. grew up around Black men in uniform. His uncles were Korean War vets; one retired after twenty-three years in the air force. Fennell joined the army at seventeen, believing it was a path toward social equality and economic uplift. "Why the hell not go into the military and serve to be able to come back and get an education and own a home—why not?" he asked. Fennell's uncle had a successful military career and benefitted greatly from the benefits of veteran status. "But my uncle is not me," Fennell explained. "I'm a generation from him. I tried it his way and it didn't work. I was exposed to a lot of covert/overt racism."[38]

From 1959 to 1964, Fennell served in the US Army. While stationed in Okinawa, he experienced a trauma that has affected the rest of his life. Towns and red-light districts outside the base were segregated. One night, Fennell crossed the color line. "I was traumatized. I was attacked—beat up real bad in the nighttime and pissed on by my attackers," Fennell said angrily. "When I reported it to the company commander, the first thing they told me was I was out of bounds. 'You weren't supposed to be down there in that area.'"

The attackers were not reprimanded, but Fennell experienced retaliation from the commanding officer, who denied his scheduled promotion. "I thought it was reprehensible," he remembered. The injustice was "eye-opening." Afterward, he was "stationed right next to a morgue and was seeing body bags every day." Drugs were readily available in Okinawa. Soon after, Fennell began to self-medicate with heroin.[39]

After getting out of the army in 1964, Fennell returned to Harlem. Reintegration "was very traumatic because I was unable to communicate the things that occurred over there because I thought that it was so horrendous. To be beat up. Degraded. I couldn't talk to my wife. I tried to heal myself. I started using," he admitted. After his discharge, Fennell "shied away from any affiliation with the military because of the shame." Then, "I got caught up in the drug game. I tried to work, but drugs became overwhelming, so I became a full-time addict." Fennell said, "The insidiousness of the drug just takes over. You have absolutely no control to the point that your freedom is in jeopardy." Heroin use was destroying his family, so he decided it would be better to leave. By 1971, "I was first incarcerated when I was 28 years old, as a direct result of my addiction. It creeps in and nothing really matters but me and the drug. The family takes second or third place. I did love my family. I do love my family. But it was up and down—jails, bails, fails for me."

Fennell spent a total of two decades in prison for drug-related charges. In the 1990s, he visited the VA and finally stopped using heroin. "Now, I want to live. I went through the withdrawals," he remembered. "I didn't have anything left to lose because I had lost everything: my family; I've got a record; I've been to prisons. What else is there for me to do but to stand up? That was twenty-one years ago." He added, "It took me twenty-eight years to get my college degree." Living in Boston today, Fennell is a writer, educator, and community activist.[40] Recently, he organized a memorial for Edward O. Gourdin, an Olympic medalist, commanding officer of the 372nd Infantry Division in World War II, and first African American Supreme Court justice of Massachusetts.

Fennell's advocacy for veterans started in prison. "There is some respect from the veterans that are corrections officers," Fennell stated. "But there is no solidarity in that relationship that would put them into an advocacy position to do more for veterans—house them by themselves and bring in people that can deal with trauma that they've been exposed to. That hasn't happened yet," he noted. In the past decade, some progress has been made to provide services to veterans incarcerated; many jails and prisons have veterans' pods, which house former military personnel in separate units.[41] Yet, due to widely differing state laws, access to these privileges remains unequal.

In the military, Fennell experienced an institutional betrayal, a fundamental violation of his ideological understanding of the United States.[42] After reporting the attack, Fennell experienced retaliation from the chain of command. "You have to careful about this United States of America—Land of the Brave and the Slave," he said. "In other countries, they're giving food in one hand, and they're taking minerals and resources with the other hand—to strengthen us and weaken them," he related, echoing Dr. Martin Luther King Jr.[43] "People don't want to accept it, but the truth will set you free." Veterans of the wars in Iraq and Afghanistan need to "know the history of how they got there," Fennell warned. "They make veterans pawns. The government could decide not to build three bombers. You know how much money that is for helping veterans?" The answer is about 1.5 billion. "Today, you're getting a backlash of ISIS and all these other groups that come from generations of war for oil, for the displacement of humanity. . . . Those things come back like a boomerang."[44]

Incarceration reproduces intergenerational trauma in families. "If you had 100,000 veterans from the Vietnam War era that were parents that got incarcerated, leaving the kids at home and . . . got a long stretch of ten years," explains Fennell. "Leave a kid at eight and come back fifteen. You try to come back as a father—to reclaim the collateral damage of your being incarcerated. A lot of these people today in their twenties, thirties, and forties had veterans as parents and grandparents. They didn't get that wholesomeness that's needed, and that prevents them from being parents. So now, you've got these Vietnam-era veterans, their children, and their grandchildren caught in a cycle." Fennell's incarceration had an immeasurable impact on his own children and grandchildren. His son, Haywood Fennell Jr., served a short prison sentence when he was eighteen years old. He later died tragically of complications from HIV/AIDS. Mr. Fennell's daughter works as a captain at Rikers Island. Their lives are caught in an undertow, pushed and pulled by the military- and prison-industrial complexes.

PART III

The son of a Vietnam War veteran, David Carlson lives in the wake of intergenerational trauma, war, and incarceration.[45] "My dad is from Mississippi. He's my Black side," Carlson said. "My dad's a Vietnam vet. He was also an infantryman. After Vietnam, he got into a criminal lifestyle. When I was born, he was a pimp, and my mom was a prostitute."[46] Carlson's father, Abra Hayes, had a brutal life in the Jim Crow South; as a child, he witnessed a lynching. "They were extremely poor. He went to Vietnam and got shot. He had a hard time coming home." After his discharge, Hayes returned to Jackson, Mississippi, where he was harassed by local police and still treated as a second-class citizen. "He moved to California because it was a little better for Black people," Carlson said, but "he could never beat the alcohol and drug addiction."

Carlson grew up amid instability, domestic violence, and drug use. He moved schools frequently. At the age of thirteen, Carlson got involved in gang violence. By fourteen, he was incarcerated in a juvenile detention center. By the time he was twenty, David sought structure, community, and discipline. Not too long after 9/11, he joined the Army National Guard.

In 2004, Carlson deployed to Iraq, and he volunteered for a second deployment in 2007. Today, he suffers from survivor's guilt and post-traumatic stress disorder. "When Sergeant [Alwyn] Cashe had got killed, that was two weeks before we left country. We had got taken off mission when he got killed." Carlson said, "It was like we betrayed them. In the moment that they needed people—not that we would have made a difference, but to suffer with them—we were back on base." Sergeant Cashe had burns over 90 percent of his body. "He lived two weeks like that," said Carlson. "Two others were killed too. An interpreter that we were all close to, he burned to death in the Bradley." Carlson remembered, "That's the end of my tour, and that's it. There was no retribution for it. That happened, and then I'm home. That really bothered me until I got reconnected with some of those guys, and I didn't reconnect with them until I was in jail." Carlson explained, "That stuck with me my entire time, and that's why I volunteered for my second tour."

During Carlson's second deployment, psychiatric trauma took a heavy toll on him. He became more isolated, aggressive, and violent. He was investigated for assaulting a subordinate. He grew paranoid. "I would go outside the wire and have Iraqis try to kill you, and then come back and have the leadership look for possible prosecutions. I had three AR 15–6 investigations. Any one of those could've landed me anywhere from demoted to private to locked up. I had the mentality that I would protect myself." His problems only worsened after the second deployment, but he did not trust the military.

As a soldier, Carlson equated mental illness with weakness, a failure of manhood. "I didn't believe in PTSD at that time," he admitted. "I had one buddy; during the first two weeks in Iraq, he got hit by an RPG." Carlson recalled, "The shrapnel went through both his feet, and he got sent back. I found out later that he had all these issues. He was an alcoholic, and I got home and saw him. In my mind, I thought he was just weak. Then, after my second tour, I started having those same issues." He believed, "If I was walking around with the appearance that I'm fine, then you should be too." He thought, "If you're a man, you're not going to have issues with this. Period." When he returned to the United States again, Carlson started to lash out more violently.

One night during an armed confrontation with police, Carlson contemplated "suicide by cop." He was arrested and confined to a VA psychiatric ward. He entered a PTSD treatment program at Fort Knox. Then, he was honorably discharged from the national guard. Carlson avoided an administrative discharge because of the advocacy of his leaders, citing his service in Iraq. Afterward, however, his mental health conditions worsened without the support of the military. He was arrested for burglary and sentenced to a veterans treatment court. While on probation, he was arrested again, this time for operating under the influence. The judge rejected him from treatment court and sentenced him to a previous three-year prison sentence.

In total, Carlson served twenty-two months in combat and over four years in prison. While incarcerated, he became more combative and undermined prison authority: "I was a predator. My whole plan was to get out and hurt the community. I wanted to destroy it. I hated the United States, and I hated everybody." "That's the way I was released, and I only lasted a few months," he said. "I ran from the cops. I was combative. I'm fortunate to not have life in prison or be dead." Carlson recidivated and spent nine months in solitary confinement. "At first, I thought it was going to destroy me, but it made me access a strength that I used to turn my life around." He started writing and eventually got connected with the VA. Through this process, he discovered a calling for advocacy.

Presently, Carlson is a law school student, a father, and a mentor at the Eau Claire County Veterans Treatment Court in Wisconsin. He advocates for a nonviolent model of rehabilitation for veterans and engages in reparative justice projects. "Policy-makers have not been held accountable for the violence they cause," Carlson noted. "There has to be retribution for that." "I've had too much violence indoctrinated into me . . . throughout my life. It won't just go away. Violence is the number one thing you've got to take out of your life if you want to make any other changes," he reflected. "One of the motivations I have for helping people is—I don't see it like I'm being a great person. I see it as I owe a lot. I owe for the rest of my life. There isn't going to be a time when I can say I have done enough because I have taken lives." Carlson said, "I owe. I am in debt. If I don't live up to that debt, and I don't keep paying back towards it—then I am not a man. I am not an honorable person."

Like Haywood Fennell Sr., David Carlson understands the inherent traumas of his life as a legacy of decades of American wars. "What we're dealing with is the consequences of imperialism, and we're still using imperialistic tactics in the Middle East. . . . We've created a severe animosity towards the West," Carlson realized. "The kids on my first tour—that saw us killing their parents and running in their homes—are now ISIS. They're of military age now," he said. "Unless there was an actual justifiable cause for being over there, we were in the wrong. And the consequences we are suffering now are because of our wrong actions, and we continue making wrong decisions." Carlson warned, "I don't see good times ahead for us because of the policies we keep enforcing and enacting on the Middle East, and even on Mexico and Central America," he added. "We support coups, allow cocaine to be distributed, and do all these things that undermine [democracy] and upset the political balance. . . . We've directly involved ourselves in places that immigrants are coming from."[47]

Today, the United States has the most expensive military force and the highest prison population in the world. The total yearly cost of mass incarceration in the United States amounts to over 180 billion dollars.[48] Nearly 60 percent of the national budget pays for more than eight hundred military bases that encircle the globe.[49] Only 6 percent pays for the VA. The costs and consequences of the Global War on Terror go mostly undebated in politics and largely ignored by the public. With less than half of one percent of the American population serving, the burdens of fighting fall on fewer families, widening the civilian-military divide. In this sense, all veterans today are marginalized in society, but some are more severely punished for their inability to cross that division.

CONCLUSION: INEQUALITY IN A TIME OF JUSTICE REFORM

Vietnam veterans and their advocates have long recognized the threat of imprisonment after war. Yet, incarcerated veterans are marginalized in American public memory. The first barrier is identifying them. Veterans in the criminal justice system do not self-identify for a variety of reasons, often related to discharge status, fear of losing VA benefits, or shame. In the 1970s, Vietnam veterans formed powerful advocacy groups, leading the fight for veterans' benefits, disability rights, and justice.[50] Vietnam Veterans of America has advocated on behalf of incarcerated veterans from its beginning, raising awareness about PTSD and crime since the early 1980s.[51] Despite these efforts, Vietnam veterans remained the single largest group of veterans in prison, surpassed only recently by Iraq and Afghanistan War veterans combined.[52]

Vietnam veterans are leading a grassroots movement for criminal justice reform, promoting mental health treatment and alternatives to incarceration.[53] First established in 2008, by judge Robert Russell, the Buffalo Veterans Treatment Court became the first hybrid drug treatment and mental health court.[54] Since then, more than five hundred veterans treatment courts have expanded across the country.[55] Today, thousands of Vietnam veterans volunteer as mentors to Iraq and Afghanistan War veterans. The shared experience of military culture opens a space for communicating and healing from trauma. Moreover, the courts provide a "one-stop shop" for veterans' services: housing, employment, the VA, disability claims, and counseling services. Unsurprisingly, it works.[56]

The exceptional recidivism rates of veterans treatment courts promise a new model of criminal justice that treats the underlying conditions of criminality. As the Incarcerated Veterans Oral History Project shows, military experiences can exacerbate underlying problems that stem from intergenerational trauma, mental health disorders, and economic and racial inequality. During the Vietnam War–era draft, 80 percent of combat soldiers were working-class.[57] Today, the all-volunteer force relies on economic incentives to fill its ranks, offering cash bonuses, job training, and education. During the wars in Iraq and Afghanistan, multiple deployments and extended combat tours increased the number of "signature wounds": PTSD, traumatic brain injuries, and cases of suicide.[58] From 2001 to 2009, opiate prescriptions quadrupled.[59] In 2009 alone, military physicians prescribed 3.8 million painkillers to soldiers. Heroin, more readily available than prescription opioids, has caused a spike in overdoses in the United States since 2016.[60] In response to the many issues veterans face after service, veterans treatment courts are leading the fight against stigmas, substance abuse, and veteran suicide. Yet equally urgent, the entire system must reckon with historic and endemic racism.

Despite criminal justice reforms, African Americans still die in police custody, on the streets, and in jail cells. Sergeant James Brown survived two combat tours in Iraq but died in a West Texas jail.[61] In 2012, the African American soldier was arrested for driving under the influence. Brown exhibited symptoms of PTSD. Five guards wearing riot gear pinned the sergeant to the floor. A video recorded his last words—"Help me. I can't breathe." In Tulsa, Oklahoma, in 2011, a Black veteran named Elliot Williams suffered a brutal death in jail.[62] He, too, had a history of mental health issues. After being pepper-sprayed and arrested, Williams behaved erratically at the jail, "crawling on the floor," and refusing to remove his clothes. Officers took "him down 'by his head and neck.'"[63] For six days, he was denied medical attention. Williams died of sustained blunt force trauma, starvation, and a broken neck. The attending nurse and jail psychiatrist accused him of faking injuries. Surveillance cameras recorded the guards taunting Williams as he lay dying. This tragic incident happened in a city where the third veterans treatment court was established.[64] At the time, Tulsa served as one of four "mentor courts," training courts across the United States to identify veterans in jail.[65] Did the veteran status of Elliot Williams matter? "In prison, you don't have *veterans*," answers Henry Burton, "only convicts and inmates."

NOTES

I would like to acknowledge my dissertation director, Dr. Christian G. Appy, for his insightful guidance and willingness to read an early draft of this chapter. My field adviser in African American history, Dr. Barbara Krauthamer, also had a significant influence on this scholarship. Thank you to the co-editor, Dr. John M. Kinder, for his ongoing mentorship and collegiality. I am also grateful for the support of Dr. Elizabeth Grubgeld and Dr. Kay J. Walter. Mary Ellen Salzano, a tireless advocate for veterans, has served as an adviser to the Incarcerated Veterans Oral History Project since 2017. Thank you to Beth McLaughlin and Adept Word Management for transcription services. This project benefitted from grants and fellowships from UMass History, the UMass Public History program, UMass Graduate School, and Special Collections and University Archives at the W. E. B. Du Bois Library.

1. See also Donald Ritchie, *Doing Oral History, 3rd ed.* (Oxford: Oxford University Press, 2015), 50.
2. I launched the Incarcerated Veterans Oral History Project in 2017 as a PhD student in history at UMass Amherst. This project documents the experiences of formerly incarcerated veterans of the wars in Vietnam, Iraq, and Afghanistan, as well as advocates and volunteers involved in veterans treatment courts. Thus far, I have recorded fifty-six oral history interviews. These oral histories will be made available at Special Collections and University Archives at the W. E. B. Du Bois Library at UMass Amherst. Each participant has signed informed consent and has had the opportunity to review the interviews with the option to delete or omit any information before publication. I have granted access to selected interviews and clips at the following site: Jason A. Higgins, "Videos," YouTube, last accessed September 2021, https://www.youtube.com/channel/UCDOhnA1c1205ZkI7ROSUsSA/videos.
3. The "wake" alludes to the work of Christina Sharpe on intergenerational racial trauma. See Christina Sharpe, *In the Wake: On Blackness and Being* (Durham, NC: Duke University Press, 2016).
4. See also David Blight, *Race and Reunion: The Civil War in American Memory* (Cambridge, MA: Harvard University Press, 2001).
5. Adrianne Lentz-Smith, *Freedom Struggles: African Americans and World War I* (Cambridge, MA: Harvard University Press, 2009), 3–4; Kimberley L. Phillips, *War! What Is It Good For?: Black Freedom Struggles and the U.S. Military from World War II to Iraq* (Chapel Hill: University of North Carolina Press, 2012).
6. See also Jennifer Brooks, *Defining the Peace: World War II Veterans, Race, and the Remaking of Southern Political Tradition* (Chapel Hill: University of North Carolina

Press, 2004); Timothy Tyson, *Radio Free Dixie: Robert F. Williams and the Roots of Black Power* (Chapel Hill: University of North Carolina Press, 2001).

7. Police killings of Black veterans ignited early opposition to the Vietnam War from John Lewis and the ranks of SNCC as early as 1965. Daniel S. Lucks, *Selma to Saigon: The Civil Rights Movement and the Vietnam War* (Lexington: University of Kentucky Press, 2014), 98, 112. For more historical depth on African American veterans and their encounters with law enforcement in the twentieth century, see Mary L. Dudziak, *Cold War Civil Rights: Race and the Image of American Democracy* (Princeton, NJ: Princeton University Press, 2000); Kevin Kruse and Stephen Tuck, eds., *Fog of War: The Second World War and the Civil Rights Movement* (New York: Oxford University Press, 2012); Chad Williams, *Torchbearers of Democracy: African American Soldiers in the World War I Era* (Chapel Hill: University of North Carolina Press, 2010).

8. See Michelle Alexander, *The New Jim Crow: Mass Incarceration in the Age of Color Blindness* (New York: The New Press, 2010).

9. David Oshinsky, *Worse Than Slavery: Parchman Farm and the Ordeal of Jim Crow Justice* (New York: Free Press, 1996), 43. See also Talitha LeFlouria, *Chained in Silence: Black Women and Convict Labor in the New South* (Chapel Hill: University of North Carolina Press), 2015.

10. Khalil Gibran Muhammad, *Condemnation of Blackness: Race, Crime, and the Making of Modern Urban America* (Cambridge, MA: Harvard University Press, 2010), 4.

11. Ibid., 4.

12. Moynihan endorsed the plan to lower military entrance exams, believing the military could provide training and skills to young African American men. Disproportionate casualties ultimately led civil rights leaders to oppose the war in Vietnam, including Dr. Martin Luther King in 1967. For further reading see, Christian G. Appy, *Working-Class War: American Combat Soldiers and Vietnam* (Chapel Hill: University of North Carolina Press, 1993); Steve Estes, *I Am a Man!: Race, Manhood, and the Civil Rights Movement* (Chapel Hill: University of North Carolina Press, 2005); Lucks, *Selma to Saigon*; Phillips, *War!*; James E. Westheider, *Fighting on Two Fronts: African Americans and the Vietnam War* (New York: New York University Press, 1997).

13. Richard Rothstein, *The Color of Law: A Forgotten History of How Our Government Segregated America* (New York: Liveright, 2017).

14. See also Rhonda Y. Williams, *The Politics of Public Housing: Black Women's Struggles against Urban Inequality* (New York: Oxford University Press, 2004).

15. John Clegg and Adaner Usmani, "The Economic Origins of Mass Incarceration," *Catalyst*, 3 no. 3 (Fall 2019): 11–22. Studying the rise of violent crime in the 1960s, Clegg and Usmani argue that class disparity had a significant impact on the rise of mass incarceration. By 1960, 25 percent of African American men between the ages of eighteen and fifty were unemployed and not in school (23). Between 1960 and 1980, homicide rates doubled. Generational poverty, segregation, and the exclusion of African Americans from the post–World War II boom created concentrated poverty and violence.

16. Donna J. Murch, *Living for the City: Migration, Education, and the Rise of the Black Panther Party in Oakland, California* (Chapel Hill: University of North Carolina Press 2010).

17. In 1968, African Americans made up 8 percent of military personnel in Vietnam; 16.3 percent were assigned to combat roles. Appy, *Working-Class War*, 32–33, 37.

18. Westheider, *Fighting on Two Fronts*, 59.

19.   Jennifer Bronson et al., "Veterans in Prison and Jail, 2011–12," *U.S. Department of Justice Bureau of Statistics* (Dec. 2015), 2.

20.   Ibid., 2.

21.   US Department of Justice, "Veterans in Prison," October 1981, *Bureau of Justice Statistics Bulletin,* http://www.ncdsv.org/images/BJS_Veterans-in-Prison_10-1981.pdf.

22.   *Veterans' Unemployment Problems: Hearing Before the Subcommittee on Readjustment, Education, and Employment of the Committee on Veterans' Affairs, United States Senate,* 94th Cong., 1st Sess., Session on S. 760 and Related Bills, October 22, 1975, 879.

23.   US Department of Justice, "Veterans in Prison." For the most recent report, see Laura M. Maruschak, Jennifer Bronson, and Mariel Alper, "Veterans in Prison: A Survey of Prison Inmates, 2016," *Bureau of Justice Statistics,* from the Veterans in State and Federal Prisons series, March 30, 2021, https://www.bjs.gov/index.cfm?ty=pbdetail&iid=7308.

24.   Henry D. Burton, interviewed by Jason A. Higgins, July 25, 2018, Amherst, MA, Incarcerated Veterans Oral History Project. Burton provided informed consent, and his family members, especially his sister, were supportive of his participation in this project. Unless otherwise attributed, all Burton quotes are from this interview.

25.   In the mid-1970s, Vietnam veterans advocated for disability benefits for incarcerated veterans. Congress held hearings on incarcerated veterans in 1979, finding that were no systemic efforts to identify or assist veterans in prison. *Hearing Before the Committee on Veterans' Affairs: Oversight on Issues Relating to Incarcerated Veterans,* 96th Cong., 1st Sess., July 11, 1979, 12.

26.   As an emergency precaution during the COVID-19 pandemic, Henry Burton was released on parole to live with his brother on March 5, 2020. "I look forward to this new journey," he wrote. "This is the first time since Vietnam, I will start a future with a right mind and heart."

27.   Elizabeth Hinton, *From the War on Poverty to the War on Crime: The Making of Mass Incarceration in America* (Cambridge, MA: Harvard University Press, 2016), 1–2.

28.   Estes, *I Am a Man!,* 123.

29.   Stuart Schrader, *Badges without Borders: How Global Counterinsurgency Transformed American Policing* (Oakland: University of California Press, 2019), 4–5. These policies "crossed the divisions of civilian and military, foreign and domestic" (15).

30.   Hinton, *War on Poverty,* 3.

31.   Jeremy Kuzmarov, *The Myth of the Addicted Army: Vietnam and the Modern War on Drugs* (Amherst: University of Massachusetts Press, 2009), 38.

32.   Alexander, *New Jim Crow,* 6.

33.   Bronson et al., "Veterans in Prison," 2.

34.   Heather Ann Thompson, "Why Mass Incarceration Matters: Rethinking Crisis, Decline, and Transformation in Postwar American History," *Journal of American History* 97, no. 3 (2010): 703.

35.   Alfred W. McCoy, *In the Shadows of the American Century: The Rise and Fall of US Global Power* (Chicago, IL: Haymarket, 2017), 86.

36.   Doris Marie Provine, *Unequal under Law: Race in the War on Drugs* (Chicago, IL: University of Chicago Press, 2007), 103.

37.   See also David Farber, *Crack: Rock Cocaine, Street Capitalism, and the Decade of Greed* (Cambridge: University of Cambridge Press, 2019).

38.   Haywood Fennell Sr., interviewed by Jason A. Higgins, July 7, 2017, Boston, MA, Incarcerated Veterans Oral History Project. Unless otherwise attributed, all Fennell quotes are from this interview.

39. Heroin use also multiplied in the United States between 1965 and 1971. See Alfred W. McCoy, *The Politics of Heroin in Southeast Asia*, with Cathleen B. Read and Leonard P. Adams III (New York: Harper, 1973), 1.

40. See Haywood Fennell Sr., *Coota and the Magic Quilt* (Boston, MA: Tri-Ad Veterans League, 2004).

41. See Bernard Edelman and Deanne Benos, "Barracks Behind Bars: In Veteran-Specific Housing Units, Veterans Help Veterans Help Themselves," US Department of Justice, National Institute of Corrections, May 2018.

42. David Wood writes about institutional betrayal as a "violation of trust" and "a most basic violation of our sense of right and wrong and can carve a jagged moral wound deep in the soul" (174–76). David Wood, *What Have We Done: The Moral Injury of Our Longest Wars* (New York: Little, Brown, 2016).

43. Fennell echoes King's criticisms of American imperialism, capitalism, and racism as espoused in his Riverside Church speech. Dr. Martin Luther King Jr., "Beyond Vietnam—A Time to Break Silence," April 4, 1967, Riverside Church, New York City.

44. See also John Dower, *The Violent American Century: War and Terror Since World War II* (Chicago, IL: Haymarket, 2017); Chalmers Johnson, *Blowback: The Costs and Consequences of American Empire*, 2nd ed. (New York City: Holt, 2004); McCoy, *In the Shadows*, 144.

45. For an analysis of trauma transmitted from Vietnam War veterans to their children, see Christian D. Weber, *Social Memory and War Narratives: Transmitted Trauma Among Children of War Veterans* (New York: Palgrave, 2015).

46. David Carlson, telephone interview by Jason A. Higgins, January 23, 2017, Amherst, MA, January 23, 2017. Unless otherwise attributed, all Carlson quotes are from this interview.

47. See also Stephen Kinzer, *Overthrow: America's Century of Regime Change from Hawaii to Iraq* (New York: Holt, 2006).

48. Peter Wagner and Bernadette Rabuy, "Following the Money of Mass Incarceration," Prison Policy Initiative, January 25, 2017, https://www.prisonpolicy.org/reports/money.html.

49. See also David Vine, *Base Nation: How U.S. Military Bases Harm America and the World* (New York: Metropolitan, 2015).

50. See also *Hearing Before the Committee on Veterans' Affairs: Oversight on Issues Relating to Incarcerated Veterans*.

51. "Incarcerated Veterans in the Criminal Justice System," *VVA Veteran* (Sept. 1984): 8.

52. The most recent Department of Justice study, "Veterans in Prison, 2016," noted an increase in the number of Iraq and Afghanistan War veterans incarcerated, as many as 28 percent and 16 percent respectively. Maruschak, Bronson, and Alper, "Veterans in Prison."

53. This is a key argument in my dissertation. Jason A. Higgins, "Stars, Bars, and Stripes: A History of Veterans in the Criminal Justice System since the Vietnam War" (PhD diss. University of Massachusetts Amherst, 2021).

54. Judge Robert Russell, Incarcerated Veterans Oral History Project, interviewed by Jason A. Higgins, July 9, 2019, Buffalo, NY, https://www.youtube.com/watch?v=jNmqqMp NH5M. Robert T. Russell, "Veterans Treatment Court: A Proactive Approach," *New England Journal on Criminal and Civil Confinement* 35, no. 2 (Summer 2009): 357–72.

55. For a discussion of Veterans Treatment Courts and limitations, see Julie Marie Baldwin, "Investigating the Programmatic Attack: A National Survey of Veterans Treatment Courts," *Journal of Criminal Law and Criminology,* 105 no. 4 (2016): 727–28.

56. See also Richard D. Hartley and Julie Marie Baldwin, "Waging War on Recidivism among Justice-Involved Veterans: An Impact Evaluation of a Large Urban Veterans Treatment Court," *Criminal Justice Policy Review,* 30 no. 1 (2019).

57. Appy, *Working-Class War.*

58. David Kieran, *Signature Wounds: The Untold Story of the Military's Mental Health Crisis* (New York: New York University Press, 2019). See also Mark A. Reger et. al., "Association between Number of Deployments to Iraq and Mental Health Screening Outcomes in US Army Soldiers," *Journal of Clinical Psychiatry* 70, no. 9 (2009): 1266–72.

59. "Substance Use Disorders in the U.S. Armed Forces," *Institute of Medicine,* September 2012, 1.

60. "Drug Overdose," Center for Disease Control and Prevention, National Center for Injury Prevention and Control, March 2021, https://www.cdc.gov/drugoverdose/data/statedeaths.html.

61. Juan A. Lozano, "Mother of Soldier Hopeful Son's Death in a Texas Jail Won't Be Repeated," *Associated Press,* December 12, 2015.

62. A complete list of references on the death of Elliot Williams can be located at "Death of Elliott Williams," Wikipedia, September, 2020, https://en.wikipedia.org/wiki/Death_of_Elliott_Williams#References.

63. Scott Allen, "Medical Expert Report Regarding Mr. Elliott Williams," March 24, 2014, available at *Document Cloud,* https://www.documentcloud.org/documents/2805982-Medical-Expert-Report-on-Williams.html.

64. Judge David Youll, "Tulsa County Veterans Treatment Court," *Oklahoma Bar Journal* 82 no. 31 (2011): 2745–48.

65. Ginnie Graham, "Court Serves with Honor," *Tulsa World,* May 18, 2010, A9.

#IAmVanessaGuillen

JASON A. HIGGINS &
JOHN M. KINDER

Mural in memory of PFC Vanessa Guillen in Houston, Texas, created by artists Roland Saldaña and Marcos Del Bosque of Artistik Misfits. Photograph by Mark Felix, August 14, 2020.

In the spring of 2020, as the first wave of COVID-19 spread across the United States, news of the disappearance and brutal murder of PFC Vanessa Guillen went viral in veteran communities. Guillen had twice reported sexual harassment by a fellow soldier at Fort Hood, Texas, but the army had failed to investigate the matter. On April 22, specialist Aaron David Robinson bludgeoned Guillen to death with a hammer inside an armory building on base. Robinson's "girlfriend," Cecily Aguilar, helped him dismember and dispose of the body, burying Guillen under concrete. More than two months later, Vanessa's body was discovered. On July 1, Robinson reportedly killed himself before police could apprehend him.[1] Guillen's tragic death might have been forgotten in national consciousness, but instead it triggered a social media movement. Under the hashtag #IAmVanessaGuillen, hundreds of women shared their experiences of military sexual trauma.[2] This hashtag created a spontaneous public archive of collective trauma, linking interpersonal histories of sexual violence and spelling out a social crisis in the US military.

Over the past decade, social media campaigns and advocacy organizations have called for investigations into specific incidents of violence and assault at military bases in the United States.[3] Most notoriously, at Fort Hood in 2020, there were five homicides, thirteen soldiers died by suicide, and eleven deaths remain unsolved.[4] Among the thirty-nine service members who died or went missing at Fort Hood in 2020, the gruesome deaths of Vanessa Guillen and sergeant Elder Fernandes—whose body was found hanging from a tree after he reported sexual assault—caused a public outcry for justice and accountability.[5] In response, an independent Fort Hood investigation concluded that the "command climate" rendered SHARP (the army's Sexual Harassment/Assault Response and Prevention program) "ineffective," and the leadership enabled a "permissive environment for sexual assault."[6] Fourteen army leaders were fired or suspended.[7] However, individual investigations such as these often occur in isolation, failing to produce effective systemic reforms.

Since the end of the draft in 1973, the number of enlisted women in the military has increased from slightly more than 1 percent during the Vietnam War era to nearly 18 percent today, yet women are regularly denied equal rights and protection. Military leadership is too often complicit, enabling sexual violence in the military. An estimated one in four women in the military is assaulted by a fellow service member, frequently resulting in military sexual trauma and post-traumatic stress disorder.[8] Victims are twelve times more likely to experience retaliation than their rapists are to be convicted.[9] The 2012 *Annual Report on Sexual Assault in the Military* documented twenty-six thousand assaults that year alone. Only 238 were convicted. Of those, 64 were acquitted.[10] Put bluntly, the chain of command protects perpetrators of sexual assault. As a result, most victims of sexual violence in the military do not report trauma for fear of stigma, ostracism, and retribution.

These issues amount to systemic inequality, due to inadequate legal protection and retaliation against survivors of sexual trauma.[11] In 2013, the US Commission on Civil Rights—the first one in nearly fifty years—found that 60 percent of women who reported sexual assault or harassment experienced "negative social, professional, or administrative consequences."[12] Survivors of military sexual trauma can be discharged for behavioral incidents and misdiagnosed with personality disorders or other preexisting conditions. This loophole allows the military and Veterans Affairs to disqualify victims of sexual assault from veterans benefits and care—a double punishment and institutional betrayal.[13]

Time and again, survivors have testified before Congress about the prevalence of sexual violence in the military. Spurred on by a grassroots veterans' movement effort to reform the Uniform Code of Military Justice, in 2013 senator Kirsten Gillibrand (D-NY) introduced the Military Justice Improvement Act. If passed, this legislation would remove the chain of command from cases of sexual assault, offering civilian oversight to ensure equal justice to victims. Amid these reform efforts, the Pentagon misled Congress by reporting inaccurate information on military sexual assault.[14] The bill failed to overcome a Republican filibuster, led by the late senator John McCain (R-AZ), a former Vietnam War POW. Since then, these problems have only worsened. In the aftermath of Vanessa Guillen's murder, the aptly named "I Am Vanessa Guillen Act" similarly seeks to reform the military justice system by circumventing the chain of command in cases of sexual assault, establishing a process for compensation for military negligence, and reforming the SHARP program to provide civilian oversight.

As the United States winds down its failed campaigns in the Middle East, the future of veterans' history appears uncertain. In the past, attention to the majority and the most representative groups overshadowed the histories of others—such as African Americans, Latinx, LGBTQ, women, and veterans with disabilities, mental health disorders, and criminal records—denying their rightful place in the American national story. Drawing on the energies of Black Lives Matter, #MeToo, and other social justice campaigns, veteran-activists are forcing the American public and its leaders to face difficult truths about the ways certain groups of military members and veterans are mistreated, marginalized, and denied equal rights. Headline-gripping stories, like those of Vanessa Guillen and deported veterans such as Hector Barajas-Varela, are presently regenerating congressional efforts to reform federal policies toward the nation's most vulnerable service members and vets.[15] But politicians can't—or, more accurately, won't—do it on their own. Scholars of war and veterans have a vital, if secondary, role in enacting social change, employing our training in support of activism, creating new historical knowledge to understand the roots of social inequality, and using institutional resources to amplify the voices of marginalized veterans.

Service Denied is our contribution to this project. In conceptualizing the figure of the "marginalized veteran," we seek to draw attention to the ways structural injustice and prejudice—from the racism encountered by African American veterans of World War I to the deep-seated stigma associated with homosexuality and bed wetting—have negatively affected veterans' lives in profound and often overlooked ways. Read collectively, the stories of marginalized veterans assembled in this book remind us that studying veterans (or, in academic parlance, veterans' studies) is never a neutral practice. If historians hope to raise up the voices of diverse populations of former servicemen and women, they must first grapple with the policies and prejudices that silence large groups of vets in the first place.

In this sense, *Service Denied* represents but a first step in a much longer journey. Even as we tried to center on the lives of certain historically marginalized veterans, we were aware of how much more work needs to be done, for example, with Indigenous veterans. Future scholars will want to look beyond the United States' "major" wars to locate veterans of the nation's irregular conflicts and proxy battles—the marines who invaded Haiti in 1915, the submariners who patrolled the Arctic during the Cold War, the "imperial grunts" currently stationed in Mongolia and on the Horn of Africa—even if such figures might not be considered "veterans" in the familiar sense.[16] Scholars will want to take seriously the millions of veterans—former cooks, mechanics, engineers, military journalists, office staff, and overseas translators—whose military experience did not center around surviving combat.

Just as important, historians will want to think critically about how veterans (individually or in groups) have wrestled with the political dimensions of their military service, for good or ill. This means asking difficult questions about the alarming number of US military veterans active in white supremacist

movements and the most virulent branches of alt-right politics.[17] Why are
neofascist groups such as the Proud Boys so eager to recruit veterans, and why
are so many ex–service members ready and willing to join their ranks? But it
also means acknowledging the veterans who derived a different set of political
lessons from their military experiences. These include groups such as Wall of
Vets, an organization of military veterans and their families that formed in
response to government "overreach and suppression" during the Black Lives
Matter protests of the summer of 2020.[18] Founded in Portland, Oregon, the
group received national headlines after forming a human barrier between law
enforcement and people protesting the murder of George Floyd by Minneapolis
police. Like other human "walls" present at the protests (yellow-shirted "Walls
of Moms," leaf blower–wielding "Walls of Dads"), members of Wall of Vets
were willing to put their bodies at risk to protect the civil rights of their fellow
Americans, just as they had when they wore their uniforms.[19]

Young and old, men and women, some wearing Black Lives Matter T-shirts,
others holding upside-down flags in a sign of distress—they stood at the
frontlines of a different kind of battle, protecting veterans of the United
States' centuries-old war to win racial freedom at home.

Wall of Vets protest, Portland, Oregon, July 28, 2020. Photo by David Killen/*The Oregonian*.

NOTES

1. Johnny Diaz, Maria Cramer, and Christina Morales, "What to Know about the Death of Vanessa Guillen," *New York Times*, April 30, 2021, https://www.nytimes.com/article/vanessa-guillen-fort-hood.html.

2. Hailey Britzky, "Service Members Are Sharing Their Stories of Sexual Harassment and Assault Using #IAmVanessaGuillen," *Task & Purpose*, June 29, 2020, https://taskandpurpose.com/news/i-am-vanessa-guillen-hashtag/; Ruthy Munoz, "I Am Vanessa Guillen," *War Horse*, July 15, 2020, https://thewarhorse.org/i-am-vanessa-guillen/.

3. The activism of women veterans, of course, predates social media. Diana Danis, founder of SERVICE: Women Who Serve, a Facebook group with over one hundred thousand followers, has been advocating for survivors of sexual assault since the 1970s. (She herself had been assaulted by a fellow soldier.) Speaking before the Senate Veterans Affairs Committee in the summer of 1992, she testified "that the circumstances and conditions leading to the assault in the military have not changed appreciably over the years, and if anything, they have worsened. . . . Over the past twenty-five years sexual trauma perpetrated against women in the military has escalated to catastrophic proportions." See statement of Diana D. Danis, "Testimony Regarding Rape, Sexual Assault and/or Harassment of Women Who Serve," presented before the Senate Veterans Affairs Committee, 102nd Congress, 35 (1992).

    More recently, a human rights advocacy group called Protect Our Defenders (founded in 2011) has led efforts to bring attention to sexual assault in the military and effect policy change. In 2013, a group of female and male victims of sexual assault in the military testified before the Senate Armed Services Committee, chaired by senator Kirsten Gillibrand as part of efforts to enact Congressional legislation. Although prior efforts have not produced effective results in Congress, Protect Our Defenders continues to advocate for policy changes and provides legal services to survivors of sexual assault in the military. See *Testimony on Sexual Assault in the Military, Hearing Before the Subcommittee on Personnel on the Committee on Armed Services, 113th Congress* (2013), https://www.armed-services.senate.gov/imo/media/doc/sexualassaultsinmilitary_subcomm_hearing_031313.pdf.

4. May Jeong, "The Only Thing I Knew Was How to Kill People: Inside the Rash of Unexplained Deaths at Ft. Hood," *Vanity Fair*, July 6, 2021, https://www.vanityfair.com/news/2021/06/inside-the-rash-of-unexplained-deaths-at-fort-hood/amp.

5. Ryan Morgan, "Missing Fort Hood Soldier Found Dead Hanging from a Tree," *American Military News*, August 26, 2020, https://americanmilitarynews.com/2020/08/missing-fort-hood-soldier-found-dead-hanging-from-tree/.

6. "Report of the Ft. Hood Independent Review Committee," *US Army*, November 6, 2020, https://www.army.mil/e2/downloads/rv7/forthoodreview/2020-12-03_FHIRC_report_redacted.pdf.

7. Tom Vanden Brook, "Panel Blasts Army Leaders, Army after Disappearance, Death of Spc Vanessa Guillen; 14 Fired or Suspended," *USA Today*, December 8, 2020, https://www.usatoday.com/story/news/politics/2020/12/08/fort-hood-panel-faults-army-ignoring-sexual-assaults-some-fired/6481836002/.

8. "Facts on United States Military Sexual Violence," *Protect Our Defenders*, May 2017, https://www.protectourdefenders.com/wp-content/uploads/2013/05/1.-MSA-Fact-Sheet-170629.pdf.

9. Human Rights Watch, "Embattled: Retaliation against Sexual Assault Survivors in the U.S. Military., May 18, 2015, https://www.hrw.org/report/2015/05/18/embattled/retaliation-against-sexual-assault-survivors-us-military.

10. Rosemarie Skaine, *Sexual Assault in the Military* (Santa Barbara, CA: Praeger, 2016), xi.

11. See also Elizabeth L. Hillman, "Front and Center: Sexual Violence in U.S. Military Law," *Politics & Society* 37, no. 1 (Mar. 2009): 101–29.

12. Shawn Woodham, *Sexual Assault in the Military: Analysis, Response, and Resources* (New York: Nova, 2014), 14.

13. See also Army Resilience Directorate, "RAND Study on Sexual Harassment and Gender Discrimination in Active Component-Army," US Army, August 2, 2021, https://www.army.mil/article/249035/rand_study_on_sexual_harassment_and_gender _discrimination_in_the_active_component_army.

14. Richard Lardner, "Pentagon Misled Lawmakers on Military Sexual Assault Cases," *Associated Press*, April 18, 2016, https://apnews.com/23aed8a571f64a9d9c81271f0c6ae2fa /pentagon-misled-lawmakers-military-sexual-assault-cases.

15. United States Government Accountability Office, "Immigration Enforcement: Actions Needed to Better Handle, Identify, and Track Cases Involving Veterans" (GAO-19–416), June 2019, https://www.gao.gov/assets/gao-19-416.pdf?fbclid =IwAR10Ed1Uf59paI9cniJWpPx2xZF_-gVfooImiT6Q6aC8Yki5l9Sx6a7RVOA. See also senator Tammy Duckworth, "Duckworth Releases New Report on the State of Deported Veterans," June 22, 2021, https://www.duckworth.senate.gov/news /press-releases/duckworth-releases-new-report-on-the-state-of-deported-veterans-.

16. The term "imperial grunts" comes from Robert D. Kaplan, *Imperial Grunts: On the Ground with the American Military, from Mongolia to the Philippines to Iraq and Beyond* (New York: Vintage: 2006).

17. Kathleen Belew, *Bring the War Home: The White Power Movement and Paramilitary America* (Cambridge, MA: Harvard University Press, 2018); "Why Are White Supremacists Trying to Recruit Veterans?" *Amanpour & Co.*, October 6, 2020, https://www.pbs.org/wnet/amanpour-and-company/video/why-are-white-supremacists -trying-to-recruit-veterans/; Tom Dreisbach and Meg Anderson, "Nearly 1 in 5 Defendants in Capitol Riot Cases Served in the Military," *NPR*, January 21, 2021, https://www.npr.org/2021/01/21/958915267/nearly-one-in-five-defendants-in-capitol -riot-cases-served-in-the-military.

18. "Who We Are," Wall of Vets Home Page, August 6, 2021, https://wallofvets.org.

19. Mike Baker, "A 'Wall of Vets' Joins the Front Lines of Portland Protests," *New York Times*, July 25, 2020, https://www.nytimes.com/2020/07/25/us/a-wall-of-vets-joins -the-front-lines-of-portland-protests.html.

CONTRIBUTORS

JUAN DAVID CORONADO is a *fronterizo* from the Rio Grande Valley of South Texas. He is assistant professor of Latino and public history at Central Connecticut State University and coordinator of Latino and Puerto Rican studies. A social and oral historian, Dr. Coronado's research and teaching interests include the Latino military experience, Chicana/o/x history, oral history, and Latina/o/x history with an emphasis on class and gender. In his award-winning book *"I'm Not Gonna Die in This Damn Place": Manliness, Identity, and Survival of the Mexican American Vietnam Prisoner of War* (2018), Coronado shares the oral histories of Latino POWs. Juan David previously served as copresident of the Southwest Oral History Association.

BARBARA GANNON is an associate professor of history at the University of Central Florida. She received her B.A. from Emory University, an MA from George Washington University, and a PhD from the Pennsylvania State University. She is the author of *The Won Cause: Black and White Comradeship in the Grand Army of the Republic* (UNC Press, 2011). This book received the Wiley-Silver Prize (University of Mississippi) for the best first book in Civil War history. It also received an honorable mention from the Lincoln Prize (Gilder Lehrman Institute) jury in 2012. She published her second book, *Americans Remember Their Civil War* (Praeger) in 2017. She has written several articles and essays on the Civil War and American veterans. She is the coordinator of the UCF Community Veterans History Project, an oral history project recording the experiences of Florida's veterans. She is a veteran of the US Army.

JASON A. HIGGINS is a postdoctoral fellow in digital humanities and oral history at Virginia Tech. He earned a PhD in history and a graduate certificate in public history from the University of Massachusetts Amherst, where he studied modern US history, global history, and African American history, and specialized in war, trauma, and veterans. Since 2011, he has completed over one hundred oral history interviews with military veterans. He earned a master's in English from Oklahoma State University and a bachelor's in English and history from the University of Arkansas at Monticello. Higgins has published writing in *War, Literature & the Arts*. He is currently revising his first monograph, "Stars, Bars & Stripes: A History of Incarcerated Veterans Since the Vietnam War," which is under advance contract with University of Massachusetts Press to be included in the veterans series.

ROBERT F. JEFFERSON is an associate professor of history at the University of New Mexico. He holds a PhD in African American history from the University of Michigan. His research focuses on the relationship among race, gender, and citizenship in twentieth-century US history. He is the author of *Fighting for Hope: African Americans and the Ninety-Third Infantry Division in World War II and Postwar America* (Johns Hopkins University Press, 2008), which was nominated for the William Colby Book Prize, and is currently working on two monographs, the first titled *American Negritude: Will Mercer Cook, the American Society of African Culture, and the Pan-African Politics of Liberation, 1957–1968* and the second *Color and Disability: Vasco Hale and Twentieth-Century America*. He has also written articles that have appeared in the *Oxford Research Encyclopedia of American History* (2021); *Representations dans le monde anglophone* (2018); *The Routledge Handbook of the History of Race in the American Military* (Routledge, 2016); *Oral History and Public Memories* (Temple University Press, 2008); the *Journal of Family History; Annals of Iowa; Contours: A Journal of the African Diaspora;* and the *Historian*. Jefferson holds memberships in the American Historical Association, the Association for the Study of African American Life and History, the National Council of Black Studies, and is a participating speaker in the Organization of American Historians' Distinguished Lectureship Program.

DAVID KIERAN is associate professor and chair of history and coordinator of the American studies concentration at Washington & Jefferson College in Washington, Pennsylvania. He is the author of *Signature Wounds: The Untold*

Story of the Military's Mental Health Crisis (New York University Press, 2019) and *Forever Vietnam: How a Divisive War Changed American Public Memory* (University of Massachusetts Press, 2014). He is also the editor of *The War of My Generation: Youth Culture and the War on Terror* (Rutgers University Press, 2015); the coeditor, with Edwin A. Martini, of *At War: The Military and American Culture in the Twentieth Century and Beyond* (Rutgers University Press, 2018); and with Rebecca A. Adelman of *Remote Warfare: New Cultures of Violence* (University of Minnesota Press, 2020). He is currently writing a history of organizational change in the US Army after Vietnam, tentatively titled *The Army's Search for Itself: Maxwell R. Thurman and the Army's Post Vietnam Metamorphosis,* and a history of the debate over amnesty for Vietnam War resisters, tentatively titled *Moral Aftermath: The Amnesty Debate and the End of the Vietnam War.*

JOHN M. KINDER is director of the American studies program and associate professor of history at Oklahoma State University. A historian of war and American society, he earned his PhD in American studies at the University of Minnesota in 2007. He is the author of *Paying with Their Bodies: American War and the Problem of the Disabled Veteran,* which was published by the University of Chicago Press in 2015. His work has appeared in numerous collections, including *Disability Histories* (2014), *Phallacies: Historical Intersections of Disability and Masculinity* (2017), and *Zoo Studies: A New Humanities* (2019). He is currently completing a book on the history of zoos and zoo animals during World War II.

STEVEN ROSALES received his PhD in history from the University of California, Irvine, in 2007 under the direction of Vicki L. Ruiz. He is currently an associate professor in the history department and the Latin American and Latino studies (LALS) program at the University of Arkansas. His teaching and research interests include the US LatinX community, US immigration history, US civil rights movements, the US military, oral history methodology, and critical men's studies, with a particular emphasis on the many manifestations of machismo. His *Soldados Razos at War: Chicano Politics,*

Identity, and Masculinity in the U.S. Military from World War II to Vietnam was published in 2017 with the University of Arizona Press. He is currently working on his next book project dealing with the continued participation of Latinos/as in the US military from the Vietnam War through the conflicts in Iraq and Afghanistan. Rosales is also a lieutenant commander in the US Naval Reserve, with over thirty-four years of honorable service.

HEATHER MARIE STUR is professor of history at the University of Southern Mississippi and senior fellow in the Dale Center for the Study of War and Society. She is the author of *Saigon at War: South Vietnam and the Global Sixties* (Cambridge, 2020), *The U.S. Military and Civil Rights since World War II* (ABC-CLIO, 2019), and *Beyond Combat: Women and Gender in the Vietnam War Era* (Cambridge, 2011). She is also coeditor of *Integrating the U.S. Military: Race, Gender, and Sexual Orientation since World War II* (Johns Hopkins, 2017). Stur is the author of numerous articles that have been published in the *New York Times, Washington Post, BBC, National Interest, Orange County Register, Diplomatic History, War & Society,* and other journals and newspapers. In 2013–14, she was a Fulbright scholar in Vietnam, where she was a visiting professor on the Faculty of International Relations at the University of Social Sciences and Humanities in Ho Chi Minh City. She is currently writing a book about general Buford Blount and the US Army's 3rd Infantry Division in the 2003 invasion of Iraq.

EVAN P. SULLIVAN is an instructor of history at SUNY Adirondack and earned his PhD at the University at Albany. His research examines the intersections of gender, disability, and modern war, with an emphasis on World War I. He is a regular writer at *Nursing Clio,* where he writes on topics such as the histories of nursing, hospitals, disability, and alternative medicine.

KARA DIXON VUIC is the LCpl. Benjamin W. Schmidt Professor of War, Conflict, and Society in Twentieth-Century America at Texas Christian University and the author of *The Girls Next Door: Bringing the Home Front to the Front Lines* (Harvard University Press, 2019). She is also the author of *Officer, Nurse, Woman: The Army Nurse Corps in the Vietnam War* (Johns Hopkins University Press, 2010), editor of *The Routledge Handbook on Gender, War, and the U.S. Military* (2017), and coeditor (with Beth Bailey, Alesha Doan, and Shannon Portillo) of *Managing Sex in the U.S. Military* (University of Nebraska Press, 2022). She is coeditor (with Richard Fogarty) of the University of Nebraska Press's book series Studies in War, Society, and the Military. She is writing a new book titled *Drafting Women*.

JOHN WORSENCROFT is an assistant professor of history at Louisiana Tech University. As a scholar, he researches and writes about twentieth-century America through the interlocking themes of policy, gender, war, the military, and society. His book project, *A Family Affair: Military Service in America* is a history of family policies in the US Army and US Marine Corps, and explores how military institutions and policies shape rights, obligations, and the meaning of citizenship in the United States. He has an MA in history from the University of Utah and a PhD in history from Temple University. Before academia, he served from 2000 to 2006 as an infantryman in the US Marine Corps. He is a combat veteran of the Iraq War.

INDEX